Dr Michel Klein

ANIMALS MY TEACHERS

THE AUTOBIOGRAPHY OF A VETERINARY SURGEON

Translated from the French by
J. Maxwell Brownjohn

COLLINS and HARVILL PRESS
London 1979

First published in France in 1976 by Robert Laffont – Opera Mundi
under the title of *Ces bêtes qui m'ont fait homme*.

ISBN 0 00 262810 4

Set in Monotype Plantin
Made and printed in Great Britain
by William Collins Sons & Co Ltd, Glasgow
for Collins, St James's Place and
Harvill Press, 30A Pavilion Road,
London, S.W.1.

I should like to thank my brother,
Dr Jean Klein, without whom I would
not be what I am.
I also want to thank
Charles Ronsac for his advice and
Albert Palle for his help in editing
this book.

Contents

Illustrations

I

In the Jaws of the Tiger

What speeds me on my way, any day or night of the week, Sundays included, to the side of an injured lion, a limping tiger, a disembowelled bear or a rhino with a whitlow? What impels me to enter the lion's cage? What is there between me and 'them'?

After more than twenty years in close contact with wild animals, so called, I cannot help wondering. What have they taught me? Are they just brutes – soulless organisms – and am I a species of animal trainer armed with a lancet and hypodermic instead of the traditional whip and stool, dominating them purely by virtue of human intelligence and technical resources?

Aren't we really closer than it seems? What about Zora the lioness, who licks my hand while I examine her injured paw: is she a mere brute? No, her tongue transmits a message of understanding, cooperation and affection. The she-elephant that gently musses my hair with the tip of her trunk while I remove a tumour the size of a doughnut from her foot – she too conveys a whole variety of things in her own way. She is telling me that we are not alien creatures, that the bonds between man and beast go deep, that we are all members of the same extended family.

It is animals as much as human beings, from the tiniest Yorkshire terrier to living colossi such as Siberian tigers or Indian elephants, that have made me what I am. It is by observing, tending and consorting with them that I have come to terms with my own humanity. Not only have they disclosed that I too am an animal, but the recognition of certain animal virtues in myself and my fellow men has made me more tolerant of our human failings.

So I believe that if wild animals claim as much of my life

as they do, day after day, it is not purely because my job requires it or because there are always bears' dressings to change, chimpanzees to poultice or hippos' abscesses to lance. It is to satisfy a passion which gradually overcame me and has never ceased to grow: to restore the animal's place in a world dominated by man, a place we encroach on by steadily destroying and looting its habitat. Man without animals condemns himself to inhumanity. My task is to protect them, draw them closer to us, promote our knowledge and love of them. An irrational enthusiasm? So say those chill critics for whom the human being can quite as well dispense with lions and tigers as with cats and dogs, but it is still my love and my livelihood.

There are mild protests when the phone rings on a Sunday morning at my home in Garches, near Paris. My twelve-year-old son Jean-François answers it with a sigh: one of our rare rough-and-tumbles has been nipped in the bud. 'It's the zoo again,' he says, handing me the receiver; 'you're wanted.' The ten-year-old twins, Florence and Isabelle, who have also been engaged in a wrestling match, break off and glance at their mother. They know I'm about to do another disappearing act.

Everybody understands for all that. My wife Michèle, who has worked with me for over ten years, is an animal lover and knows the score. As for my children, they spend too much of their lives with animals – our own cats and dogs as well as the young lions, tigers, cheetahs and monkeys temporarily housed in our garden for convalescence or observation – not to accept that their father has work to do, even on a Sunday.

So what's on the agenda this morning? The lion's tail? That can't wait, certainly. The tiger's jaw? We'll see; I may not have time. The ostrich's wing needs a quick once-over too. So does that little eland with the bloodshot eye and wobbly legs. While we're at it, we ought to make a decision about those two young lions; they're looking worse than ever. Oh yes, and the tigress is still losing weight. All right, spare me the rest, I'm coming. We'll see what we can do.

So much for a typical Sunday morning. Five minutes later I was on my way to the wildlife park at Thoiry. It was only 8.30 a.m. I planned to be back in time for Sunday lunch, the only midday meal I ever have a chance of sharing with my family. Where man and beast are concerned, my job is one in which the former proposes but the latter disposes.

Two men were waiting for me at the lion house. Thoiry's wardens know the temperaments, moods and afflictions of their sixty healthy lions. They are fond of them and treat them so admirably that our work together is an unfailing source of pleasure. We entered the zoo's inner sanctum, the part from which visitors are excluded for their own good as well as that of the inmates. This is where the sick and injured come to be nursed and recuperate, where the incurables die and the neurotics – zoos have them too – are isolated, where lionesses give birth untroubled by the attentions of curious onlookers whose presence may easily scare or provoke them into killing their young.

I began by visiting the largest patients. These were two lions on the verge of adulthood, one male and one female. They were dozing at the back of their cage among the excreta that had accumulated despite regular cleaning because neither animal was assimilating its food. Their tawny coats had almost disappeared, giving them a woefully naked appearance. Their blackish skin was wrinkled and too roomy for their wasted muscles. There was almost nothing leonine about them, except that they still bared their fangs and roared at our approach, halfheartedly but with considerable resonance. Their discoloured and sunken eyes had become almost as black as their skin – the saddest and most dejected orbs imaginable. The male had preserved a residue of mane which made him look even more pitiful than his mate. It was impossible to persuade them to stand by calling or prodding them with a stick; they roared again but refused to stir. I hosed them down to clean them and encourage movement, but it was no good. Before long they closed their eyes and accepted their shower-bath with total resignation. However, they had to be transferred from the restraint cage to make room for the lioness requiring surgery. They roared feebly as the three of us half lifted, half propelled them along with pieces of wood. The lioness eventually managed to stand. She collapsed, then recovered and took one step before flopping back on her mate. He rose on his hindquarters and shuffled along with our poles supporting his weight, forelegs flailing the air. He was more than half paralysed and ataxic.

Could something still be done? The outlook was grim. I

had sometimes saved animals that looked very sick indeed, but these two seemed to be at death's door. We had been treating them for three months, vitamins, tonics, trace elements, extra rations – but to no avail. I was inclined to think that it had something to do with the exceptionally cold and rainy spring. They had suffered more severely from lack of sunshine than the other young lions in the enclosure where they were reared. The remedy? A massive dose of ultra-violet rays, but it was too late for that in their case. So what were we going to do with them? A vet's duty is to preserve life rather than hasten death, but in this instance I felt the two poor creatures should be put out of their misery. However, the final decision rested with the management.

While waiting to be introduced to my next patient, a young lioness, I turned to look at her. She was watching us placidly from a cage adjoining the restraint cage which the other two had just vacated. Her tail had been severed almost flush with her rump, bitten off by another lioness. Although she did not seem to be in pain, the wound was not a pretty sight: a big bloody stump fringed with shreds of flesh, already partly necrosed. The trouble would not cure itself. Unless I operated, gangrene would set in and spread like wildfire.

We transferred the lioness to the restraint cage after cleaning it thoroughly. This was where I would give my patient her anaesthetic injection. She would then be laid out for surgery on a trestle table in the centre aisle.

The mobile partition was adjusted so as to immobilize the lioness as far as possible. She was in excellent health despite her wound and resisted fiercely. To keep her head and jaws away from me, a warden distracted her with a piece of wood which her sharp teeth reduced to splinters. My problem was to insinuate a noose between the bars, imprison one of her forepaws without getting my hands clawed or bitten, and pull it clear of the cage. This was a tricky manoeuvre and had to be repeated several times. Success at last. Two men hauled on the rope and secured it to the bars of a neighbouring cage. The lioness could not withdraw her paw but continued to jerk and shake it, temporarily preventing me from administering an injection.

The first step was to quieten her. I talked to her and gently stroked her paw while one of my assistants continued his diversionary tactics with the piece of wood. The paw relaxed a little. I slipped a rubber tourniquet round it and probed for the vein, half sensing rather than actually feeling it beneath the thick skin. I had to inject by guesswork. Easier said than done. My patient was still busy gnawing the stick, but her head and teeth were perilously close. The other paw was free to lunge at me through the bars. Finally, although the lioness became less restive, she continued to struggle and deafen me with her roars. Injecting an animal under these conditions is a very tricky business, and I couldn't afford to make any mistakes. The anaesthetic was a barbiturate of the thiopental family. If it missed the vein it would cause necrotic phlebitis. This produces a cavity in the flesh and is extremely difficult to cure.

Therefore, my aim had to be perfect. The wardens stood silent and motionless. They knew that nobody must talk to the lioness but me, partly to reassure her but also to help me gain a measure of psychological ascendancy. I inserted the needle into the supposed axis of the vein at a prescribed angle, withdrew it slightly to correct my alignment, then thrust it home and aspirated. Blood streamed into the barrel of the syringe. I was well and truly in the vein and could proceed with the anaesthetic injection.

Twenty seconds passed. The patient went limp, but I saw at once that something was wrong. I put my hand on her chest. Her heart had stopped beating. An overdose? No, apnoea – respiratory failure. I had to work fast.

Hurriedly, we opened the door and heaved the inert 400-pound animal on to the operating table. Her tongue was lolling between her open jaws. Two big tears oozed from her eyes, which were open and motionless – a normal reaction on the part of the lachrymal glands. Every second counted.

Using both hands, I opened the jaws still wider and pulled on the tongue. Meanwhile, my two assistants applied rhythmical pressure to the animal's chest. Air hissed into the two deep bellows and issued noisily from the throat. I manipulated the jaws, alternately opening and releasing them. I brushed an eyelid with my fingers. It reacted: life was still present. All this happened very quickly. Twenty seconds later, breathing recommenced. I too breathed again. Losing a patient on the table would have earned me no medals.

Before long, one paw stirred a little. Now was the time to insure against unwelcome surprises. Additional ropes kept the hindlegs splayed and clear of the wound. I attached the syringe to a forepaw with a reserve of anaesthetic, the needle in the vein, so that I could inject more of the drug if my lioness showed signs of coming round.

I was 'on site' at last. My first job was to cut away all the necrosed tissue, but I had to do more than that or I would not have enough skin to cover the wound.

Circumstances compelled me to take up where the tail-biting lioness had left off; in other words, to remove the little that remained. The root of a lion's tail is conical in shape and firmly implanted in its croup. The first coccygeal vertebrae, which are very substantial, have to support and activate a supple whip measuring a good yard in length and tipped with a tuft of black hair. The tail not only serves as a balancing aid during acrobatic movements but provides a means of expression. Among animals, the tail talks. My patient must have 'spoken' out of turn and metaphorically had her throat cut.

These relatively bulky vertebrae, with their overlapping arrangement and complicated processes, are linked and kept in almost constant motion by muscles, tendons and ligaments which make their amputation a difficult and laborious pro-ceeding. It took me a good hour to detach the two crushed vertebrae neatly, without damage to the remaining articular surfaces, and leave a healthy area behind. Osteomyelitis, or chronic infection of the bone, is hard to treat.

I now had a flap of skin large enough to cover the wound. It only remained for me to bathe it with plenty of water containing a special antiseptic detergent. Next came needle-work. I left an aperture to serve as a drain, swabbed the area once more, and my work was done. Within a few weeks, the lioness would look as if she had been born without a tail. Visitors would be puzzled. So would the other lions, which might present a danger to my youthful patient. Lions detest anything out of the ordinary, so we would have to take care when the time came.

I straightened up, my back aching after an hour and a half's exertions over a table of inadequate height. A group of young lions in the cage on my right, mainly female, snorted as though relieved to witness the end of the operation they had all been watching, nose to bars, from a range of· five or six feet. I recognized a former patient who had been almost as bald two weeks ago as the pair of young lions I had examined before the operation. She looked much better. Her coat had almost regrown and she seemed considerably more cheerful. I clicked my tongue and smacked my lips at her, partly in friendship and partly for relaxation's sake. She received these salutations by clambering over the heads of her companions, who had also crowded closer to the bars.

The cage containing the two moribund lions presented a less cheerful picture. They too were facing their fellow feline, who still lay limp on the table, but they neither snorted nor jostled. They simply stared in an apathetic way that made me wonder what they were thinking – what form their forebodings took. The lioness, who was reclining against her mate's flank, seemed to have revived a little. She licked his shoulder repeatedly as though to comfort him *in extremis,* but he did not react.

In a cage on the left, facing that of the young lionesses and just as close to the operating table, Saphir paced to and fro. I stretched to ease my aching back, and he growled. I raised my arms above my head. He roared and hurled himself at the bars, rising to his full height and thrashing the air with his paws. Poor Saphir was as mad as any deranged member of the human race. Attempts had been made to habituate him to other lions, but he proved wholly unsociable, fighting all comers and spurning the advances of females until the zoo authorities were compelled to put him in a cage by himself. Here he suffered from periodic fits which made him leap around and climb the bars in a truly insane manner. Even his mask had a lopsided look expressive of mental disorder. Saphir was acquired from one of those self-styled zoos that have recently incurred so much criticism in France. This particular establishment had closed down as a result of a television programme presented by Brigitte Bardot. The *Association des Parcs Zoologiques* had undertaken to accommodate all animals from 'zoos' faced with closure, so Saphir had ended up at Thoiry.

Housed not far away was another hapless relic of one of these zoos, a large but rather hump-backed and knock-kneed lioness. Like Saphir, she was condemned to solitude and debarred from the relative freedom enjoyed by the other lionesses in their big enclosure. Being a stranger, she would probably have been killed. Her predicament, no less than

Saphir's, exemplified the difficulties of adapting animals to a new environment or group.

My patient was still sleeping peacefully. Four men lifted the table and carried it to the entrance of her cage. Between us, we hauled the limp body inside. I turned the lioness so that her head faced downhill and she could evacuate saliva without risking suffocation, gave her a farewell pat and wished her a speedy recovery.

Meanwhile, I had been joined by Raoul de la Panouse, one of the zoo's directors. We held a brief discussion in front of the cage containing the two chronic invalids. They watched us, raising their heads a little to draw back their lips and growl feebly. The verdict was unanimous: they were past saving.

A sad but unavoidable business, so the sooner it was over the better. We began with the lioness, who was closer to the restraint cage where the deed would have to be done. Once more we lifted and propelled her along, this time towards her final moments on earth. She mustered unsuspected reserves of strength, clung to the bars and gnawed at them, growling incessantly. She was finally separated from her mate. He growled too, raising his tremulous head without actually focusing on the scene that unfolded beside him. At last we got the lioness wedged and immobilized between the two partition walls. Although she continued to resist, far less effort was needed to haul her paw through the bars than for that of the lioness with the severed tail. On with the tourniquet. I located the vein beneath the black and hairless skin and inserted the needle. The same barbiturate as for the operation, but a much stronger dose laced with a muscle-relaxant. The dying creature would not suffer. Another few seconds and it was over. Everybody looked relieved.

We removed her from the cage and hauled her aside under the gaze of Saphir, who, sane or insane, appeared unsurprised by the spectacle. And yet . . . One of my assistants called out 'Look!' Sprawled on her flank with her tongue lolling, the lioness had preserved a flicker of life. The heart continued to beat – visibly – beneath the ribs protruding from the wrinkled black skin. Though seemingly at death's door, she had resisted a massive dose of barbiturate.

She was still alive but as good as dead. Turning to her mate, we propelled him towards the restraint cage. The lion was bigger and heavier than the lioness. He roared but put up less of a fight. He even succeeded in raising his hindquarters and taking a couple of steps. His uncoordinated and ataxic movements almost suggested that he was cooperating in the belief that further resistance would be futile and undignified. It proved unnecessary to put him right inside the cage with the mobile partition. He surrendered his paw to the noose with little or no resistance. I felt for the vein. No roars; not even a growl. He rested his head against the bars. His eyes were closed when he received the *coup de grâce*, whereas those of his mate had remained wide with terror to the last. He did not open them again. The nervous and muscular collapse of death was even less perceptible in his case than in that of the lioness. He had already given up.

I still had to gain a rather more precise idea of what killed the animals, for the lethal injections had only stolen a brief march on nature. I had to ascertain whether my theory about their physical deterioration was correct or whether it stemmed from something more localized, for example, an infestation of parasites. Autopsies are regularly performed when animals die because their cause of death may provide pointers to the protection of the living.

The young lioness's heart was still beating. A second injection arrested it for good. I examined her carcass first. Thorough scrutiny of her vital organs yielded nothing – no obvious infestations or lesions of any significance. My original hypothesis still stood: the two animals had been inadequately equipped for life by their genetic antecedents. Without the care of man, they would probably have died much sooner.

I stripped off my rubber gloves. The young females in the next cage had again followed the entire operation, their muzzles pressed against the bars and their plump paws dangling over the edge. How full of life they looked, and how richly they deserved every care, if only because of the vital spark within them! I couldn't resist going over and giving them a little pat on the paws. Much excitement, frolicking and jostling.

Were they saddened by the sight of the two inanimate carcasses? Not that I could see; they appeared quite indifferent. Were they aware of death at all? Who could tell?

Enough of the lions' house for one morning. I made my way back past Saphir, who growled at me, and the big hump-backed lioness, who was asleep. A little farther on I came to the maternity wing; three lionesses, each in a separate cage with her young. Two of the litters were feeding. In the third cage, some slightly older cubs were chewing their mother's tail and scuffling with ferocious squeaks. The lioness patiently endured their attentions. Up on the corrugated roof of transparent plastic a bird was pecking at something unidentifiable in a ray of sunlight, making a noise like a pneumatic drill. In the midst of life . . . It was nearly midday. I was growing hungry, but the tigers were waiting, not to mention the ostrich with the broken wing.

The ostrich enclosure was on the way to that of the tigers. My patient had been shut up as an aid to convalescence, unlike her free-ranging companions. For some weeks, one of them had insisted on mounting guard in front of the lion enclosure and charging anyone who left his car inside the fence, in other words, any member of the staff. A strange whim, but there was no way of reasoning with the bird or intimidating it. It charged with a haughty and – in our eyes – idiotic expression, leaving us with no choice but to dive into the car and slam the door in its face.

The injured ostrich was a more timid type. We let her out of her pen and into a yard where we could observe her at our leisure. She circled the yard at a run. The plaster encasing her broken wing was in good condition. I felt rather pleased with my handiwork. The wing had been immobilized against the thorax, which was fully enclosed by a plaster cast that picked out the ostrich's breastbone and stressed her elegant lines. My patient was mystified by our visit and took fright, as though stalked by hunters. In the end she lay down and huddled against the yard door. We entered by another door, intending to lead her back into her pen. Now that we were almost within arm's reach, however, the bird decided to ignore our presence in the belief that she was perfectly concealed. We decided to leave her in peace.

On to the tiger enclosure, which was half a mile from the ostrich house. Here I was confronted by two grave problems, in other words, matters of life and death. One related to a Siberian tigress and her young, the other to a big Siberian male named Bouboule.

The tigress had recently given birth to four cubs. One of them, a female, was injured when a door accidentally closed on her left forepaw, causing a double fracture. I had operated to insert a pin in the foreleg. The danger in such cases is that a mother will reject her offspring or try to remove all traces of an operation by nibbling and licking the wound. I had been duly careful to suture the skin from the inside so that no stitches protruded. I also dispensed with a dressing and ensured that the cub was returned to her mother the same day.

Despite all these precautions, my worst fears were realized: the tigress rejected her cub. The little creature whimpered, rolled on its back and made repeated attempts to suck, but in vain: the mother pawed it roughly aside. She would undoubtedly have killed it if they had not been separated. For three days the warden in charge of Thoiry's tigers re-introduced the cub to its mother, but her reception of it became progressively more hostile. In desperation, I had taken it home.

No sooner had this problem been temporarily solved than another reared its head. The mother was losing weight. She had turned melancholy and was devoting less care to her young. She prowled the wire mesh separating her from the four males in the enclosure beyond her cage, indifferent to her offspring, or sprawled on her side with muffled growls of boredom. What was her trouble? We debated the problem. According to one school of thought, the trouble stemmed from a premature recurrence of oestrus, or heat. If so, she had to be put back in the males' enclosure or she would pine away and endanger her own life as well as that of her young.

I did not endorse this diagnosis. The tigress might have experienced a certain increase of oestrogen, which would account for her lovesick behaviour and loss of appetite, but I strongly doubted if ovulation had taken place and she was genuinely fertile. This phenomenon would not normally have occurred at the present stage. Still, we could try putting her back with the males and see what happened.

At once a new difficulty loomed. Mate the tigress by all means, but how, and with whom? Putting the mother and her litter in the big enclosure with the four males might provoke fights between the latter and prove fatal to the cubs. Installing the mother and her offspring in a separate enclosure with a single male would be just as risky from the cubs' point of view. Which male, anyway? The gentlest and least likely to harm the baby tigers was Bouboule, the injured Siberian. But what would happen after the mating, when he rejoined the others? Already something of a target for their bullying, he would inevitably be killed.

We continued our conference outside the mother's enclosure. She watched us, lying on her side with her nose against the mesh. From time to time she emitted the sort of lip-flutter with which tigers express friendship, rather as domestic cats do when purring. Quite close to us inside their wire mesh enclosure, the four Siberian males had ambled up in quest of diversion. I purred at them and passed a few friendly remarks. They returned my greeting by rubbing their heads against the wire and fluttering their lips.

Finally, I recommended putting the mother and her cubs with the strongest male. The design of the tiger enclosure, which could be divided into two sections, made it possible to separate them from the others.

Next day the female and her young were introduced to the male. Irritable and impatient as he was, he did the cubs no harm. However, his equal reluctance to touch the tigress confirmed that she was not genuinely in season.

Now for a look at Bouboule. Hidden in the ruff on the left side of his lower jaw was a wound that refused to heal. Should I intervene or let nature take its course? The first step was to try and discover the exact nature of the injury. There was no question of lifting the ruff for a closer look, of course, so my preliminary examination had to be carried out by subterfuge.

The idea was to lure Bouboule close to the wire netting and induce him to pace slowly along it. How? With the help of a dog. We had one handy: Icare, a black-and-tan Beauceron belonging to Thibault d'Orléans, a son of the Comte de Paris.

Like any dog, however big and strong, Icare was terrified of tigers and ignored a preliminary summons to approach the fence. He clamped his tail between his legs, so Raoul had to use a little friendly persuasion. The tigers, who were ambling along some distance away, galloped up at once with Bouboule timidly following in their wake. Icare looked browbeaten but finally obeyed his adoptive master, whom he trusted implicitly. All we had to do now was walk the dog along the fence in a direction that would enable me to examine Bouboule's wound. Highly intrigued, the tigers accompanied us on our stroll in single file, jockeying for position. Bouboule brought up the rear.

My preliminary examination proved inconclusive. All I could tell from this closer inspection of Bouboule's bloodstained ruff was that the wound might well be serious. So was his position in the tiger community. His injury was weakening him. The others were bullying him and stealing his food, which he no longer dared to defend. The more his timidity increased, the more exposed he became to maltreatment by his own kind. Sooner or later they would kill him. The tigers of the jungle are solitary, unlike lions. In captivity they may some day adapt to communal living, but the game is far from won. In any case, Bouboule's recovery was an essential condition of his survival within the group.

I had to try to examine Bouboule at even closer quarters. We coaxed him into his cage inside the tiger house, and I entered the cage next door. Good boy! He sat down on the floor of the cage, right up against the bars that separated us, as if anxious to make my work easier. I squatted on my heels and stroked his whiskers with a stick. He didn't object, just opened his jaws and gave the stick a gentle bite or two. This gave me time in which to inspect his teeth. They looked sound enough, so the wound could not be attributed to a dental abscess. I lifted his ruff with my stick but could see nothing, even though he offered no resistance. I spoke to him and he fluttered his lips. Bouboule was genuinely docile. I sent for a hose and sluiced the affected jaw. Although I could see no more than I had before, the shower would at least do something to clean the wound. Still stoical in his suffering, Bouboule did not bother to rise and evade the jet of water. He drank a little, turned away and closed his eyes. Eventually he retired to another part of the cage and presented his back to us. I was little the wiser, yet the infection would only grow worse if left untreated. Two days later I returned to examine Bouboule under a general anaesthetic and, if need be, operate. Bouboule was suffering from an infected bite in the masseter, or masticatory muscle. I lanced and disinfected it, and it healed without trouble. Lying in his cage three days after this operation Bouboule licked my hand through the bars. A few weeks later his behaviour within the group was noticeably more stable. The others had stopped attacking him.

What time was it? 3 p.m. My wife and children – my Sunday lunch! There were still the elands, but they could wait till tomorrow. High time to head for home.

A storm was brewing back home in Garches. Mimine, the rejected baby tigress with the fractured leg, had been playing up and making messes, and my animal-lover of a wife was beginning to lose patience. I promised her it was only a question of a few more days – just long enough to get Mimine fit again. The only solution for the moment was to keep her at home with us. Where better? She had plenty of company: the two Pekingese, the Burmese cat, the poodle that didn't like human beings but had no objection to baby tigresses, and, last but not least, Rinka, the big Alsatian bitch that had promptly adopted the newcomer as her own.

This was lucky for the tiger cub. Responding at once to the bitch's advances, Mimine had installed herself between Rinka's paws, where she purred affectionately and butted her from below. For her part, Rinka licked and groomed Mimine without being in the least put off by the cub's emaciation, dull coat and tinea – all of them conditions that had beset her since she was rejected by her mother.

No sooner was I home than I had to treat her. It was time for Mimine's tinea tablets. I had to get six down her, which was easier said than done. The whole family assembled in the kitchen. So, attracted by the rumpus, did the rest of the animals. The little tigress squirmed on the tiles, squawling, spitting and snarling in her usual fashion. It was all the three of us – Michèle, Jean-François and I – could do to hold her down and open her mouth. I got my way in the end, but I could only induce her to swallow the tablets by thrusting them down her throat, one by one, with a pencil.

Mimine was a real she-devil. She still had her milk teeth, being less than three months old, but they were needle-sharp and she used them as spiritedly as she wielded her big paws with their fast-developing claws. These were one of the causes of Michèle's bad temper, for Michèle was still smarting from a minor act of spite inflicted on her before my arrival.

Young, cheerful and well disposed towards animals, Michèle invariably wins their affection. Mimine, however, had yet to fall under her spell. A little while earlier she had been stretched out on the kitchen tiles surrounded by all the other animals, unenthusiastically chewing one of the four or five lumps of meat she should have devoured with relish. She made no move when her Alsatian foster mother snatched one piece away, nor when the timid poodle robbed her of another. She merely closed her eyes when cuffed by the Burmese cat, who took the liberty of gnawing the piece she

24

had already started on. She didn't even retaliate when the two Pekingese came and abstracted their own tithe from her meal, but my wife had only to pass within arm's reach – innocent, one assumes, of any designs on Mimine's raw steak – for her to lash out and draw blood from the nearest leg. Even the most confirmed animal-lover may be forgiven for an outburst of temper under such circumstances. Mimine was well aware of the mood she had provoked, and this was no doubt one of the reasons for her unpleasant behaviour while I was administering the pills. For all our efforts to rekindle her love of life, and despite the maternal affection bestowed on her by Rinka, we failed to save her. Melancholia, coupled with the ailments that ensued on her mother's rejection of her, carried Mimine off a few weeks later. Any relief we may have felt was far outweighed by our sorrow at her passing.

Mimine was not the first to give us trouble in the kitchen, the garden or even in our bedroom, to which right of access is regularly claimed by lion and tiger cubs as well as dogs and cats. Frida, a young but already sizeable tigress, escaped from the garden one day. We searched for her everywhere, but in vain. In the end, I toured the neighbourhood warning people not to be alarmed or call the police if the animal turned up: I would deal with it myself.

Just before five next morning I received a telephone call from my next-door neighbour. He thought my 'cat' was holed up in a hedge and had heard it 'miaow'. I took a torch and went to look, still in my pyjamas. Frida was almost as invisible as she would have been in the jungle. Grabbing her by the tail, I hauled her backwards through the dense undergrowth and into our garden. She was too terrified to put up a serious struggle. Once inside the garden she yielded to a few well-chosen words of persuasion and consented to return to the room which served as her quarters at night.

But the most memorable wild animal in our home was Sacha, the lion. Sacha was the fourth and smallest cub of a lioness I had cured of toxaemia. He was also the runt of the litter, in other words, a surplus cub which the mother instinctively rejects because of its vulnerability and small size. In this case the mother had pushed him out of the cage with her paw, and he had fallen into the gutter below.

My wife retrieved Sacha, more dead than alive, and decided to try to save him. The same day – it was 14 July, the national holiday – she wrapped him up in cotton wool like a premature human baby and bore him off to our Mediterranean vacation home. There he received intensive care with a drip* of dextrose and amino-acids in the jugular. To convey the extent of the nursing required, I should point out that each infusion took an hour, that the young lion had to be watched every minute of that time, and that the process had to be repeated three times a day.

The whole household was on duty, including my wife, my mother-in-law and Jean-François, who was then about eight. This regimen continued for ten days, but it did not end there. From the third day, the drip was supplemented with artificial feeding. Six times a day, as in the case of bottle feeding, a tube had to be introduced into Sacha's little stomach to dispense cow's milk enriched with elements giving it the same formula as carnivore's milk. All in all, nursing the cub called for nine separate operations daily, and Michèle who shared them with me on a fifty-fifty basis, miraculously contrived to maintain her hectic schedule as a dedicated mother of three who looked after her children, played and swam with them, and single-handedly ran a home into the bargain. The true animal-lover must not only like animals but be ready to take on the full responsibility for them.

The outlook remained dubious in spite of our efforts. Sacha was so miserable that even Rinka, the bitch we hoped would foster him as she had already fostered numerous young animals, declined to cooperate. We were compelled to perform the equivalent of the first maternal task: licking. This is at once a caress, a form of contact and reassurance, a hygienic and sanitary measure, and an aid to defecation. In the latter instance, a finger dipped in oil applies gentle pressure to the anus with slow circular movements imitative of the maternal licking that induces a motion and subsequently cleans it away. Sacha started out with severe diarrhoea and became toxic. In short, his life hung in the balance for a fortnight.

My children watched over him anxiously. My son kept him clean with cotton wool. Before long our perseverance and patience and the love of the entire family brought results. The diarrhoea ceased. Rinka began to take an interest in Sacha,

* A drip, or perfusion, is the method of administering fluids and essential substances, such as salt or dextrose, intravenously – drop by drop – to establish normal blood pressure etc.

sniffing and licking the little creature, and Sacha instinctively realized that he had found a new mother. We fed him with a dropper, then with a bottle.

Brigitte Bardot, who visited us late in July, helped the convalescent by giving him a bottle of milk. Whether or not he appreciated this signal honour, he continued to improve, and by the time we left Porte-des-Issambres at the end of August he was a healthy young lion cub. While waiting for the train we dined at the station restaurant, where everyone admired him and spoiled us on his account. I shared a sleeper with Jean-François and Sacha, who slept in my son's arms. Calls of nature presented no problem because he was already clean at night. Next morning he was regaled with a bottle heated by the sleeping-car attendant.

Under the guidance of Rinka, his adoptive mother, Sacha took possession of the house and garden at Garches. He decided to relieve himself on the front steps the very first day. Although this remained his favourite spot until the day he left us, he once forgot himself so far as to make a puddle in one of our drawing room armchairs. He was five months old by this time, and growing big and strong. My wife decreed that he should henceforth sleep outside with Rinka, whose kennel was large enough for both of them, but Sacha disagreed. As soon as he grasped that his house privileges had been withdrawn he started to cry.

I know of no more heart-rending sound than the groans and roars of a young lion which has picked up some of the vocal characteristics of its canine foster mother. Unable to endure it any longer, I got out of bed and crouched in Rinka's kennel, trying to console Sacha and reconcile him to his fate. It was December by this time, and my ministrations lasted a good hour. Sacha finally calmed down and buried his nose in Rinka's fur like a puppy, although he was already bigger than her. His former sleeping quarters had been our bedroom – preferably our bed itself. It would have been beneath his dignity to sleep on the tiled floor of the kitchen. He might aptly have been called an eiderdown lion.

Sacha worshipped Michèle, who had, in a sense, restored him to life. His great game was to rise on his hindquarters and clasp her from behind. Michèle, with Sacha's big fat paws encircling her waist or chest, had only to say 'No claws, Sacha!' and he would retract them at once, though they were already sizeable and his fond exuberance was such that he tended to play with them out like any affectionate cat. Ordered to restrain his playfulness, he butted his mistress in the back with his muzzle, causing her blouse to ride up and enabling him to caress her delicate skin with a tongue rougher than sandpaper. She then had no alternative but to disengage herself, gently but in haste.

Before Sacha's arrival and during the early months of his stay with us, we also had to cope with the whims of a young female chimpanzee named Charlotte. I had been landed with her when she was three months old and very sick. The same old story: a self-styled animal-lover who had thought how nice it would be to keep a little ape but soon grew tired of the creature and couldn't wait to get rid of it.

At that age a little ape is far more demanding than a lion cub or even a human baby. It can only survive in contact with its mother. Unless it can cuddle her the whole time, it pines away and dies. Michèle consequently spent her entire day, whether at home, at the clinic, or visiting friends, with the chimp clinging to her hip or thigh. Piercing cries were the immediate consequence of any attempt to put Charlotte down. At night she slept on the eiderdown, nestling against a foot or leg. If she grew fretful, as she sometimes did, we had to soothe her by stroking her head or foot.

Charlotte had been bottle-reared like a baby. She started with nine feeds a day and graduated to six, and each bottle meant a change of diapers. Michèle drew on the stock left over from our twins. Charlotte was genuinely like a fourth addition to the family. She wore the children's cast-off pullovers and jeans, took her bath with the twins and soon learned to eat at table with us.

Like the other animals of the house, Charlotte had a passion for her mistress. Michèle treated her firmly, giving her the occasional smack and tweaking her ears. A chimpanzee's affection for a human being is inseparable from respect. Charlotte was far less attached to my sister-in-law, who erred on the indulgent side, and would sometimes try to bite her.

Charlotte learned how to use a spoon and fork with alacrity. Although there were still times when she tried to dip her hand in her plate, she would glance at Michèle and quickly pick up her fork again.

Sometimes she was punished. 'You shan't eat with us tonight,' my wife would say, 'you've been too much of a nuisance'. Charlotte's response was to seek my help. She would jump on to my lap, seize my fork and start eating from my plate as a token of goodwill.

She played boisterous games in the garden with the other animals, though she did have a tendency to use our two Pekingese as balls and throw them into the air, which they much disliked. On other occasions she thought she was in the jungle. She would race upstairs, grab one of the curtains and – to the huge delight of our children – launch herself into space. The curtains gave way, one after the other, as a result of being mistaken for tropical creepers, and Michèle soon stopped replacing them.

Charlotte lived with us for nearly two years, happily and in good health. She was still quite small – chimpanzees take a decade to reach maturity – but extremely venturesome and not easily intimidated. Sacha soon found that out.

One day, Michèle was sitting in the kitchen with Charlotte comfortably installed on her lap. Sacha, now five months old, ambled lazily in with friendly intent. The big lion cub was used to Charlotte, with whom he had lived almost since birth, though he treated her with greater reserve than his playmates the dogs. This time, seeing the chimp on the lap of his beloved mistress, he began by showing a remarkable degree of tolerance. He sniffed the hairy little thigh on a level with his nose and licked it. He gave it another lick, and another.

Although Sacha was no stranger, Charlotte took fright and cowered against Michèle. Still good-humouredly, Sacha continued to lick her thigh. Then as though in quest of an even closer understanding he took it in his jaws. Whether or not he squeezed a little, this was too much for the chimpanzee. She leaped up and stood there on my wife's lap, fur bristling and chest distended – a very impressive performance, even in a little ape. Finally, with a scream of fury, she sprang at Sacha's head.

The lion was terrified by this bold and instantaneous response. He ran off, yowling, and sought refuge – as he often did – between the paws of Rinka, the foster mother whom he had now outgrown, while Charlotte triumphantly resumed her favourite place on Michèle's lap.

But Sacha, although he behaved like a clumsy kitten, grew

and grew. At seven months he still found it natural to jump on the kitchen table and sweep things aside with his paw so as to make room for himself. By this time, he was so big that two swipes of his paw were enough to clear the entire table. We kept asking ourselves how much longer it could go on.

Sacha was the most human of lions – a lion that had never seen another wild animal in his life, having been pushed out of the cage with his eyes still closed – but he was becoming a nuisance and even a source of alarm. However much he tried to model his growls on those of his 'mother', the Alsatian bitch, he would sometimes bare his already sizeable teeth and give vent to a roar which, though doubtless innocent of malice, was nonetheless awe-inspiring. My children had never teased him. They adored him, but we could all see that he was becoming difficult and dangerous. Isabelle and Florence were obliged to protect themselves with a large dustbin lid when Sacha playfully chased and upended them. The time had come to say goodbye. Sacha's future lay with others of his kind.

It was an epic departure. A truck came to Garches to collect him, and the transfer should – in theory – have gone without a hitch. The truck contained a cage; Sacha would be lured inside, QED. Unfortunately, matters proved to be less simple.

The truck drew up in the road beyond the garden gate. The door was opened by the man in charge of the operation, an animal trainer, assisted by his wife. Michèle headed for the garden gate with Rinka. Full of curiosity, Sacha followed. Rinka was encouraged to enter the truck, which she readily did. Some pieces of meat had been placed on the floor, and Rinka started wolfing them. Sacha was standing with his paws inside the door, eager as usual to follow his foster mother's example, but the door had not been opened wide enough to admit his broad shoulders – the first false move – and he could not get in. Besides, something seemed to be troubling him. With the help of the trainer, who was carrying a stick, Michèle gently tried to push him. Looking genuinely angry for the first time ever, Sacha turned on her with a roar. She and the trainer stepped back and Sacha escaped into the street.

He had been scared – doubly scared by another two false moves. Standing with his forepaws on the floor of the truck, ready to jump inside and take his cue from Rinka, he had suddenly caught a whiff of something unwonted and alarming:

the smell of lion. The truck was, in fact, carrying another lion. Although some bales of straw separated its cage from the one destined for occupation by Sacha, they concealed the animal from view without masking its scent. The smell did not alarm Rinka, who lived with a lion. Sacha, who was still more of a dog – and a humanized dog – than a feline predator, found it terrifying. One whiff was enough to make him turn tail.

Finally, there was the trainer's stick. Sacha had never before been threatened or prodded with a stick. To him, sticks were playthings. He chased and retrieved them like his canine foster mother. Now, for the first time, a stick had assumed a sinister significance. For the first time, Sacha was entering the vicious circle compounded of fear and aggression.

Michèle, who had promptly set off in pursuit, managed to catch Sacha by the tail. She talked to him and asked him to come home like a good boy. Sacha merely snarled and refused. He continued on his way, towing Michèle behind him. Still clinging to the lion's tail, she trotted along for quite a distance. Fortunately, the roads around my home are very quiet. The few observers of this strange spectacle quickly made themselves scarce.

Sacha finally consented to return. Another attempt was made to get him aboard, this time with the rear of the truck flush against the gate to prevent another escape. No luck. Sacha was growing more and more irritable and the trainer more and more perturbed.

I was not present at this embarkation attempt, which should have gone smoothly, and it was late afternoon before I reached the scene. Meanwhile, alerted by my wife, I had sent for a small travelling cage, which we placed in the road about twenty yards from the truck. I filled Sacha's bottle with milk – he was still devoted to it, even at eight months – and used it to lure him inside. I bolted the cage without more ado and we lifted him into the truck. Sacha, whose only desire was for human society, departed for good.

He had the utmost difficulty in accustoming himself to a lion's existence. I was then associated with a wildlife park at Fréjus, in the South of France, which seemed to offer him the prospect of a good home, but he had some distressing frustrations to overcome before he settled down. The first stemmed from a belief that he had caught sight of Rinka on the other side of his wire fence. He flung himself at it, roaring and wailing with despair. It was not Rinka but her daughter Popie, a bitch belonging to my brother-in-law, Robert Bruneliere, who was assisting me at the park. Popie was terrified and scampered off with her tail between her legs.

Sacha's hopes revived once more when my brother-in-law and his wife, Marie-José, entered the enclosure to bid him good day – not really such a rash thing to do because Sacha was still a very youthful lion. My sister-in-law was wearing the same scent as my wife. At once, Sacha leaped at her and hugged her. Once he realized that she was not his beloved he backed off and gave a menacing growl. Robert and Marie-José had to beat a hasty retreat.

Sacha had just completed a new stage in his leonine education. Would he show hostility to dogs and human beings from now on? As if he felt that life under these conditions was not worth living, he began to pine and refuse food.

In response to an SOS, I set off for Fréjus at once. I spent a long time talking to Sacha and fondling him. I also installed Cora, a lioness of the same age, in his enclosure to keep him company, but to small avail. Cora simply devoured her companion's rations as well as her own. Emaciated and ill groomed, Sacha made little attempt to stop her and continued to go downhill.

Now it was my wife's turn to make the trip to Fréjus. She approached the fence and called Sacha's name. The lion froze. 'What is it, my pussy cat? Are you missing your bottle?' Not a muscle moved. Had he forgotten everything? Had he rejected his human ties? Had he become a true lion at last?

Next day, another visit. 'It's me, Sacha. Don't you remember?' This time the living statue became a living projectile. Sacha leaped at the fence with roars of excitement. He galloped off and returned in three great bounds. He clung to the wire and rolled around in an absolute ecstasy of affection. Of course he remembered; lions have long memories. The shock of their first reunion had literally paralysed him.

Sacha regained his appetite within hours. Now a large and handsome male, he lives at Peaugres, near Annonay. Although he has never really accepted the society of his own kind, Michèle refuses to see him again. That last visit to a friend she was forced to abandon after saving his life proved equally distressing to both parties. There would always be some kind of barrier between them, so why pretend otherwise? It was better to make a clean break.

Should we have left Sacha to die in the gutter where his mother had left him? This is a valid question, and one that arises every time human beings rear a wild creature or any animal from which they must one day take their leave because it has grown too large or dangerous. Where Sacha is concerned, I saved him with my family's help because I am on the side of life rather than death.

As to his future, I am satisfied that we have secured it to the best of our ability. Although Sacha could only have lived out his natural existence as king of the beasts in the savanna of Africa, he will at least have led a worthwhile life. What is reprehensible is the irresponsibility of those who adopt a young animal and then get rid of it, no matter how, when it grows up. Fortunately, the field of human-animal relations is favoured with more responsible people than one might think, and sometimes with individuals whose nobility of character far transcends the norm.

The wild animal and the human being occasionally develop a love and affection that surpasses the ties between house pets and their owners. Speaking for myself, I am very attached to my cats and dogs, but I have to acknowledge that our relations with Sacha attained an even greater intensity.

There are always wild animals in my life, not to mention my garden, where four-legged lodgers spend weeks or months devastating the rose beds in company with our cats and dogs. I have a recurrent dream of re-creating that Eden where man, lion and gazelle dwell in peace and speak the same language. I suspect that years ago this dream was a real factor in my choice of profession. Other factors were more earthbound but nonetheless significant, like my brush with some chickens in 1940 at the start of the German occupation. That incident occurred in a context so dramatic that it was destined to play a more important role in my life than circumstances seemed to warrant.

2

From Submachine-gun to Syringe

What made me a veterinary surgeon and an animal conservationist? First and foremost, two hundred chickens and the fact that I was at a loose end.

I ended by recognizing that I had a vocation too, of course, but that took time. My vocation took root, not without difficulty, in my personal and social background. I was the baby of the family. One of my brothers, Jean, is fifteen years my senior and was already married, qualified and practising medicine in Paris by the time I reached adolescence. He has always been the spreading oak whose branches shelter me in stormy weather.

Another of my brothers is a chemist and one of my uncles a dentist. Finally, I come of Jewish stock.

I discovered during my childhood that, to some people, Jews were a pet aversion. This discovery prompted all kinds of rebellious behaviour from fighting at school to wielding a submachine-gun in the Resistance. Now that I confine myself to the lancet and syringe, I wonder if protectiveness towards animals was not another form of protest. I think that in some measure I strove to treat animals like human beings by shielding them from cruelty, contempt and indifference because some people were inhuman enough to treat their own kind like animals or worse. Protecting animals may thus have become equated in my mind with the protection of man.

But in 1940, when my brush with the chickens occurred, I had no particular interest in animals and absolutely no thought of becoming a vet. Being good at maths and physics, I planned to attend the air force academy and satisfy my hankering for a life of action and adventure by becoming a pilot. I had passed the first part of my university entrance examination and was studying for the second part in Paris when everyone's plans were disrupted by the German offensive of May 1940. Together with numerous other evacuees, I and my family sought refuge at Vic-Fezansac, a small village in the Department of Gers, north of the Pyrenees.

I was nineteen. I had been temporarily reprieved from academic drudgery, only to be burdened with serious worries of a different kind. I had been in school at Bernay in Normandy when the Germans made their breakthrough at Sedan. Mounting my little *pétrolette*, I rode it to the hospital at Alençon, where my brother Jean was assigned as a medical officer, to ask what to do. We discussed the future, of which I took a gloomy view: if the Germans won the Jews would be massacred. My brother, who still regarded me as a little boy, slapped my face. How dared I say such a thing? What about the Maginot Line and our armies? What about France?

I set off again on my motorcycle. Jean remained in Alençon to the end, helping to evacuate the hospital. The last to leave the station when the Stukas and Heinkels bombed it, he was hit in the spine and sustained two lumbar fractures. My pessimism seemed justified. Even in our temporary refuge in the south, the position – especially for Jews like us – had become precarious in the extreme.

But the weather was glorious and a holiday atmosphere reigned in spite of everything. I was in direct contact with the countryside. I had nothing much to do but a little swotting for my *baccalauréat* in case the examinations were ever held, which seemed unlikely. And so, telling myself that any future I might have would necessarily be spent in a rural environment, I roamed the byways round Vic. In the prevailing mood of universal anxiety, I felt that true peace, security and humanity could only be found on the modest farms which I visited to buy food for my family.

Thus it was that one day, going in search of milk and eggs, I made the acquaintance of Mario, an Italian tenant farmer. Mario did a little market gardening and a little vine growing, kept four cows and owned about two hundred chickens which had the run of the farmyard. I soon discovered that he was the scion of a monumental immigrant family. He had no less than twenty-two brothers and sisters, some of whom were also local tenant farmers, paying rent in kind. Mario was a very decent fellow. He never refused to sell to refugees and made no attempt to exploit them. He could not, however, supply as many eggs as he would have wished because his hens were sick and dying. What of? He had no idea. He would have consulted the vet, but the local man had been taken prisoner and there was no replacement. Consequently, his hens went on dying.

I took an interest in the matter, less from any love of chickens than because I liked Mario. There is no doubt that I was also prompted by a sense of curiosity, a spirit of initiative and a fondness for tinkering with things. My tendency has always been to look for the remedy or solution to a problem, so I wanted to discover what was going on inside the creatures and put it right.

Having learned to strip rabbits and poultry for the pot since our exodus, a job which other members of the family detested, I was at least partially equipped to perform an operation for which nothing in my childhood or adolescence had prepared me but which now seemed essential. I removed one of the dying hens from the farmyard and essayed a kind of autopsy.

Mario's interest in the hens had been revived by my own and he cooperated with alacrity. He treated me like a serious-minded and well-meaning lad, not a young city slicker playing at being a doctor. We soon discovered that the cause of the trouble was something he remembered hearing about in the past: tracheal worms. These feed on the bird's blood, causing severe coughing, choking, infection of the respiratory tracts, and – in many cases – death.

All that remained was to discover a cure and apply it. After making inquiries on all sides, I got hold of a back number of an agricultural journal which dealt with diseases in poultry and, more specifically, with the one that was killing Mario's hens. It was a very commonplace infection called gapeworm. As for the treatment, details of this were also supplied. It consisted of disinfecting the premises, administering intratracheal injections and putting a vermifuge in the hens' drinking water.

It was a laborious and tiring business, but I felt no inclination to give up. The prospect of beating the disease and helping Mario stimulated me. Disinfection was a big enough job in itself. Townee and peasant, we tackled it side by side. After scattering ferrous sulphate over the entire surface of the contaminated area, or nearly half an acre of farmyard, we turned the surface with spade, hoe, and, in places, pick-axe, to bury the hens' droppings, sprinkled the yard again and then levelled it with a roller.

Although it may have been less tiring, the second part of the operation was trickier. This meant giving every hen and chick an injection of carbon tetrachloride in the trachea, or windpipe. I had never administered an injection nor ever dreamed of doing so, even when playing doctors and nurses as a child – swapping punches was more in my line. However, since injections were the way to put things right, inject I must.

I bought a syringe and the requisite chemicals. I carefully re-read the article in my agricultural journal, which gave the proper dosages and described the method of treatment. Then, with Mario's help, I tackled my first patient. I was scared stiff and would have kicked myself if I had killed the bird, which was a white hen. Mario imprisoned its wings in one hand and held the neck fully extended with the other. I had to inject into the trachea itself, between two rings and as close as possible to the larynx. The needle had to be inserted at a certain angle, then adjusted slightly. This was an expert's job in itself, but I aimed with care and pushed the needle in. Aspirating a little, I found that air flowed freely into the barrel of the syringe, which proved that I was well and truly in the windpipe. I expelled the fluid. Would the hen drop dead? No, she spluttered with indignation behind the netting where Mario had deposited her and soon started coughing violently. This was the predicted result. Anaesthetized by the injection, the worms had become detached from the lining of the trachea. As if she had swallowed the wrong way, the hen was hawking and expelling them.

There was nothing for it but to press on. After treating a few more adults, I set to work on the chicks. This was far harder. Week-old chicks have a very soft windpipe which must be visually located through the skin. The other essential is to inject a suitable dose. Too little and the chemical fails to act sufficiently; too much and you drown the chick by filling its lungs.

Counting hens and chicks, Michel Klein the would-be aviator stuck his needle into about two hundred windpipes. Mario and I devoted several days to the job. The outcome? Highly satisfactory. A few more hens died, but not as a result of my treatment. The vast majority of the ailing birds re-covered. Although we were not in a peak laying season they resumed their labours with some enthusiasm. Mario was most appreciative. I had helped to save his poultry with no motive other than the pleasure it gave me to save the creatures. I had made a friend at the same time. Some months later I attended one of his Mama's grand reunions and was the only outsider present.

True, my minor victory over the parasitical invaders of Mario's poultry was a mere drop in the ocean of defeat which engulfed our country that summer. Oppressed by the worries that afflicted everyone and my family in particular, I attached no more importance to it than it deserved. By working with Mario and getting to know his brothers and sisters in the neighbourhood, I developed a lively interest in farms and their animal inhabitants. Many young urban holidaymakers have said the same, of course, but how many actually put their hand to a pitchfork or splash around in liquid manure? It was not all hot air in my own case. Like everyone at this period, I yearned for security and a return to the land, but I quickly transformed that yearning into action: I became genuinely peasant in spirit. The results were soon apparent.

Circumstances notwithstanding, a *baccalauréat* examination was held that autumn at Toulouse. I safely passed the second part. What to do now? The air force academy was out, of course, so a friend of the family made another suggestion. Why not apply for admission to the veterinary college at Toulouse?

Veterinary college. Horses, cattle and pigs, cowsheds and stables. Well, why not? I had always enjoyed physics and chemistry. I had just discovered a taste for country life and I was good with my hands. Impelled by a kind of instinct for self-preservation, I was growing more and more convinced of my need for close contact with nature. Very well, I would study to become a vet.

For some months I concentrated on learning my trade at the college in Toulouse. This was still the era of the cart and plough-horse. We were often taken to the tow-horse school on the Canal du Midi, where many animals developed 'grease', or seborrhoea of the foot. Theoretical and practical instruction at the college centred on calves and cows, the animals which at that time constituted the basis of the rural economy, but on one occasion a circus brought us a sick lion cub. Its coat was patchy and redder than it should have been. It was also thin and walked with difficulty. I did not treat it myself and had no inkling that lions would some day loom so large in my life.

I felt at ease with animals. Their complaints did not turn my stomach. As often as I could, I went to visit my friend Mario and his numerous brothers and sisters. Being a veterinary student, I made myself useful by helping to tend their animals. I also became friendly with Pierrot, the son of the rope and twine dealer who lived opposite us in Vic. He chattered to me and took an interest in my doings. Pierrot could only have been eight or ten at the time, but he afterwards became a vet himself. I later discovered the extent of the liking, affection and instinctive appreciation felt by children for those who tend animals and protect them. Today, in my veterinary and conservationist endeavours, I find that children often provide a valuable source of help.

But animals and children were not the only creatures I encountered at this period. More importantly, there were enemies in the shape of Nazis. During spring 1941, when an opportunity arose to join in Resistance operations, I leaped at it. The opportunity stemmed from personal contact with Vila Rachline, an industrialist friend of the family who soon became a leading member of the Resistance like his brother Lucien, later known in France under the name of Lucien Rachet.

I grabbed the chance not only because I was adventurous by nature but because I had all sorts of things to save, starting with my own skin. I was fair-haired and did not look 'Jewish', nor did I display any of the behavioural characteristics – for instance meekness and subservience – which anti-Semites ascribe to us. For the Gestapo and its French allies, however, I was very much a Jew. And so, whenever Jews were persecuted, I fought back. I had always reacted in this way, ever since my childhood, and would lash out at school if one of my friends was called a 'dirty Jew'. If my brothers were to be killed I would join them, but gun in hand.

Under these circumstances, my studies necessarily took second place. I attended courses, took an interest in them and passed examinations, but it was the operations I took part in as a member of the Buckmaster network that claimed the bulk of my energies: Intelligence work, liaison missions, air drops, organizing safe houses for fugitives, concealing and transporting men and weapons, gathering information and forging papers for those who had to hide or run, and numerous other assignments.

My principal contact and the man whom I assumed to be in local command was an Englishman whose alias was Martin. At this period, in 1942, he passed himself off as a captain in the French army reserve. His French was so flawless that I would never have taken him for an Englishman. A tall thin man with fair, slightly ginger hair combed down on one side, he was extremely discreet and spoke very little, which may explain why I failed to notice the almost imperceptible accent he must have had. I did not receive any instructions from him direct nor, incidentally, did I ever discover the nature of the orders he issued or to whom they were addressed. I knew him simply as *le capitaine*, who sometimes spent the night in my tiny student's room in Rue Montcabrier, behind the veterinary college. My uncertainty did not, I think, testify to the network's organizational perfection and stringent security so much as to the still vague and extremely embryonic nature of our system.

My room, which became the focus of many comings and goings, was a port of call for fugitives of two kinds. Some were Jews who were trying to reach Spain and had been directed to me for forwarding to an assembly point near the frontier, while others were people about whom I knew nothing but whom I was likewise under orders to conduct farther south. Some of these were Allied airmen.

I only went back to my lodgings to sleep, but did not spend every night there. In company with several others including my brother and Vila Rachline, the man who had recruited me into his network, I had access to a safe house in the Grand Rond district of Toulouse. I often used it, primarily for security reasons but also because it was a more convenient rendezvous for dates with my girlfriend. The day I spent at lectures or in the bars of the neighbourhood, notably the Café du 10 avril, near the college.

This was where I often took delivery of my charges. One I remember particularly, although he did his utmost, like others of his kind, to pass unnoticed and create as nondescript an impression as possible. He was sitting at a table in the Café du 10 avril with a cup of tisane in front of him, observing his neighbours with feigned indifference. He did not look English to French eyes, but there was an indefinable hint of disguise about his grey suit and the shabby overcoat draped across the chair beside him. Somebody must have tipped him the wink, because he soon came and joined me at the bar, where I was drinking a PGK, or Picon with grenadine and kirsch. He began by asking me if I knew Michel Klein and mentioned that Vila had sent him.

All this was said in passable French. We left at once and I took him to the Grand Rond apartment. He had earlier called at my lodgings in Rue Montcabrier. The landlady, Madame Besset, eschewed all knowledge of my activities on principle, but she did know more or less where I was during the day. Although nothing specific ever passed between us, we tacitly trusted one another. I had never asked her to, but Madame Besset directed my visitors to the college and the Café du 10 avril, and that was how the newcomer had found me. Our entire operation preserved an amateurish flavour, as I have already said, but that was inevitable in the early days.

Something else may have contributed to my landlady's soft spot for me. I used to make her little presents from my personal black market. People were hungry in 1942, and the veterinary school's dissecting room was an occasional source of supply. The cows they brought us were technically unfit for human consumption, but some of them had met an accidental death as a result of swallowing nails or fragments of wire. At all events, my friends and I seized the opportunity to purloin five or ten pounds of meat whenever we could. This enabled us to hold periodic feasts in my little room in Rue Montcabrier, present my landlady with the odd steak and even ingratiate ourselves with the townsfolk by making profitable exchanges which sometimes proved beneficial to our clandestine operations.

I should add that my current girlfriend also played a very useful part in my activities, in which black marketeering and resistance to the forces of occupation sometimes went hand in hand. Being secretary to the managing director of a wholesale groceries chain, she managed to get me listed as an agent. In this capacity I received cartons of condensed milk and other provisions. These riches opened numerous doors to me when I went to reconnoitre likely dropping-zones in Gers and decide what areas might be suitable for the establishment of maquis groups.

41

At least my fugitive British airman would not die of hunger in our Grand Rond apartment. How long before he could be shepherded to the frontier? I had no idea. At this stage, towards the end of 1942, my own sector had yet to acquire any well-organized escape routes. Every success was a feat of improvisation. I waited for instructions, but it was not beyond doubt that any would reach me.

The first requirement was to clothe the fugitive in something less at odds with current Toulouse fashions in dress. His grey suit gave him a rather spurious air. A fellow-lodger named Raymond Harter, who worked as an engineer at the aircraft factory in Blagnac and was himself a member of the Resistance, dug out a sweater and some slacks. Thus attired, the Englishman could pass for one of my student friends. To entertain him a little, I took him into town with me. This was rather unwise, but we were always taking risks which professional agents would have been careful to avoid. I particularly recall taking our visitor to drink some indescribable concoction at a bar owned by Tony Murena, a celebrated accordionist who employed an exceptionally pretty barmaid.

We finally managed to devise a scheme whereby our Englishman could slip into Spain. One link in the chain was Nicolas, a friend who had some reliable contacts at Saint-Girons about twenty miles from the Spanish border. From there the route ran via Seix, our last assembly point and the place where 'ferrymen', or guides, embarked on the final stage through the mountains. My own mission ended at Seix.

It was in this way, blundering from one improvisation to another, that we gradually built up a more or less coherent escape network. The organization was not, however, devoid of blemishes or instances of childish stupidity. Nobody adapts himself to a life of secrecy overnight, and my room in Rue Montcabrier eventually attracted attention.

The first alert sounded when I was summoned to police headquarters. A denunciation: I was a Jew who lived in illegal circumstances and received a stream of visitors. The police gave me a thorough grilling. I did not find it hard to guess the source of the mischief – an elderly couple living in hostile and suspicious seclusion two doors away from my room. I defended myself fiercely, claiming that I was a sociable type who had every right to entertain his friends. The *flics* could not have been too keen to lock me up after all, because they released me.

Our second scare was caused by a police raid on the district, complete with house-to-house calls. Vila Rachline happened to be with me that morning. By then, my room had become a miniature arsenal. My clandestine visitors sometimes left their guns there, and I myself owned two. Four or five ill-concealed weapons always reposed beneath a plank at the top of my wardrobe where the most perfunctory of searches would have unearthed them at once.

Vila Rachline and I were determined not to be taken alive. In the excitement preceding the entry of the police, we each had time to grab a gun and pocket it.

The police were French, but accompanied by Germans. As luck would have it, they took no special precautions. Instead of searching us they asked for our papers and left it at that. Vila's were forged but convincing. My own were still genuine. The police examined them idly. Like my interrogators at the station, they did not seem particularly aggressive. After asking two or three questions, they left. We had escaped by the skin of our teeth. So had they.

A third alert, this time crucial. I had spent the weekend closeted with a girlfriend at the Grand Rond apartment. I neither knew nor wanted to know what was happening in the outside world. I had no suspicion that the Gestapo, not the French police, would descend on Rue Montcabrier at 6 a.m. that Monday. They were looking for me. Instead, they arrested the son of a woman neighbour, Christian Marnier, to whom I had lent my room. He secured his release shortly afterwards, though not without difficulty, when the police realized their mistake. Nobody in Rue Montcabrier knew of my clandestine retreat in Grand Rond, but everyone was aware that I attended veterinary college on week days.

That Monday morning – it was 12 April – I strolled into the dissecting room, yawning. I was alone when my friend Robert Bellec came to warn me that the Germans had sur-rounded the school, that they had just arrested Professor Petit, the principal, and Monsieur Dupin, the secretary, and were looking for me everywhere. I thought I was done for. The storeroom contained weapons and some plastic explosive earmarked for an attack on the aircraft factory at Blagnac.

43

The material had been dropped by parachute at Moissac. On the previous Friday, some Wolf Cubs had brought it to the school and concealed it in the medieval dust of the store-room.

I asked Bellec to hand over his identity card. He agreed at once but for which gesture I would not be alive today. Then I asked him to fetch Bitoun.

Bitoun was a Jew from Philippeville in Algeria and a class-mate of mine. He came running. I put him in the picture.

'I'm a Jew like you' – he looked dumbfounded – 'and I'm also a member of the Resistance, so pin your ears back.'

Very briefly I explained that I was going to try and escape, but there were arms and explosives in the storeroom and it was absolutely essential to retrieve them sooner rather than later. I devised a plan. Bitoun listened intently as I sprang it on him, pushing him in at the deep end before he had a chance to prepare himself. He was just the type of man who was regularly described by Nazi sympathizers as cowardly and pathetic, but he didn't hesitate for an instant and carried out my instructions to the letter.

Armed with Bellec's papers I headed for the school gates. The entrance was guarded by a German soldier, rifle in hand, and the janitor. Fortunately, the latter was fairly new to the job and didn't know all the students by sight.

'Where are you off to?' he demanded. 'Nobody's allowed out.'

'I'm only going to post a letter.'

'Can't be done. Hang on, aren't you Michel Klein? You're just the person they're looking for.'

I guffawed. 'Me, Klein? I'm Robert Bellec.' I dug in my pocket and produced Bellec's identity card. The janitor hesitated. At that precise moment my parasitology teacher, Monsieur Martin, entered the lodge with Monsieur Dubac the bursar. Martin took in the situation at a glance.

'What's the trouble, Bellec?' he asked curtly.

I repeated my story. Reminding me that it was absolutely forbidden to leave the premises, Martin authorized me to go and post my imaginary letter. The janitor bowed to higher authority. The German soldier did not appear to have any very strict instructions, thank God. I made a decorous exit. As soon as I reached the cover of the tree-lined avenue, I started to run like mad.

44

It was 9.30. I was safe for the moment, but the prime essential – getting the arms and explosives out of the college – had still to be achieved. It would also be necessary to remove any evidence that might implicate the principal and secretary. I had arranged with Bitoun to return at lunchtime, when surveillance would probably have relaxed. At 12.30 Madame Dupac the bursar's wife would be standing in the courtyard near the entrance, holding a newspaper. If it was unopened, the Germans were there in force. If she had opened it and was reading, the coast was clear. In the event of an emergency she would fold it.

I reached the school at 12.30 sharp. There was a German sentry outside the gate, but I could see into the courtyard. Madame Dupac was browsing through an open newspaper. I walked in and headed for the principal's office. The Gestapo had put seals on the door. I broke them, slipped inside and removed every compromising article; forged identity cards, rubber stamps, stencils for the production of our clandestine news-sheet on the school's duplicating-machine. During the morning Gilbert Bitoun and Madame Dupac had filled two suitcases with plastic explosive. I took one and Bitoun the other. We walked out, I in the lead and Bitoun a minute later, like any two students off to visit their families. The sentry made no attempt to stop us.

We were extraordinarily lucky. Lunchtime had been the ideal moment. It seems that the Gestapo had come to arrest three people: Petit, Dupin and myself. One of us had got away, but they banked on picking me up later. With two out of three in the bag, they had thought it unnecessary to keep the school under close surveillance.

I had won the rubber. The two precious suitcases were temporarily deposited with a friend, Harter of the Prunus network, but Petit and Dupin remained in the hands of the Gestapo. They were 'interrogated'. Who is Michel Klein? Where is he? Torture failed to loosen their tongues and both were deported. Thanks to their steadfast courage and determination, they were among the few survivors of the German death camps. As for my friend Bitoun, he got away scot-free and we met again after the Liberation.

Meanwhile, the Gestapo plastered my name and photograph over the walls of the Gare Matabiau and other public places. It was now April 1943. I said goodbye to school and

45

my veterinary studies, at least for the moment. Trying to re-establish contact, I found that our network had been dismantled. Arrests came thick and fast, but several people managed to escape. One of them was my chief, Vila Rachline. He continued the struggle but was arrested and shot at Lyon on 6 June 1944, the very day of the Normandy landings.

Against all the odds, I picked up a Resistance thread and was sent to work as a farmhand on a remote smallholding in the Auvergne. The idea was not only to put me out to grass but to employ my services in organizing a maquis group which would, after their dispersal, absorb the inmates of the Brioude youth camp. The two thousand youngsters housed there were on the verge of being sent to Germany as labour conscripts.

Although the farmer knew I belonged to the Resistance, I performed my farmhand's duties in full. I slept in the stable with the oxen and rose at dawn to harness them. I drove the cart into the forest, felled timber and hauled it back to the farm. I chopped wood, harvested peas, milked cows, fed pigs and generally worked like a slave. I was really put to the test. As with Mario, however, I was in my element. It was there on the farm that I, a native of the city, felt truly at home. Thousands of Jews living on kibbutzim in Israel, have, I imagine, undergone a similar experience. I told myself that I was a real, not make-believe countryman. The only person who failed to appreciate this was the farmer's wife. She thought I ate too much, spent too much time listening to the radio and didn't look the part. She had no idea who I was, unlike her husband, so she found me vaguely suspect.

One Sunday morning she told me to fetch some bread from Chapelle-Laurent, eight miles away. I wheeled the bicycle out of the barn, but she changed her mind at the last moment and told me she was going herself. I soon discovered that the cupboard where I kept my few possessions had been boarded up. Questioning the farmer, I gathered that his wife had been hoping to prevent me from removing my things while she went to inform the police that there was a shady character living on her premises. That left me no choice. I wrenched the nails out, retrieved my suitcase and set off on foot in the opposite direction, towards Massiac, where I knew the gendarmes were well disposed and aware of my existence. I spent that night at the police station, but not under lock and key.

The noose drew steadily tighter, however. The networks had taken a hammering and no one felt safe any more. I became convinced that my best plan would be to slip into Spain in the hope of reaching Britain or Africa.

One of the men with whom I had maintained contact throughout these troubled times was Monsieur Serville, a friend of Harter and, like him, an engineer at the Blagnac aircraft factory. Serville approved of my plan and helped me to carry it out. He put me in touch with two other members of the Resistance who had also blown their cover and were left with no alternative but to skip the country, a teacher and an ex-officer of the 41st Engineers.

We holed up in a derelict building which Serville had pointed out to us near Sainte-Croix and made our preparations. Our first task was to build up a stock of food, but all we could obtain was some lump sugar, sausage, flour and butter. Using these ingredients and an old bread oven in the ruin, I baked a number of slab-cakes the size of a prayer book. Our daily ration for the journey was set at one of these cakes, two lumps of sugar and one slice of sausage per person. To keep ourselves warm – it was September 1943, and the Pyrenean nights would be cold – we each cobbled together a patchwork quilt out of scraps of material gleaned from various sources.

Our intention, once across the border, was to get as far as possible into Spanish territory before giving ourselves up. If the frontier guards caught us near the border we would risk being summarily returned and thus fall straight into the hands of the Gestapo. Armed with a compass and a map, we travelled at night wearing socks to muffle the sound of our footsteps. During the day we went to ground and slept. Each of us carried a kilo of sugar, a sausage and thirty-five cakes, so we reckoned that our supplies would last us five weeks.

The first step was to cross the frontier. Our rendezvous was Seix, where we were to be met by a guide who would take us by night to a pass on the Spanish border.

Three parties took to the mountains that night. Two of them numbered about ten each, including some Jews. The third consisted of us three, who enjoyed slightly preferential treatment thanks to our friendly personal relations with local members of the Resistance.

There was one guide to each party. The three groups were

to assemble at about 2 a.m. in a shepherd's hut some 6000 feet up and a good three hours' walk from the frontier. From there on, it was every man for himself.

No serious incident marred our progress. Happy to have reached the hut unscathed, we indulged in a rather risky display of exuberance. The first guide to arrive called out, '*Halte-là. Qui vive?*' We identified ourselves by replying '*Vive de Gaulle*', as arranged, but we also fired a few shots, which made a terrible racket in the mountains. Our guide loosed off a couple of rounds himself. We found this highly entertaining, but the other escapees, who were unarmed and felt a good deal less cocksure than we did, called us all the names under the sun and were justly enraged by our horseplay.

We and the guides did our best to reassure the members of the other two groups. Although we swore there were no Germans close enough to hear, they were only half convinced. This incident established a kind of complicity between us and the guides. Producing a scratch meal of bread, Pyrenean cheese (I have never forgotten the taste of that cheese!) and brandy, they invited us to join them. Our spirits, which had been high, rose still higher. So did theirs. They asked us to bequeath them our pistols, arguing that we would not need them because we were crossing the frontier. After some discussion we agreed to hand over our guns when we reached the pass that marked the border.

We set off again. Warmed by the brandy, we almost forgot that the object of our climb was to get us out of France. A good three hours later we were close to the summit of Mont Vallier on the side of a natural amphitheatre at the foot of which lay a German frontier post and two lakes whose sparkling waters could just be detected in the gloom. Our guides knew every twist and turn of the route.

Every pistol and rifle was cocked and ready to fire as we cautiously spread out and worked our way round the lip of the amphitheatre in single file. We had adopted this formation so that, if we were attacked, the noise of our firing would convey the presence of a substantial armed force. There were no signs of life at the post, but this was no place to linger. We reached the pass and walked a few hundred yards beyond it. Then, after a final swig of brandy, we handed our guns to the guides, who retraced their steps.

There was less of the night left than we had foreseen.

Sheltering behind a rock, I burnt the forged identity card I had procured after the Gestapo's descent on the school in Toulouse. We headed into Spain and walked till 8 a.m., when daylight compelled us to take cover as planned.

We were captured during our fourth night on Spanish territory. We had reached a village perched high in the mountains and were wondering whether to walk boldly through, braving the lights, or skirt it. Suddenly, in the silence and darkness that surrounded us, I felt the muzzle of a rifle prod my ribs and heard some words in Spanish. Fingers closed round my left wrist – the one I wore my watch on. Its luminous hands had betrayed our presence.

We were taken to another small village and confined in a barn which had to serve as a makeshift prison. The alcalde came to question us escorted by a well-meaning lawyer who acted as interpreter. My two companions passed themselves off as Canadian airmen and I as an Englishman. This worked – for the time being. I suppose we must have been the first French frontier-jumpers to surface in that remote spot. We were promptly and courteously transferred to a hotel in the neighbouring township, where our captors treated us to a comfortable room and regaled us on anchovies and olives. Our spirits recovered fast.

Next day the fairytale came to an end. We were transferred again, this time to the prison in Lérida, which housed hundreds of Frenchmen who likewise claimed to be Canadian. Our heads and other body-hair were shorn and our personal effects confiscated. No more anchovies and olives, just stew with rice, beans and a sprinkling of the innumerable local bugs. What was to become of us?

For my own part, I had concocted a story which proved to be a winner. I was a British airman who had been shot down over France, and my name was Michael Hartley. It so happened that I had spent a holiday with some people named Hartley as a child, and that they had a boy of my own age whose name was Michael. I also had an excellent English accent and could write the language proficiently.

The Spanish authorities would not allow us to send mail. Fortunately, the little money I had secreted was enough to finance a trip to Barcelona by a Spanish political prisoner who enjoyed outside working privileges. He undertook to ensure that a letter from me to the British Consul reached its intended destination. Written in good English, this missive must have created a good impression. Just over a fortnight later, the consul's representative arrived to collect me and two other Frenchmen. Exactly seventeen days after my arrival, we became the first prisoners to secure our release.

Once in the consul's office, however, I felt bound to come clean. There were too many gaps in my story for it to have withstood careful scrutiny. My candour met with a very chilly reception, though the consul did agree to intervene to secure the early release of my two original companions. He also told me to retain the name Michael Hartley and suggested that I contact the military attaché at the British Embassy in Madrid. I assume that this relatively benevolent attitude was due in part to my record of service with the Buckmaster network, which maintained links with British Intelligence.

Had I ever been a budding vet? My recent past already seemed light years away. Thanks to some discreet wire-pulling by the British military attaché, I became Michael Hartley, executive secretary with the Gresham Life Insurance Company in Madrid. My job was to make English translations of Spanish insurance laws for transmission to head office in London. Although I did not know a word of Spanish when I arrived in Spain, I had devoted my seventeen days' detention at Lérida to learning as much as I humanly could in so short a time. I have some aptitude for languages and did not fare too badly with my translations, but accuracy was of secondary importance because their real and only purpose was to serve as vehicles for coded messages.

The mere fact of being 'British' was a calling-card that opened many Spanish doors at this stage in the war. Furthermore, I lost no time in looking up a number of valuable contacts who knew relations of mine, some belonging to prominent Jewish families to whom I could divulge my true identity. As the months went by, I became acquainted with numerous members of Madrid's social set. Not unnaturally, I enjoyed myself. I went to cocktail parties and dined at Chevasson's, an excellent French restaurant. I also got to know Madame P., who harboured Frenchmen *en route* for London – for instance Maurice Schumann and a member of the Rothschild clan – just as she was soon to harbour Pétainists and Laval himself after the latter's flight from France. Having so often flirted with death and worse during the past three years, I almost felt in holiday mood.

At the same time, all this socializing in the midst of war began to prey on my mind. I tried to join the French paratroops, then the British, then the Jewish contingents serving with the British Forces in Palestine, but it was no use. The British were already displaying a reluctance to see any more Jews on Palestinian soil. Having explored other channels with an equal lack of success, I sought oblivion in a love affair. A delightful girl had entered my life. She was nineteen years old and had just won acclaim as the star of an anti-Semitic film entitled *Raza*, though she herself was innocent of any racist ideas. I loved her and she returned my love with interest. I think she would have loved Michel Klein as much as she loved Michael Hartley.

The only fly in the ointment was her father, a diplomatic courier whose job took him to various European capitals and had, in particular, earned him the 'privilege' of several encounters with Hitler at Berchtesgaden. My relations with him remained amicable until he discovered that the ties between me and his daughter were more than merely social. He considered the idea of marriage but rejected it at once. Michael Hartley had a French Catholic mother, which would do at a pinch, but his Protestant father made any union with his daughter impossible. What attitude would he have taken if he had known my real identity? He had no knowledge of the Jews – no physical perception of them, so to speak – but that did not prevent him from being a rabid anti-Semite. To him the Jew was an abstraction, a soulless, incorporeal, insensate symbol of evil. He was the first to acquaint me with the existence of German death camps. I don't know how he pictured them but I don't think he knew – or wanted to know – what really went on there. I myself found it hard to believe in them and was greeted with scepticism when I conveyed the diplomat's story to the British military authorities in Madrid. Ever logical, he strongly condemned the papal nuncio at Bratislava, whither he had also carried the 'bag', for having given asylum to some Jews. In the dispassionate tones of one referring to so much garbage, he went on to describe how other Jews had recently been thrown off a bridge into the Danube.

I had to listen to these stories without exploding. Michael Hartley would not have been entitled to vent the indignation proper to Michel Klein. Of the British, French and Spanish circles I frequented, some were pro-Nazi and others not, but I almost universally encountered a virulent or latent anti-Semitism which sickened me but had to be tolerated for diplomatic reasons. You never knew which side a fellow conversationalist was on.

I also became acquainted with a variety of secret goings-on which did nothing to improve my morale. I knew, for example, that German aircraft laden with gold and valuables stolen from Jews used to land in Portugal before flying on to South America.

The military authorities systematically rejected all my requests for a return to active service. I approached two senior officers, one French and one British. The first opposed my departure despite the approval of the second. I never discovered their reasons, but I was compelled to remain where I was.

How, after all these upheavals, was I ever going to regain my balance and apply myself to the profession I had started to learn? 1945 and the end of the war saw me back in Paris, but was I still the same person? If the truth be told, I had no idea who I was – other than a former veterinary student without roots, qualifications or a sense of direction. Would I have the will-power to resume my studies and complete them? I was twenty-four and destitute. What was I to do? How would I earn a living?

I was reunited with one of my sisters, an ex-deportee who had survived after five attempts to escape. She told me that she had seen our parents, with whom she had been deported, disappear into the shower hut where those who were condemned to death by the SS received their lethal dose of gas. All the horror of the past four years surged over me once more, amplified by a thousand stories of which each was more gruesome than the last. We seemed to be accursed. The future took on a sinister hue. I felt that society would never recover from the shock it had just sustained. I was convinced, despite the defeat of the Nazis, that anti-Semitism and persecution had barely begun. I found plenty of confirmation. During a sojourn in the Hôpital Rothschild, for example, I met a young man who told me an extraordinary tale. He was the son of a militant German communist from Breslau who had fled to the USSR. He was also a Jew, and he described massive deportations of Jews from Latvia to Kazakhstan, where thousands of his co-religionists, stripped of all they possessed, had lived in holes scraped out of the very ground. Many had died. It was only by dint of good luck and immense determination that he had managed to reach Israel on foot by skirting the Caspian Sea and trekking across Iran and Iraq. Anti-Semitism in the Soviet Union too? So it wasn't a Nazi monopoly . . .

The whole situation was unbearable. I felt shocked and revolted. Should I remain in France – should I leave for Israel? My elder brother Jean, the doctor, exerted a steadying influence on me. With his help I regained my stability.

I enrolled at the Maisons-Alfort veterinary college near Paris. I had little choice and equally little faith in myself. Another two years' study followed by a thesis seemed an interminable prospect. Luckily for me, I tend to take an interest in anything I put my hand to. Despite my misgivings, the work grew on me. I became an enthusiastic student with a consuming desire to learn. Almost before I knew it, I was at work on my thesis, an extremely interesting assignment which I tackled under the aegis of a world celebrity in the field of endocrinology, Professor Henri Simonnet. This was a contribution to the study of the part played by various hormones, notably in the functioning of the mammary glands. By applying an ointment containing oestradiol (a synthetic hormone) to a mare's udders, for example, we induced her to yield enough milk to feed her foal. The same mare had lost all her previous foals for want of milk. In another of our experiments we succeeded in getting a billy-goat to lactate. He produced 10 ounces of quite normal milk daily. Nowadays, of course, this all sounds out-of-date and old hat.

I did not seem to have lost the spirit of invention and inquiry which had prompted me to treat my old friend Mario's chickens – a corollary of the alertness and vigilance that had more than once saved my life during the war. At this precise juncture, I and my fellow-toilers in the laboratory were abruptly put to the test by a dramatic problem.

Professor Simonnet, who was supervising my thesis, fell gravely ill. Some pundits from the Académie de Médecine examined him, but in vain. Our professor's condition deteriorated and he became comatose. After taking various specimens on our own initiative, we managed to isolate Pfeiffer's bacillus, then considered fatal.

However, a cure had just been discovered in the shape of streptomycin. At this time there were only 12 grams in the whole of Paris – 12 grams for the treatment of hundreds and thousands of sufferers whose needs were just as pressing as those of Professor Simonnet. We could never have obtained the requisite dose in time, so we made do. We managed to procure a few grams of the rare product and saved our professor from certain death. His was a deserving case. Thousands of patients owe their lives to his research on vitamins and hormones, not to mention other fields of study.

Although hard work proved an aid to rehabilitation, the man I had been for four long years was always on the verge of revolt. I had a tendency to kick against the delays, constraints and injustices of peacetime.

3

Wild Oats and Bran Mash

After completing my studies I was taken on as an assistant by a fellow student at Toulouse, who was three years my senior and had a country practice at Montoire. There in the world of horses and cows, calves and foals, I quickly rediscovered the peace and contentment I had known a few years earlier on Mario's farm.

My employer came from Martinique. He already had a thorough knowledge of his profession and practised it with extreme conscientiousness. It was not, I suspect, altogether coincidental that I made my debut with him. I may have been giving myself every opportunity to prove myself a man in his eyes, not just a Jew.

I lived at my employer's home. Our transport consisted of two old and unreliable cars; there weren't any new ones to be had. We shared a Peugeot 201, a Citroën Trèfle and a brace of ancient police motorcycles. Thus equipped we rode from farm to farm, separately or in convoy.

The work was endless, and whole nights could be devoted to the care of a single horse. For me, it was like bathing in a sea of decency, well-being and genuine contentment. Montoire was in the administrative department of Loir-et-Cher, a predominantly agricultural area. Although it seems only yesterday, the farms were still worked with horses and oxen, so a country vet had plenty to do. I seldom spent more than two nights a week in bed; the cowshed and stable claimed the rest. If I went to the cinema on a Saturday or Sunday I never saw the end of a film. I could not visit my girlfriend without leaving a note of my whereabouts. I received my board and lodging and an assistant's salary. No days off and no fixed working hours, but no cause for complaint either. I was lucky enough to be learning my trade under someone who was not

55

only a friend but an outstanding man, and the work fired me with enthusiasm.

It was not just a matter of giving the odd injection or writing out a prescription, then heading leisurely for home. The old motorbike might first have to negotiate a rutted and slippery track, more often than not in the middle of the night. Half the time the lights failed, leaving me to steer by guesswork and the beam of a flashlight. The brakes were as good as useless and the tyres so worn that they punctured incessantly. Sometimes I rode cross-country. One day while riding down a farm track I let go of the handlebars to consult my visiting list. I came a cropper, naturally, and the bike dragged me ten yards through the mud before coming to a standstill.

I finally reached the farm, where my boss was impatiently awaiting me. All the inhabitants were up and about. The paterfamilias was there and so was his wife. Even the children had assembled in the cowshed or stable, quite as interested and inquisitive as their elders. The horse had colic and might be dying; the cow was having difficulty calving. This was very serious. Important items of capital equipment were in danger, so the entire family followed the vet's work closely and co-operated to the best of its ability. The mother brought hot or cold water on request, the daughter fetched a bottle of oil, the son held the animal's head while an enema or injection was administered.

They were peasants. So, in this context, was I. We weren't sentimental or squeamish; we understood each other perfectly. There is nothing poetic about the sight of a cow lying on her flank in a mass of excrement. I was an equally unpoetic sight, lying on my side, stripped to the waist with my face against her hindquarters and my arm buried shoulder-deep in her genital tracts, being pushed so that I could probe even deeper. Vets who do this kind of work today wear plastic aprons and shoulder-length gloves, but no such refinements existed in those days. We performed internal examinations with our bare arms washed with soap and coated with rape-seed oil.

In this case I could not insert my hand into the animal's uterus. What was the matter? Contractions were occurring, but to no avail. Diagnosis: the uterus was twisted and, thus, sealed. The remedy was a rather spectacular form of manipulation.

Like the cow, the vet lies on his side. He inserts his arm

56

into her rectum and grips the uterus. The object is to rotate the animal round this fixed point so as to 'unroll' the uterus and relieve the torsion – a process effected with the help of several men, who push and pull the cow by the feet while the vet maintains his pressure.

There is another method which can be tried in advance of the foregoing. For the purposes of this technique, which I practised at a later stage, the animal remains standing. Inserting one hand in the rectum, you try to turn the matrix by imparting a series of limited movements. This is very difficult, however. Counting the calf and the placentas, plus their waters, not to mention the uterus itself, the vet has to shift a mass weighing 200 pounds or more. If his strength and dexterity prove insufficient, he must fall back on the first method.

Even in the absence of uterine torsion, there were occasions when a cow could not, for one reason or another, give birth. Bovine Caesareans being still a thing of the future, you then had to engage in a truly Herculean task which nobody in the cowshed found gruesome because it alone could save the life of the mother, who would be very tired by the time you resorted to such an operation. This consisted in dismembering the calf – sometimes already dead – and extracting it from the uterus piece by piece. You did the job with a wire-saw or a small curved blade, wielding it blind and at arm's length while you lay in the blood- and dung-saturated straw with your nose glued to the cow's rump. The weight of the calf crushed your hand against the pelvic bones, your fingers grew numb and your hand became paralysed. It was an exhausting task which lasted two hours on average and seemed twice as long. Meanwhile, every move you made was closely followed by the entire family.

There was still the afterbirth. Normally, expulsion would occur unaided. If it failed to, the vet had to step in. This called for a strong stomach because the placenta would already have begun to decompose and the smell was enough to make you turn tail. No time to dwell on sweeter scents. The present objective was to get at the putrified placenta at the base of the uterus. It was attached to it by cotyledons (little pear-shaped vessels) of which every last one had to be detached by hand. There were about a hundred of them. As an accompaniment to your labours the cow would console herself by expelling a variety of excreta which one or other of your helpers wiped

57

away with swabs of fresh straw. It was not only an arduous procedure but a dangerous one, because you ran the risk of contracting Malta fever or picking up a staphylococcal infection.

But perhaps the longest and most exacting task was the treatment of horses suffering from colic, a common disorder which often proves fatal if left to take its course. Colic is a vague term applied to intestinal spasms due to various causes. They are sometimes so violent that the gut becomes knotted, in which case death ensues.

There was no question of giving an injection and retiring to bed. Horses demanded very lengthy and difficult treatment. You either administered antispasmodics or, by contrast, sympathomimetics which increased peristalsis and thereby stimulated evacuation. You could also make punctures in overdistended intestinal coils, either through the flank or with the trocar shielded by your hand and your arm thrust as far as possible into the rectum.

Enemas, too, were often used. A pail or two of cold salt water worked best. To avoid getting yourself 'photographed' – or receiving the liquid full in your face – you wrapped the tube in a thick cloth and kept it firmly pressed against the base of the tail. Once the enema had been administered you withdrew the tube, keeping the cloth in place over the anus, and quickly lowered the tail to retain the entire input. Then you stood the horse on a slope, facing downhill, to help the liquid penetrate. Next, you ensured a good mix by getting it to trot on the flat. Typical sequence of events: the animal slows to a walk and halts. You wait. You sense that its gripes are returning. It paws the ground or tries to lie down, turns to examine its belly from one side or the other. All at once it starts to sweat – copiously. You can tell that it is in pain. Your hopes fade but you redouble your efforts. To dry off the sweat you rub down the animal's belly and flanks with straw and apply heated bricks or old flatirons.

On night calls I often ended by falling asleep in the straw, tired out. But the horse would soon display renewed symptoms. That meant waking up, giving more injections and getting it to swallow another dose of medicine.

A vet needs all his experience, skill and sense of touch to ascertain the nature of a colic. The intestines are a world in themselves, and various forms of colic can develop there.

You have to palpate, explore, probe, percuss, look and study the animal's behaviour. Colic in horses is a real test of veterinary skill. The most subtle procedure is diagnosis based on segmental innervation. You feel the horse's flanks and can tell from its reactions which part of the abdomen constitutes the site of the spasms. My employer's predecessor used to aid his diagnoses by dangling a pendulum over the animal's belly. Although some people smiled at such practices, their derision did not prevent the vet with the pendulum from obtaining good results. As for my boss, he was a first-class man. Of the four hundred horses we treated for colic in a single year, all but four recovered.

I felt happy and at home in a world where intellectual and emotional honesty reigned supreme. You did not cheat on a sick horse, a cow in calf, or the farmer who anxiously shared in your labours. You did not cheat on anyone and were judged according to your merits. After a night of toil – a cow delivered, a horse saved, a farmer and his family satisfied – I tasted real contentment.

The farmer's wife having brought a pail of hot water and a towel, I would wash in the warmth of the cowshed or sometimes in the yard where, even in winter, I never felt the cold. Then came that token of gratitude and friendship, potluck in the farm kitchen with the entire family and any neighbours who had come to lend a hand. In winter there would generally be a cauldron suspended in the big fireplace, and simmering inside it a tasty soup containing beans, meat and fat bacon. The farmer would go and fetch a bottle for the concoction of *chabrol* – soup laced with wine – and everyone cheerfully set to. In the wine-growing district of Chablis, where I worked later on, the farmer would often be a vine grower or *éleveur*, to use the local term, and he never failed to dig out one of his best bottles. Very often, too, the snack was eaten in the wine-cellar itself.

When a peasant trusted you, he did so unreservedly. I was once called to a farm near Montoire where I had already treated several animals. Instead of being taken straight to the stables, however, I was shown into grandpa's bedroom. I knew the old boy well. He downed his mug of brandy every morning, had all his own teeth, few wrinkles and an iron constitution, but today he was laid up. He pulled back the covers and showed me his leg. He had varicose ulcers.

'You treated our horse,' he told me. 'You're quite up to treating this leg of mine. I'm eighty-two. I've never been to a doctor yet, and I'm not going to start now.'

Was I to disappoint him, tell him I couldn't engage in the illegal practice of medicine? Of course not. I was a youngster and he an old man. There was no point in arguing. I treated his ulcers with amniotic powder obtained from the lyophilized placenta, at that time a rarity, and they healed.

One morning at Montoire, when I went to collect my car from the garage, I saw a farmer having his petrol tank filled. My boss and I had been doing shift work at his stables for the past forty-eight hours. Both his horses were suffering from colic. All our efforts had failed to save the first – it was one of the four we lost that year – and the second had developed colic while we were treating its stable companion.

My farmer friend, who was attired in his Sunday best, prepared to drive off. I expressed surprise. Why wasn't he at his horse's side? Looking rather sheepish, he eventually confessed that he was off to Châteaudun to see a lady crystal-gazer. She would lift the spell that had been cast over him and was making his horses ill.

'But don't tell your boss,' he added, still looking a trifle shamefaced.

Naturally I passed the story on. That evening we both called at the farm to check on the surviving animal's progress. The farmer was back from Châteaudun. Being a clever psychologist, my boss wormed the truth out of him without giving me away.

'You should have warned me,' he said. 'If I'd known you were under a spell I'd have lifted it right away, but it's not too late. We'll do it now. I know about these things; my grandfather was a magician.'

Coming from a Martiniquais, his remarks sounded plausible. He proceeded to stage an elaborate candlelit ceremony in the stable, complete with much bobbing and bowing, marching and countermarching. At the end of it all, our rather puzzled client took it for granted that his evil spell had been lifted. I need hardly add that we continued to administer the proper treatment as well.

My satisfaction with this way of life at Montoire was enhanced by the absolute trust that reigned between me and my friend and employer. But the old devil that had been bred within me by war and persecution, though usually dormant, sometimes stirred in his sleep. Although I lived and worked with farmers, I remained in touch with the city, with my relations in Paris and the outside world. The press and radio occasionally rekindled memories and reopened wounds I had thought healed. There was, for instance, the trial of the man I had arrested in the boulevard Saint-Michel. His political connections did their best to minimize the charges brought against him. The main prosecution witnesses should have been myself and Dupin, the secretary of the Toulouse veterinary college, who had survived deportation, but we were not even called. I was periodically overcome by a renewed temptation to simply pack up and go somewhere – anywhere.

Meanwhile, I took a holiday. This marked the end of my probationary period. It is customary for a young vet to do a stint with an older colleague before joining another or going into practice on his own. For the moment, however, I was looking no further ahead than my holiday. I left for the South of France with some friends whose dog I had treated. When we arrived at the Côte d'Azur, my friends booked in at the Carlton in Cannes. I did likewise, even though I was only an assistant vet. It was the first holiday I had taken since the war. There in the luxury of the Carlton I experienced another kind of contentment, one I felt entitled to. One evening over a large scotch, as I was mentally toying with the idea of giving up my veterinary practice and finding a more lucrative career, my face began to smart and tingle. It was a brutal call to order. Within a few hours I was covered in pustules. A cow I had helped to deliver some days earlier had left a memento in the form of a severe staphylococcal infection, almost as if she wanted to convey that I belonged on the farm and not on the French Riviera.

I undertook locum duties in the neighbourhood of Paris. For the first time I was standing on my own two feet. The realization that I could soon become a complete vet grew stronger the more I deputized for experienced colleagues. And yet, just as I was really getting into my professional stride, a chance encounter once more put my future career in doubt. On this occason fate assumed the guise of an American named Arthur, a rather devil-may-care young man who was purser of a ship chartered by the US Army for troop-carrying purposes. My family had asked me to entertain him during a leave he was spending in Paris with an Australian sailor. He was an ideal boon companion. I let him drag me into all kinds of wild escapades and elaborate practical jokes, for which he had a genius. He also had a brazen effrontery which took him sailing very close to the wind, legally speaking.

Fortunately we preserved just enough common sense to keep on the right side of the law. At this time, having fun was our sole aim in life. But even while pursuing this rather aimless, empty-headed and irresponsible existence, I far from broke with my profession. I continued to do locum work based in Paris. What was more, like a man clinging to a lifebuoy, I prepared to go into practice on my own.

My favourite animal at this period was the horse, so I decided to install myself at Alençon, in a cattle-farming district where horses remained numerous despite the increasing mechanization of agriculture. It was time to stop sowing wild oats. I had rented a house in Alençon, purchased equipment and ordered the contents of my dispensary. Next Monday, after a last weekend of freedom, I was leaving Paris.

Arthur and I had been invited to spend the weekend in Switzerland with a British general in the International Refugee Organization, a UN agency which took care of displaced persons or war refugees who were unable to return to their own countries. He was responsible for a fleet of twenty-eight vessels which transported them to new homes all over the world.

In the course of conversation that weekend, our host tapped me on the shoulder and said:

'So you like travelling, do you? All right, we'll see what we can do.'

I was back in Paris on Monday morning and getting ready to catch a train to Alençon when the phone rang. It was the general's secretary.

'Bob [the general] has hired you,' she said. 'It's a plum job. Make sure your passport's in order and take the 5 p.m. train to Bremen next Saturday. You'll be met at the exit. You're leaving for Brazil.'

Brazil! So what I had dismissed as an idle remark had proved to be genuine. Which was I to choose, Alençon or Rio de Janeiro, the profession I was ready for or something quite different? Temptation reared its head once more. Was I really so set on being a vet? Was I really the type to put down roots?

Living life to the full meant roaming around and seeing the world.

I quickly extended the validity of my passport. Forty-eight hours later I had sold back my new equipment and cancelled my tenancy, and on Saturday I caught the train for Bremen. It was a complete leap in the dark. I might be going for good.

From one day to the next I became an IRO official accredited to the governments of South America and charged with helping to organize the resettlement of European refugees in that part of the New World, primarily Brazil. For two years I shuttled back and forth between America, Europe and Australia, which was also accepting refugees.

Vets being versatile creatures, I even became a marine architect and converted a seaplane carrier into a vessel for the transportation of refugees. It was hard to avoid making comparisons between my new status and that of an assistant vet. My job entitled me to a large salary, lavish expenses, periodic bonuses and a terminal grant when I finally left the organization.

But despite all these advantages and the sometimes exciting aspects of the life I led, I remained dissatisfied. My activities often seemed sterile. I felt more rootless than the people in my care. There were times when I thought nostalgically of the profession I had abandoned, of the farms of Loir-et-Cher, of the simple, honest, close-knit families that had shared my nocturnal labours in cowsheds and stables, some medieval, and the dawn breakfasts with their warm and friendly atmosphere. Unable to renounce that world entirely, even during my peregrinations across the American continent, I continued to keep abreast of developments, attend seminars and familiarize myself with the latest veterinary techniques. I sometimes attended courses at Cornell and the Philadelphia veterinary school. Noting how much more advanced veterinary medicine was in the United States than at home, I yearned to spend some time there. My sister Alice, who had lived in the States since 1930, urged me to stay for good, but by then I had become disenchanted with my life as an international bureaucrat and tendered my resignation.

Life in France seemed best after all, so one day in August 1952 I returned to Paris. The capital was holiday-stricken and denuded of friends and relations. I saw nobody I knew until, in the Place de l'Hôtel de Ville, I bumped into a contemporary whom I hadn't seen for years. He had just blown a tyre and was changing his wheel in the broiling sun.

It was a comforting reunion, but one which could have broken up – as such reunions generally do – after a friendly exchange of news. In the solitude of a Parisian August, it struck me as providential.

My ex-chum, who was in business, had an office above the Lido in the Champs-Elysées. There on a table he showed me a roll of material resembling the transparent adhesive strip of which countless varieties are now in general use.

'Terrific stuff,' he told me. 'I'm going to make a fortune out of it.'

I told him I had seen similar tape in the United States. That gave him an idea. What about going into business together? We would be the first arrivals on the French market. He needed someone competent and reliable to form a company with. I was just the person.

I fell for the scheme at once. Circumstances had presented me with another challenge. There was a problem to solve, a task to fulfil.

I made it my business to fulfil it. Anyway, the sticky tape idea was a good one, so why not?

I tackled this manufacturing venture in total ignorance, just as I had tackled Mario's chickens a few years earlier. Almost unaided, I set about solving technical problems of daunting complexity.

It was a titanic task. Everything had to be learnt, discovered or reinvented. I became a one-man band. We needed a fitter, a lathe operator, a welder, a chemist and so on. Compelled to be all these things myself, I delved into countless textbooks and manuals. I made friends with machine-shop proprietors who gave me the technical know-how I required and produced a few components for me. Little by little I became as well informed as any professional.

The craze lasted four years – four years in which I worked twelve or fourteen hours a day. And for what? A technological success: a handsome machine 36 feet long and 3 feet wide designed to turn out high-class adhesive strip in a satisfactory manner.

It worked; there was ample room for our product on the market. But it was then, with success in my grasp, that I drew back. Was this what I wanted? After four years of gruelling work all I had done, in essence, was to accept a challenge which could help to fill the vacuum in my life. I had stuck it out. I had once more proved what I was capable of, but ought I to follow the road any further? No, earning money interested me only to the extent that it was complementary to the task I had set myself. I sold my plant and changed course.

My varied experiences had left me very unsettled. For ten years I had been drifting like a rudderless boat at the mercy of the winds. I had no idea where to go, what to do, what to aim for. Everything seemed futile and devoid of interest. Was I genuinely unstable, as I sometimes tended to think? I was thirty-four years old. It was high time to make up my mind, high time to stop taking gambles every time they came along. The alternative was to resign myself to a sort of vagabond existence punctuated by peaks and troughs. At the same time, I felt a keen desire for continuity and a settled life. What was the answer?

I reverted to what came most naturally to me, the profession that had already brought me such profound peace and content- ment. My brother Jean had never approved of my industrial venture. 'Why mess around with all that sticky stuff?' my sister-in-law Simone used to ask me brightly. 'You're a vet with a decent profession at your fingertips.' In fact, even during my four years in business, I never entirely lost touch with the living world of animals. Although nobody knew I was a vet, I would occasionally treat a neighbour's dog or cat. I also acted as locum to a country vet from time to time, partly because I was short of cash and partly, I think, because it satisfied a genuine need.

One fine day I made up my mind I had been, was, and would remain a vet.

To brush up my knowledge, I went back to the college at Maisons-Alfort and took a refresher course. Then, like any young graduate, I re-entered the service of my original em- ployer. Already an excellent vet when I worked for him ten years before, Pierre had made still further progress while I was knocking about the world. I was starting from scratch. I explained the position to him, and he had sufficient faith in me to take me back as a probationer.

I didn't exactly jump for joy when I reached Souligné- sous-Ballon, in the Department of Sarthe, that Sunday in spring. The drive there in my little 4CV convertible had given me time to think. I weighed my achievements in the balance and found them wanting. Harshly as I judged myself, however, my morale was not at rock bottom. I was returning to the familiar peace and security of the animal world like a prodigal son. Besides, my years of absence had not been wholly wasted. I had gained experience, seen and learnt a wide variety of things – tested my powers of adaptation.

I would have to tread carefully. It would not be easy, and I made no attempt to conceal my faint misgivings when Pierre started briefing me at lunch the first day. He would be there to advise me, but only at a distance. The fact was that he had become allergic to penicillin. It brought on severe asthma attacks even when confined in a sealed flask or present as a trace substance in mixtures and ointments. This sensitivity later compelled him to give up his country practice. For the time being, it would be my job to look after the farm animals which he was no longer able to visit or treat in person.

What animals? Many of them were racehorses, which presented problems of a specialized and delicate nature. As for the local cows, they were Maine-Anjous, a breed of heavy beef animals bearing large calves which often proved incapable of unaided delivery.

But there was another problem. Our practice shared the veterinary field with a dozen bone-setters or gelders – *empiriques* (quacks), as they were locally known. These unqualified practitioners, many of them experienced and capable men, were legally permitted to practice under certain conditions. In principle, scientific and technological progress gave the vet a big advantage, but the *empiriques* had also made progress and often employed techniques which were officially forbidden them. Their clients had confidence in them. Quite frequently the vet was not called in until things went wrong, less to save an animal which the farmer had already written off than to save the meat. Only a vet could authorize its commercial sale.

All things considered, it seemed that I would be up against stiff opposition in a contest which promised to be unequal from the start.

Pierre's briefing made my heart sink. I hoped to have a few days in which to find my feet and get back into the swing, but fate decreed otherwise. I was promptly thrown in at the deep end.

The phone rang at 2 a.m. on the very night of my arrival.

'An urgent foaling,' I was told. Just what I had been afraid of, first because I had never handled one and second because I attached an almost sacred quality to foaling and regarded it as one of the most difficult tricks of the trade.

I had barely slept for an hour when the call jolted me awake. Yawning, ill at ease and rather apprehensive, I stowed my bag in the car and set off. I had to negotiate a ten-mile maze of minor roads and rutted lanes before reaching the stables. Here I was greeted by an intimidating sight.

As usual on such occasions, the entire family had assembled. I was introduced by the farmer to a trio of large and muscular individuals all considerably sturdier and taller than myself. They wore corduroy trousers, rubber boots and shirts with rolled-up sleeves. The look in their eyes conveyed that they were men of intelligence and experience. I was face to face with three *empiriques*!

There was plenty to be nervous about. I would have to succeed where these men, whom I reckoned to be competent practitioners with twenty or thirty years' experience behind them, had just failed. It was a crucial moment.

We gathered around the mare. What was wrong? Nobody was very explicit, so I had to find out for myself. I got into my working clothes, stripped to the waist, disinfected and lubricated my right arm. The mare was standing with one man at her head and another holding a foreleg off the ground to prevent her from lashing out. She was already so tired that I had little to fear in this respect, but textbook precautions are always worth observing. I proceeded to explore her genital passages with my arm buried shoulder-deep.

All eyes were fixed on me – eleven pairs of them – and everyone remained silent while I felt the foal in the animal's uterus. Countryfolk are courteous and tactful on these occasions. None of my audience asked any stupid questions, but their concerted gaze was a lot more intimidating than the risk of a sudden kick. After all, what was I to them? They knew 'Monsieur Pierre' of old. I was an anonymous creature who didn't rate as a proper vet. I wasn't even a junior partner or assistant, just a temporary sidekick.

This is not to say that I meant nothing to them. They entertained no particular mistrust or hostility towards me, but their attitude was guarded. They were waiting for me to act. The three *empiriques* would not, perhaps, be sorry if I

67

failed as they had done. For the moment, however, they were neutral – not that this prevented them from showing a measure of good will. Work came first. One of them, a big strapping fellow with ruddy cheeks, shoved me hard against the mare's rump so that I could thrust my arm still deeper inside.

Throughout this time, the mare continued her attempts to expel the foal. Each contraction immobilized my arm and hand by crushing them against the pubis, but I finally managed to detect what was happening. A foal normally emerges with its head and forefeet leading, like a diver, but this one was, in a sense, looking back over its shoulder. To make matters worse, the head seemed too big and one of the forelegs was flexed. I tried to manipulate it but the knee joint was locked. We were undoubtedly dealing with an abnormal foal.

I explained the situation. I could already detect a hint of respect in the watchers' eyes, but they were waiting for a solution to the problem. In theory, there were two: Caesarean section or embryotomy. In practice, only embryotomy was feasible. At that time, in 1955, it was far from common practice to induce general anaesthesia in a mare – the only thing that would have enabled me to section her under satisfactory conditions. Without this precaution, any movement on the mare's part might have expelled the intestines from the abdomen and would almost certainly have caused fatal peritonitis. A horse's peritoneum (the membrane lining the abdominal cavity and covering the organs it contains) is extremely fragile – far more so than in human beings and other animal species. The least contamination will set up a fatal infection.

In order to save the mare I would have to dismember her foal, which was not viable in any case, and extract it. The first step was to administer a regional anaesthetic, a tricky procedure which exceeded the competence of any *empirique*. Here again, as in diagnosis, the qualified veterinarian enjoys a fundamental advantage. Epidural anaesthesia calls for an injection into the spinal column at the base of the tail.

I injected a massive dose of novocaine to ensure that the uterus was thoroughly relaxed and enable me to remove the foal. The disadvantage of this excessive dosage was that the anaesthetic affected the mare's hindquarters and made her lie down. All my ensuing labours would have to be performed lying in the straw with my head against the animal's rump.

I introduced a wire-saw into the uterus. This is a cutting

wire with a toothed edge and two handles which remain outside to enable it to be worked back and forth. The trick is to insert it by hand without injuring the genital organs in the process. The loop must then be inserted as far as possible, passed round the area to be cut, and secured with the aid of Thygessen's apparatus, two metal tubes which enclose both ends of the wire and protect the adjacent organs while it is being operated.

I lay on my side in the straw. Though stripped to the waist, I was soon bathed in sweat. The mare's proximity made it very warm in the loose box. A vet's arm is never long enough, so one of the men had to push me the whole time to enable me to gain an extra inch or two. Although there were no more contractions, thanks to the anaesthesia, the very weight of the foal and the mare's internal organs was enough to compress my hand and arm while I inserted the saw in the uterus and someone else worked the handles from outside. My fingers grew numb to the point of paralysis, and I had to withdraw my arm every five minutes to massage my hand and rest it. I was rather like a wrestler in an armlock. My struggle was, in fact, a trial of strength as well as skill. Instead of wrestling in a nice dry ring, however, I was lying in filthy straw. Throughout my exertions, the mare kept showering me with urine and sending me presents of dung. It wasn't exactly comfortable, but I can't say I minded too much. Even at that close range, I quite enjoy the smell of horse's dung and urine.

Once the wire-saw was in place I withdrew my arm and used both hands to saw, taking it in turns with one or another of my assistants but continually checking to see that it remained in position. Sometimes it got jammed, pinched between tendons or fragments of bone. Again I had to plunge my hand into the uterus, this time holding a small incurvated knife, to clear the whole obstruction. Sometimes, too, the saw snapped. This meant groping about inside and starting all over again with a replacement.

It was a really back-breaking business. Preliminary success at last: I managed to sever one shoulder and extract a foreleg. I now had more room to loop the saw round the neck and cut through the cervical vertebrae. Once freed, however, the head refused to come. What was the trouble? Excessive size: the foal was hydrocephalic. I had to make a sagittal or midline section, an irksome and infuriating job. The head kept shifting and jammed the saw, so I had to hold it by hand while some-one sawed from the outside.

The foal's pelvis presented a similar problem. It was too broad to negotiate the narrows formed by the pubis and the sacroiliac arch. A final section severed one of the hindlegs together with part of the pelvis. This enabled the whole of the remainder to be extracted.

After completing the 'delivery', I made sure there was no bleeding and that the vagina, cervix and uterus had suffered no injury. The vagina had dried up during the operation, so it had to be lubricated with several pints of oil and some anti-septic gel. Despite these precautions, the mare's genital area was in a bad state. The contractions had made it sore, and the haematomata covering it looked as if they had been inflicted with a clenched fist. To soothe the mucous membranes I introduced another generous dose of antiseptic gel followed by some antibiotic pessaries. The effects of the anaesthetic were likely to linger for another two hours, so the mare would be spared the worst of the pain before she regained her feet.

It was 5 a.m. All finished. Grubby and bathed in sweat, I emerged from the saturated straw and abandoned myself to the delights of a stand-up wash in a pail of hot water. The farmer's wife proffered some nice dry sweet-smelling cloths. I got dressed and went to receive my reward, an early breakfast in the farm kitchen. Eleven good-humoured faces gathered around a big cartwheel of a loaf, Calvados and bottles of red wine. Everybody registered satisfaction. The mare was safe. Our efforts had not been in vain.

But I was happier than any. I had not lost my touch. Far from proving a handicap, industrial work had increased my dexterity. Although I was starting all over again, I had acquired more self-confidence. I had been scared before the ordeal but not during it. My drastic re-introduction to professional life left me feeling satisfied and equal to any problems that came along.

The next day, Monday, brought another test of skill. This time the challenge was a pregnant cow. She was ready to calve but had stopped feeding. Something was wrong, the owner told me anxiously. Did it portend a difficult delivery, or what?

The cow was carrying her head low. I detected a slight swelling on the dewlap, the big fold of skin running from the throat to the chest. Some kind of cardiac trouble? I auscultated and then percussed the animal, but not with two fingers as a physician sounds a human patient's chest. I dug my fist under the last rib and supported it there with my knee. Sometimes a pole is used. This time my fist was good enough. The cow gave an agonized moo. I examined her from the calving aspect. Everything seemed to be going well. Conclusion: the cause of the trouble was very probably a nail or piece of wire which had lodged in the vicinity of the heart. She must have swallowed it several weeks ago. The movements inside her rumen, or first stomach, had carried the piece of wire or nail towards the left anterior portion of the stomach. This had eventually perforated, causing localized peritonitis. If it were not removed, the foreign body would continue its progress towards the heart and do fatal damage.

The only answer was immediate surgery.

I reported my diagnosis to Pierre. It would be a major operation made even trickier by the fact that the cow was at term and about to calve. Pierre's reluctance to delegate the job was obvious. As tactfully as he could, he proposed to enlist the services of a more experienced colleague. Emboldened by my success of the previous night, I refused point blank. Either I operated alone or I went. My determination must have impressed him, because he gave way.

I got to the farm at eight the next morning. It was a small, somewhat dilapidated building with a stable door, a pot of flowers on the windowsill and a dung heap in the yard – a modest establishment with eight cows and two horses. The sun was shining brightly. The whole family – father, mother and three children aged between ten and fifteen – had been mobilized for the occasion. So, as usual, had a number of neighbours.

I had not come alone this time. Some vets enlist their wives to help them. Not being married at this stage, I had brought along a girlfriend whom I introduced as a veterinary student. Monique was a physiotherapist, not a budding vet, but she worked at the Cochin Hospital in Paris and was no stranger to surgical operations. She knew how nurses worked, what instruments were used and how they should be presented to the surgeon. Equipped with this knowledge, she made a deft and able assistant. For good measure, she called me 'doctor'. I could tell at once that this title was not lost on my audience. Around here, vets were called 'monsieur', so who was

71

this sidekick of Monsieur Pierre's to be addressed as 'doctor', like a big-city practitioner?

The farmer and his wife emerged from the cowshed leading my patient, who was looking even sorrier for herself than the day before. They tethered her to a ring in the wall and stationed themselves at her head and tail respectively. A bed of straw was arranged around the animal. I had previously sent for two pails of water, one hot and one cold, together with a sponge and some cloths. Monique laid out the sterile instruments on a covered packing case and the non-sterile equipment, pliers, razor blades and so forth on a box beside it.

I knew the operation in theory, having rehearsed every phase of it the night before. All I now had to do was take the plunge, in other words, dive into that vast organ which constitutes the rumen or stomach of a cow and find an insignificant little piece of metal.

Everybody has some idea of the human stomach, but the layman finds it hard to conceive of a cow's bulk and the dimensions of its internal organs. The rumen alone has a volume of 17 or 18 cubic feet, and it was in or around this that I would have to rummage with my fingers, working blind.

I began by administering a local anaesthetic of xylocaine. This took the form of twenty-odd injections following the line of the 12-inch incision which would be made in the flank, high and to the left, to provide access to the rumen. Then came an epidural anaesthetic, as in the case of the mare the day before. This time, however, ease of access prescribed a dose that would not cause the cow to lie down. We pulled on our gloves, which were still not in widespread use in animal surgery. The incision had to be vertical so that the immense. weight of the rumen would tend to close the wound, whereas a horizontal cut would have torn it open still further. I sliced through a layer of muscle over an inch thick. My task was to reach the peritoneum, the fine membrane enclosing all the organs in the abdomen, without detaching it. The incision had to be accurate to within a millimetre.

Inserting my entire arm into this big 12-inch slit, I pushed the rumen aside and explored the abdomen. I felt the calf on the other side. I groped along the rumen on the side nearest the heart and encountered clots of fibrin – a sign that I was getting warm. At last my fingers detected something: a nail whose point had pierced the rumen, the head remaining inside. It had perforated the diaphragm and grazed the pericardium, the membrane surrounding the heart. The point was titillating this entire area and subjecting it to painful tension. The nail itself was quite sizeable – perhaps three inches long.

I was in luck. So was the cow. If the nail had passed right through, inflammation of the pericardium would have been more advanced, probably accompanied by purulence, and nothing could have saved the beast. I now had to remove the nail, but not from the outside. The head would make an even bigger hole in the rumen as it passed through, and the contents would be discharged into the peritoneum. I would have to extract it from the inside after first emptying and cleaning the entire organ. To help me locate the nail head more easily, I began by pushing the point inwards.

Before opening the rumen, I cleaned its exterior and sponged the retrodiaphragmatic cavity between the base of the rumen, the diaphragm and the sternum. At last I opened it up, securing it with clips to the surrounding skin and muscle to prevent it from 'capsizing' inside the abdomen and voiding its contents there. These I proceeded to empty by hand – not just a bowlful but several brimming buckets.

Rather anxiously, I ran my fingers over the base of the voluminous sac. The head of the nail was hard to locate, especially as the lining of the rumen is honeycombed with alveoli, but I was in luck once more. My fingers soon encountered four pieces of wire at the place where I guessed the nail to be. I felt again. The nail was there. The pieces of wire which had served as a guide were clustered round it. I had only to remove them.

These fragments of metal can travel round the rumen for a long time, propelled by the ruminal movements, without doing any harm. Some are eliminated, but others may become lodged in the honeycomb lining. Because peristalsis continues to exert pressure on them, they end by piercing the rumen as the nail had done.

I pursued my search to ensure that nothing was left behind. There was always the chance of finding a hairball or two. Formed by a process of gradual agglomeration, these can circumnavigate the rumen indefinitely without causing any trouble and sometimes come to light during autopsies or in the slaughterhouse.

I completed my voyage of exploration. No more pieces of wire; no hairballs either. Everything was going well. I could sense growing approval in the eyes that rested on me. All that remained was needlework: five layers totalling about fifty stitches. The rumen required two rows superimposed to form a sero-serous seal, with the edges of the seam turned inwards. Then came the peritoneum. Then a layer of muscle. Finally, the skin.

The cow and I had both made it. I prescribed a muzzle during her twenty-four-hour postoperative fast followed by a diet of bran and barley mash to provide nourishment for the calf's benefit. Some antibiotics too. Monique and I gathered up our equipment. It was all over. The farmer's wife anxiously inquired if the calf would be all right. I told her there should be no problem. 'Thank you, Doctor,' she said.

Monique glanced at me.

Two days later a problem did crop up after all. The cow was too weak to expel her calf.

My third test: a Caesarean. Yet another operation I had never performed – one which was then a comparative rarity and had to be carried out on an animal debilitated by recent surgery.

Fortunately, I emerged with flying colours. The cow, the calf and my professional reputation all survived. Pleased as I was with my success, I still had much to learn and relearn before I became an experienced professional, as I would soon find out.

One day I was summoned to the aid of a sick calf. The farmer led me to his cowshed, which housed two rows of animals separated by a central walkway. The calf was in the second stall on the right. It was feverish, so the farmer had draped a sheepskin over its back to protect it from the cold. He removed the fleece when we entered and tossed it into the manger.

This gesture startled the calf's neighbour, a cow with big horns. One toss of her head dislodged the beam, doubtless worm-eaten, to which she had been chained, and which formed the edge of her manger. The farmer and I were between her flank and the calf. As she turned to flee down the central aisle, the cow upended my companion with her beam and chain. I tried to seize her by the horns but was brushed aside in my turn.

74

I received a butt in the chest which winded me and knocked me down. The cow charged towards the exit. Then a sudden whim caused her to turn back. Lying there on the mud floor, bruised, soaked and unable to move, I saw her looming over me. She lunged, trying to gore me.

The farmer had meanwhile regained his feet. He managed to shove the cow away and released me with the aid of his wife, who had been milking farther down the aisle. Then he helped me up, only to find that I couldn't stand. My legs weren't working.

Together the farmer and his wife half-carried me to the farm kitchen, where they sat me down on a chair. I didn't feel too bad, but my legs still refused to obey me. I was completely dazed and feared the worst.

The farmer went to fetch a doctor from Ballon, four miles away. I asked his wife for a cloth and some cold water, intending to make myself a compress. It was less a rational attempt at treatment than the whim of a man in shock. She came back with a saucepan and a handtowel. Still half dazed, I calmly removed my trousers, gazing at the farmer's wife with a vacant expression. I don't know what she thought, but as soon as I raised my shirt to examine my stomach I detected a glint of alarm in her eye. She retreated hastily, and I didn't see her again until her husband returned.

A little later the doctor drove me back to Pierre's house. I was still paralysed. That evening, ensconced in a wheelchair, I was put aboard the train to Paris, where my brother whipped me into hospital.

It was nothing serious, thank God. The cow had merely inflicted massive bruising, and the blood-filled contusions had temporarily paralysed my legs by pressing on certain nerves. Ten days later the bruises had dispersed and I was able to return to Souligné-sous-Ballon.

Did this little *corrida* put me off cows for life? Far from it. Not long afterwards we received a call from the same farmer. It was the animal that had gored me: she had developed some warts in her teats, and they were making her rather edgy.

Was I edgy too?

Having asked myself this question, I found I could answer it in the negative. It was the farmer and his wife who looked nervous when I got to the farm – nervous on my behalf, so I had to set their minds at rest. I petted the cow for a minute or two, checked that the worm-eaten beam had been replaced with a new one, hobbled my patient's hindlegs – cow-kicks are peculiarly treacherous because they describe a sideways arc – and set to work. The object was to curette the warts after drawing off the milk with a teat syphon and infusing the teats with a local anaesthetic.

The cow was as good as gold. I didn't feel at all apprehensive, a fact which reassured me about my relationship with animals. Physically, the earlier incident might have had serious consequences. Psychologically, it might have put my future career in doubt; I could hardly conceive of a practising vet who felt ill at ease with animals and was scared of touching them. The perfect peace that reigned between me and my erstwhile attacker was a practical demonstration of the profound accord between myself and 'them'. It was real confirmation that I had chosen the right path in life.

4

Youyou and Me

The cow's horns did, for all that, have a significant effect on me. They prodded me even harder into considering whether to leave the provinces in spite of my deep attachment to the countryside.

'You'd do better to switch to small animal practice,' Pierre said occasionally.

In other words, go and look after cats and dogs in the city. Why should he have advised me to move when my preference was for horses and cattle, stable and byre? Why, when I was just starting to build up a good store of experience in my chosen field? Why? Because the rural scene was changing fast. The tractor was replacing the drafthorse and the industrialization of stock farming called for prophylactic measures rather than the services of a traditional country vet.

Besides, other people kept asking me what I was doing in the country. I was the young man who had roamed the world from Madrid to Buenos Aires via New York, hobnobbing with the kind of people – generals and ambassadors – who are rarely seen soiling their shoes with cow dung. Although this did my reputation no harm, it did prevent me from becoming all I wanted to be in the eyes of others: a straightforward country vet.

For me, the problem was a very serious one. However cosmopolitan I might seem, I yearned to be a countryman. I had planned to work in the country ever since 1940. My ultimate dream was to be a farmer, and my choice of profession had been a circuitous attempt to fulfil it. I couldn't even conceive of being an urban vet, so how could I leave the provinces? How on earth could I ever practise in town?

But that was where the future lay, and the forces that were recalling me to the city had never been wholly subdued by

77

those that attracted me to the land. Yet again, chance resolved the issue.

While I was attending some specialist courses at Maisons-Alfort, a fellow student asked me if I would stand in for a vet at Bois-Colombes during August. I agreed. At my colleague's request, I went to see him the day before he left. He was going on holiday, leaving me his house and his mother-in-law. I found that he possessed no dispensary to speak of and gathered that he had very few clients either. He performed no surgery. As soon as a dog showed any signs of illness, he resorted to the final solution.

Actually, my first patient turned out to be a horse, and it was partly thanks to this animal that all the canine pets in the neighbourhood descended on my temporary consulting room. The horse belonged to a market gardener from Gennevilliers who had been advised to call in the colleague I was replacing.

I was pleased at the prospect of treating a horse and even more pleased to discover, on arrival, that I was still in the country despite my suburban surroundings. I found myself in the paved courtyard of an old farm. On one side stood the wash-house where radishes, beetroots and lettuces were rinsed before sale, on the other the stable housing the sick drafthorse. There was a delicious scent of earth, vegetables and dung. I felt thoroughly at home although factories loomed close at hand and buildings were going up in the vicinity.

The owner, too, was a thoroughbred agriculturalist even though he lived and worked within spitting distance of Paris and drove to Les Halles every evening to sell his produce. He was not a relic of another era but a sturdy man of thirty. We were soon on the same wavelength.

He took me to see his Percheron. I noted at once that the big horse's eyes and penis were yellow and that his urine was a deep orange, indicating jaundice. I gave him copious drips, and after ten days of treatment he began to recover. His owner followed his progress with satisfaction. I returned from every visit laden with lettuces and bunches of radishes. My client sensed that he was dealing with someone who shared his genuine love of animals and the land. We became friends and have remained so to this day.

My success with the Percheron brought me several cat owners from Gennevilliers, but cats from Bois-Colombes also took the road to my temporary headquarters. For my

78

first feline patients I prescribed preparations for human use on sale at the chemist – an unusual practice in that part of the world. I had also come equipped with my instrument bag and was persuaded to undertake a few operations – yet another novelty. Before long, I was swamped with ailing cats and dogs.

Small animal practice was a new field from my point of view. Our staple subject at Toulouse had been the horse (today it is the dog), and all other animals were studied on a comparative basis. However, I was now experienced enough to tackle animals unfamiliar to me. My colleague expressed satisfaction on his return, but my own satisfaction was greater still.

Was I really going to set up on my own at last? I examined a few likely prospects, preoccupied by an urgent desire to go on holiday. I had a girlfriend, a car and a little spare cash. Studying a map of Spain I decided that the coast around Alicante looked attractive. I guessed it might offer some good fishing, so we went. My hunch paid off. Once there, I found that chance had guided me to a spot frequented by Jacques Cousteau.

By the time I got back to Paris, the only property still available was a small surgery in the Batignolles district. It was an unprepossessing establishment which averaged less than one client a day. I had been offered the place before leaving but had not even bothered to view it. Since then it had closed down. What if I took it all the same?

It was a gamble, but I felt the time had come to stop changing horses midstream. I had to settle down somewhere and stay put.

I duly bought the place. It boasted a facia inscribed in letters two feet high. I had them sanded off. I was not going to put up a plate or facia of any kind. My clientele would be based on recommendation, personal contact and good will.

So that was where circumstances, Mario's hens included, had installed me by such devious means: in a little urban surgery in Paris, settling for small animal practice. My intention was to stay for some time, and despite many subsequent changes, I have been in practice there for over twenty years.

My predecessor had employed a male nurse who asked me to take him on. He also tried to sell me an instrument of torture – a castration box for cats which his predecessor had used. Until the last century, cats haunting the banks of the

Seine used to be neutered with the aid of a sack or a length of stovepipe. A tomcat imprisoned head downwards in either of these could not bring its claws to bear. You simply pulled its tail to make the testicles protrude, slit the skin of the scrotum, gripped the testicles between your fingers and tore them out 'by elongation', thus avoiding the risk of haemorrhage.

The castration box, which was still in general use when I set up shop, represented only a minor technical improvement on this barbarous method. It was a box so designed that the cat remained inside while its tail and testicles protruded. This enabled the vet to pluck out the animal's testes without being hampered by its struggles.

But the Middle Ages were over. I had no intention of using such a method. Given the resources available to us, there was no justification for castrating an animal without a general anaesthetic. I declined both the services of the male nurse and the use of the castration box.

Before long, a number of permanent lodgers insinuated themselves into my professional and private life. The first was a parrot left with me by a woman because it had taken to pulling out its own feathers. She found the sight distressing. I liked the bird and wanted to identify the cause of its relentless devotion to this strange form of striptease. It was undoubtedly a neurotic behaviour pattern. Was its cage too small? If so, was it worried because its plumage brushed against the bars? Was it suffering from claustrophobia? Boredom? A dietary deficiency? Whatever the trouble, I removed it from its cage and installed it on a large perch in the waiting room, where it would never lack for company.

The bird's condition improved. It became calmer and more cheerful. I discovered that it could whistle the 'Marseillaise' and delighted in saying 'Shut up!' and *'Merde!'* to clients in the waiting room, who were enchanted. It could also imitate a group of people laughing in several voices. What was more, it had a sense of the ridiculous. When a woman client's voice was too loud or shrill, it emitted a strident laugh. The parrot's timing never ceased to amaze me. I became convinced that it did more than mimic what it heard and possessed greater intelligence than people imagined.

A little later I acquired a myna to keep it company. Together, they put on a double act which went down well with the occupants of the waiting room. Frequent exposure to telephone conversations had caused them to memorize certain phrases. '*Allo, docteur?*' the myna would cry. '*N'est pas là,*' came the parrot's response.

The children of the quarter were quick to take an interest in my two birds. Every day after school, some of them visited the waiting room to make the birds talk, whistle the 'Marseillaise' and cackle with laughter. This additional distraction proved very welcome to my lodgers. Just before four o'clock, they embarked on a major wash-and-brush-up in the bowl of water I had given them. Then, well before their visitors' arrival, they began to imitate childish laughter. My own belief is that they could hear the children emerging from the nearby Lycée Chaptal well in advance of the human ear.

Sometimes I was brought an animal and asked to destroy it. If I refused, it might be left in my care. That was how I came to inherit a young cercopithecus – a long-tailed African monkey – whom I christened Julot. Julot, who spent the day tethered to the radiator in the consulting room, had very bad manners. One day he snatched a female client's earring, popped it in his mouth and secreted it in one of his cheek pouches. No amount of persuasion would induce him to spit it out.

Julot used to masturbate lustily. He derived particular inspiration from a very pretty and sexy-looking girlfriend of mine, who induced an erection whenever she played with him. One day she was sitting in the consulting room about 10 feet from Julot's radiator. Between this and the desk stood the table where I was busy examining a spaniel. My friend picked up the phone and started speaking. Whatever the effect of her voice on Julot, he started to masturbate. A moment later he came with such force that his semen flew over my head, the cocker and the table, to complete its trajectory on my girlfriend's dress. Her reaction can well be imagined.

Another time, a woman client was leaning over the examination table, chatting to me. Her skirt was on the short side, so Julot jumped off his radiator and bit her in the buttock.

There was absolutely no doubt that women excited him, but he showed just as keen an interest in my nurse's white poodle bitch, a very elegant, flirtatious and feminine little creature called Jisca. Julot's feelings for her were more than friendly. He spent a deal of time touching her backside and sniffing his hand with an inquiring air. It was a hilarious gesture. The monkey genuinely looked as if he were seeking sexual relations with an animal of another species. On the other hand, he may simply have been playing for laughs.

I also kept a turtledove which had the freedom of my consulting room. Her favourite perches were the top of the dispensary cupboard or, less often, the telephone. Contrary to my expectations, she did not let fly at random but deposited most of her droppings on the top of the cupboard, which I lined with fresh newspaper every day. She also liked to perch on the cupboard door when I opened it. I put a newspaper at the foot, and this became her other main depository. I think she realized where, and where not, to go.

The dove was a great source of annoyance to Julot, who invariably tried to grab her when she flew past and often managed to pull out a feather. One dark day he caught and plucked her clean in a matter of seconds. Much to our sorrow, she died.

Nevertheless, Julot had a keen sense of right and wrong. He spent the lunch hour chained to the top of some stairs which led down to the basement, where we took our meal. A woman client turned up but was too scared of the monkey to negotiate the stairs. I offered Julot a piece of bread. He sidled close enough for me to take him by the arm to let our visitor pass. Then I forgot to give him the bread. Justly incensed, he sank his teeth in my palm. I bear the scar to this day.

Sadly, it might be said that Julot died of greed. Another woman client had brought me some surplus medicines, thinking they might come in handy. Among them were some sleeping pills, which she left on my desk. Julot, who always filched anything he could, had already managed to get himself drunk by swigging the surgical spirit in my wash bottle. One lunchtime he slipped his chain. The padlock had not been properly secured, so he made the most of his heaven-sent opportunity. The pills being-sugar coated, he wolfed the lot.

Beyond compare, the star of all my animals and the one I loved best was Youyou, a black and tan shepherd dog from Beauce with sorrowful eyes and an endearing face.

The purpose of Youyou's first visit to my consulting room was to spend his last moments on earth there. He limped in with a mournful air, dull of coat and eye, one leg dragging, accompanied by his master and mistress. They were a young respectable-looking couple who seemed as dejected as their dog.

'You see?' said the man. 'You'll have to put him down.'

He gulped hard, and his wife started to cry. The dog stretched out between them and my desk, indifferent to what was going on. Put him down, I thought – just like that?

I had steadfastly refused to destroy animals during my spells as a locum whenever the owners' motives were insufficient – most commonly, a wish to go on holiday unencumbered by a pet. On the other hand, canine euthanasia was money in the bank.

Determined not to crack under pressure, I questioned my clients. They had been involved in a road accident in the provinces. The dog sustained a fracture of the left femur. Despite surgery and the best of postoperative care, osteomyelitis developed. This is an infection of the bone marrow which often proves incurable, and some veterans of the 1914–18 war had never got rid of the infection after being hit by shrapnel. The owners had left Youyou in kennels for eighteen months, being often on the move, but his condition deteriorated. He was steadily losing weight, had three suppurating ulcers on his thigh, and suffered from chronic diarrhoea. Things couldn't go on this way, the man said. They were sick with worry themselves, quite apart from the fact that they had already spent a great deal of money on treatment. They made a fair living but they weren't millionaires, so they had decided to end the dog's suffering – and their own. While driving to their home near Barbès, they had spotted the barely legible words *Clinique Vétérinaire* on my stone facia.

The owners sounded very convincing, but was there really nothing more to be done? I couldn't bring myself to destroy the dog. The more I saw of Youyou, the more I liked the look of him. Instinctively, I refused to kill a creature that might still have years of life ahead.

What was to be done? The man and his wife gazed unhappily at one another, reluctant to press the point, so I made a suggestion. Why not leave the dog with me? Before putting him down I would make a last attempt to cure him. Fees? We could discuss that later. I promised to keep in touch.

They patted the dog in a rather shamefaced way before tearfully taking their leave. Youyou, who had been lying down, merely sat up when they walked to the door. He was too weak for any greater display of emotion. I also believe that his nobility of character, which I was soon to discover for myself, imposed a certain degree of self-restraint.

So what had I taken on? The signs were most unpromising. Could a dog – even a young dog like Youyou, who was only two years old – recover from osteomyelitis? I felt an instinctive urge to fight for his life, first and foremost because I had taken a liking to him but also because I have never been able to resist the challenge posed by a problem, especially one that looks insoluble, or by the need to improvise and experiment.

Poor Youyou went back on the operating table. I took specimens for the preparation of cultures. Research into antibiotics was all the rage at this period, so I made widespread inquiries in the hope of finding one that would act. I asked my friends in the laboratories if they could suggest a new product and prevailed on them to study the germs we were isolating. I also tried an autovaccine. I opened Youyou's ulcers several times and scraped them, but nothing really worked. For some weeks he improved slightly and my hopes revived. Then the ulcers started suppurating again. Youyou lost weight. The diarrhoea returned and his limp became more pronounced. It was most discouraging.

During these experiments Youyou lived at the surgery, where I used to leave him overnight. There was no cage, so he came and went as he pleased. He behaved well and did no damage in spite of his ailments. At the end of the day he used to watch me leave with an inquiring air, never barking, always the soul of tact. One evening, moved by affection and a sneaking sense of pity, I said 'All right, come along!' and took him home to the small studio apartment where I then lived. It was an effort, for all that. What with his ulcers, his diarrhoea and his dragging leg, Youyou was not the most appealing of companions.

Winter came. I had been trying hard to save the animal for nearly a year and was close to giving up. So was Youyou himself. Quiet and reserved though he was, he started to tremble and bark as soon as I approached to give him an injection. It became increasingly difficult to get him on to the examination table. He resisted with all the strength of his large breed and tried to bite me.

As a last resort, I decided to operate. This was yet another occasion on which I had to make do without the benefit of

84

prior experience. An x-ray of the dog's thigh revealed a hole in the femur. I proposed to open him up again, scrape and clean the cavity even more deeply than before, and then make a graft with a fragment of bone removed from the pelvis or one of his ribs.

I took every care to work in aseptic conditions, which were absolutely essential if I was to have the slightest prospect of success. The operation might not work, but I should at least have given Youyou one last chance.

Although I cannot claim that the entire quarter took an interest in Youyou's operation, plenty of people were ready to hold his paw and offer encouragement. The neighbours knew of his trials and tribulations, and I was not the only one who found him endearing. Across the way from my surgery lived a dachshund patient of mine whose mistress often asked for news of Youyou. Her third-floor apartment overlooked the windows of my consulting room, which was at street level. A blind shielded it from the gaze of passers-by, but only to shoulder height. I learned some days later that my neighbour had followed the entire operation through binoculars.

I knew I had to work with extreme care. If I left any trace of infection in the bone or marrow, however small, it would spread once more. The affected areas were slightly greyer than the healthy, but it was not easy to distinguish them. To help me see better, I procured a pair of glasses with special magnifying lenses like those used by ophthalmic surgeons.

The cavity in the femur looked very nasty. I enlarged it, scraping out the bone with a curette. I removed the infected marrow, cut away all the damaged tissue and painted the area with tincture of iodine. Instead of making a graft at once, however, I closed the wound.

There was nothing to do but wait.

A month passed without any sign of renewed infection. I postponed the graft again.

I was far from certain of success, being aware that the trouble might well recur at any time in the next few months, but the weeks went by and Youyou continued to improve. I was not only gratified but a trifle surprised as well. I had been prepared for failure. Why had the operation succeeded? Perhaps because Youyou was exceptionally tough, perhaps because I had taken a gamble on scraping the bone thoroughly

85

and removing so much of it – perhaps too, because Youyou and I had both been lucky.

There was still no relapse after six months. I regarded Youyou as cured. Now in the best of spirits, he never left my side, escorting me home every night and sleeping at the foot of my bed. If I took him along when I went to the cinema, he guarded my car without a single whine or bark of protest. He was a perfect companion: attentive and affectionate, always well behaved, never overexuberant or boisterous. In the days of his illness I had been dutiful enough to take him home with me, rather against my will. Now everything had changed. Youyou was my pride and joy.

However, I had made his owners a promise when they left him in my care. I wrote and told them that their dog was cured and they came running. We met in my consulting room. Youyou went over, sniffed them and wagged his tail. His mistress started to cry just as hard as she had done when she left Youyou with me so many months ago. I asked the couple what they planned to do. They exchanged a glance, then said they wanted him back. How much did they owe me? I told them I didn't know exactly. Youyou had been with me for over a year. I had given him a lot of treatment, x-rayed him, made cultures and autovaccines, operated on him.

Throughout our conversation, Youyou lay between me and his former owners on the floor of my little consulting room. His ears moved as we spoke, and I could have sworn that not a word escaped him. I was standing in front of my desk with my clients seated facing me.

Suddenly but unhurriedly, Youyou rose. He walked over to me and sat on my foot, leaning against my leg. I instinctively got the message. Youyou had just made his choice. He had told me, 'I'm yours, not theirs.' He wasn't a client's dog any more, he was mine. I couldn't give him back or exchange him for a sum of money. Youyou's simple gesture had made me realize the depth of my affection for him.

His owners were a decent couple. I put it to them that the dog had just indicated our proper course of action and asked them to let me keep him. Although the wife shed a few more tears, they agreed. The fee they had offered me represented a great financial sacrifice. They wanted to do the right thing by the dog, but the fact remained that they had grown accustomed to his absence.

86

Who could have been indifferent to such a dog? I was happy to keep him not only because of my affection for him but also because he was now an inseparable part of my life, professional as well as personal. This was the slightly selfish aspect of my attachment to him. Youyou, who had become extraordinarily popular in the neighbourhood, functioned as my unpaid PR man. Everyone at the local café knew who he was and what he had been through.

'Tell us, Youyou,' the initiates would say, whereupon You-you would sit, gaze at the leg which had caused him so much pain, and proceed to vocalize. I am convinced that he under-stood every word. He had often heard me describe the various forms of treatment I had given him. On one of these occasions, his eyes seemed to convey such an interest in the story that I broke off. It was as if he wanted to present a personal account of his feelings. That was when I first said, 'All right, *you* tell us.' And, to my great surprise, he began to 'sing', glancing at his thigh meanwhile. From then on, he would repeat this trick when asked to do so by his human friends.

Youyou remembered everything. If I said 'You want an injection?' he started to tremble; if other people said it, he would attack them. His behaviour was always perfectly gauged, perfectly controlled and adapted. He had the run of the neighbourhood, my sole proviso being that he remain on the same side of the street. To the best of my knowledge, he never broke this rule. His lavatory was the gutter of a small street leading off the boulevard, where the traffic was light. He never performed on the pavement itself.

Youyou's serene temperament and ease of manner with other people were miraculous. Although I was his master and came first in his affections, he was always polite and sociable towards others, even when they were obviously not to his taste. He was a model of instinctive dignity, but he expected other people's manners to be as good as his own.

Despite his manners, Youyou showed a natural protective-ness towards children. I shall never forget his behaviour at the home of Brard, the Gennevilliers market gardener whose horse I treated. The Brards had a baby. One day, for whatever reason, I raised my arm above its cradle. Youyou promptly started growling. Even coming from me, it was a forbidden gesture. Just to make sure, I repeated it. This time Youyou leapt at me and pushed me aside, still half convinced that the

87

threat was genuine. I raised my arm a third time. Although he was too intelligent not to grasp that I was play-acting, he reacted despite himself. Anyone else would have been ill advised to try such an experiment.

Youyou assumed the guardianship of our firstborn, Jean-François, as a matter of course. My wife and I, who were then living in a small apartment, sometimes employed a neighbour's daughter to baby-sit. Youyou did not utter a sound when she arrived, but one day he flatly refused to let her leave. He growled so fiercely when she approached the door that we had to come and rescue her. It was a sheepdog's reaction: when the sheep are in its keeping, no member of the flock may stray.

One of Youyou's fans was a magistrate friend of mine. One day, he came and asked me if he and his wife might take Youyou for a walk in the Bois de Boulogne. Instead of bringing him back that evening, however, they phoned to suggest keeping him till the following afternoon – partly, perhaps because they had just lost a beloved Airedale of their own. Youyou, who rarely raised his voice, greeted me next day with a barrage of furious growls and barks. I had earned myself a proper telling-off.

Youyou was so sociable and well behaved that people often borrowed him for the sheer pleasure of his company. I knew he was sure enough of my affection not to pine in my absence and so, being perennially short of space I did not mind gaining a little extra elbow room by entrusting him to others as fond of him as I was myself.

One afternoon I received an urgent call from a Madame X. I went to see her the same evening. The address turned out to be a shabby block in the 15th arrondissement of Paris. I was received in a two-room apartment by a monumental and imposing figure of a woman aged about fifty and weighing at least 200 pounds. Madame X introduced me to her 'companion', who was as thin, furtive and timid as her employer was vast and imperious. I was then taken to my patient.

Dozing on Madame X's bedspread was an enormous female mongrel, a cross between a mastiff and a hound, a creature built on the lines of its mistress, with a coat of many colours including yellow and white. My examination revealed endometritis and metroperitonitis. The bitch needed surgery at once. Her troubles must have been brewing for a long time, but now she

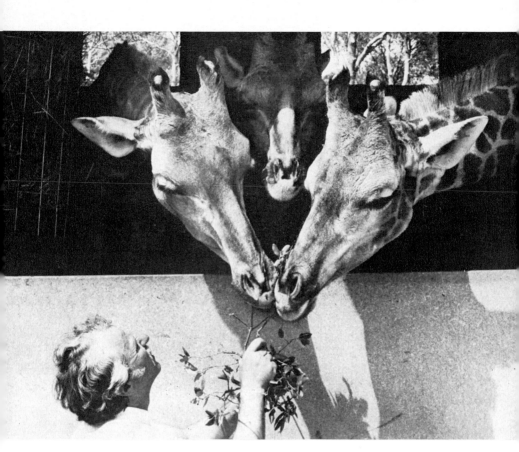

Making friends with three giraffes *(photo Figaro)*

The author anaesthetizes Cora, a 20-year-old lioness (*J.J. Morer*)

Cora on the operating table for a hysterectomy (*J.J. Morer*)

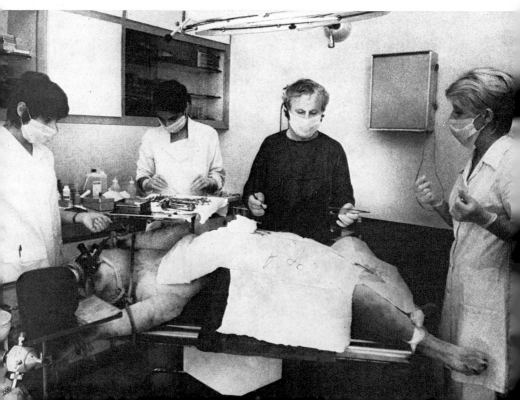

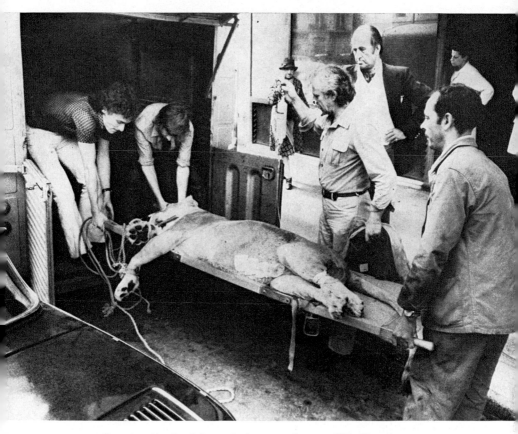

Cora is taken back by ambulance to the zoo *(J.J. Morer)*

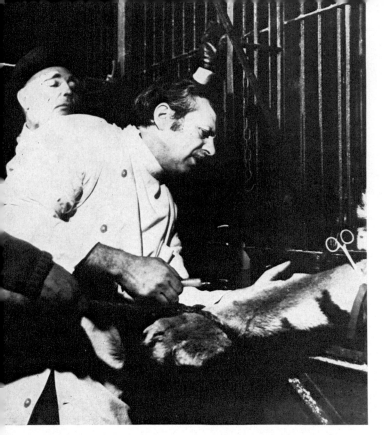

An intravenous
injection into a tiger's
paw (*L'Aurore*)

A tranquillizing injection before a medical examination in the cage (*J.J. Morer*)

was close to death. Although I was due to leave Paris at dawn next day, I decided to postpone my departure. I operated for the removal of a pus-filled uterus which must have weighed eight or nine pounds, and the dog survived.

After the full recovery of her pet, on one pretext or another, Madame X continued to haunt the surgery. She never came empty-handed and showered us with gifts. Needless to say, she fell for Youyou and would come to take him for walks with her own dog. One day Madame X held a big party at the house of one of her friends, a well-known architect, and asked if Youyou might accompany her. The guests were greeted by a butler. Every time the bell rang, Youyou escorted him to the top of the stairs that led to the reception room, then followed him downstairs and repeated the trick when the next arrivals came. I was assured that his dignified bearing had lent added lustre to an elegant occasion.

However, Youyou soon found another protectress who was destined to play an important part in his life. I often spent weekends at Courchevel, a popular ski resort, and always took him along. He roamed the resort freely, of course, but I never worried because he always reappeared at the day's end. Although everyone knew and liked him, he made a special hit with the proprietress of La Cordée, whose beloved greyhound had recently died at the age of fifteen. She always gave my Beauceron a warm welcome, and Youyou returned her affection. One weekend, just as I was leaving, she begged me to let him stay for a while. She had felt lonely since the death of her greyhound – and besides, she needed an efficient watchdog until she acquired a replacement. Youyou would be happy with her, she was positive.

I left him there for several weeks, then took him back, then left him again. One day, Youyou went to Courchevel for good. He was obviously happy in his new surroundings, which afforded a space and freedom of movement denied him in Paris. Would he grieve at my absence? Past experience proved otherwise. Youyou's emotional stability and sense of inner security would have enabled him to adapt to any new master or mistress who earned his affection. He had a big heart and a generous nature. It would have been unworthy of him to feel any kind of jealousy, and nothing about the atmosphere in which we had lived together justified the growth of such a

89

sentiment. Tolerance and friendship prevailed because they went without saying. Youyou was no more of a pampered 'only child' than any of my animals. His attitude towards me rather resembled that of a grown-up son towards his father. Everything about Youyou was in perfect harmony: freedom and obedience, love and independence.

I was soon to discover that I had far from ceased to figure in his life. I saw him whenever his mistress stayed in Paris, which was quite often. He would then spend several days with us, being made much of and no doubt reminded that my affection for him remained undimmed. One weekend I set off for Courchevel. I got there late at night after a difficult drive through rain and snow. Nobody had been warned of my arrival, so I decided to stop off at a chalet belonging to some friends who lived on the far side of town from La Cordée. The front door was unlocked. Rather than wake anyone, I sneaked in and commandeered a guest-room overlooking the terrace. Before going to bed I left the window ajar in my usual fashion.

Next morning I was butted awake by a dog. It was Youyou, whose instincts had alerted him to my presence. Sensing that I was in the neighbourhood, he had gone off in search of me and found his way to my terrace unaided. I should add that this was the first time I had slept at the chalet and that I had never even visited the place in Youyou's company.

Another weekend he went one better. It must have been a year later, by which time Youyou was entirely at home in the mountains. I reached Courchevel one rainy afternoon at the end of the season. Nobody was expecting me, as before, and I descended without warning on some other friends. This time I was in an apartment block with three flights of stairs and four doors on each landing. My friends' apartment was on the third floor.

We were chatting over a drink when something or someone scratched at the door. My hostess opened it to reveal Youyou, sopping wet and furiously wagging his tail. Once again he had been roaming the town, and once again something had alerted him to my presence. Nobody could have mentioned it in front of him because nobody knew I was there. If they had, he would have cocked an ear and gone looking for me at once. That, I venture to say, would have reflected but little credit on a dog of Youyou's omniscience. What we, as human beings, found so remarkable and mysterious was that he had once more sensed my proximity without hearing a word that might have put him on my track. He had trailed me to a large apartment block, taken the right staircase and scratched at the right door. It was quite a feat.

In one way or another, Youyou continued to show his enduring love and affection for me. I saw him often. Looking more and more regal, he presided over a carpet in front of the hotel's big open fireplace. Here he lay in a majestic pose, one forepaw flexed and the other extended. He would rise when I appeared and walk discreetly over to present his compliments. I suspect that if I had said 'All right, come along,' he would have followed me despite the affection he bore his new owner.

Youyou had found happiness. He divided his time between Courchevel, where he spent five or six months each year, and Paris or Castellane, but I often had him to stay for quite long spells.

He remained a very handsome dog to the last, with only a sprinkling of white hairs around his muzzle. What did I mean to him by then? I don't think I ever became a stranger. But once, while he was following his mistress down my garden path after a visit, the sight of him midway between me and her – I was standing on the steps to see them off – reminded me abruptly of that day in my consulting room when he had hesitated between me and his original owners. 'Youyou,' I called, but this time he did not come and lean against my leg. He paused and turned to look at me. Then, with the unhurried tread of an old gentleman, he caught his mistress up.

Not long afterwards, his mistress asked me to board him at Garches while she went on holiday just as I had entrusted him to her in the past. It was early summer. Youyou was now fifteen years old and did not get around much any more. What he liked best was to lie on the sandy path, warming himself in the sun. One Saturday afternoon my wife had been cutting some roses a few yards away. Bending down to give him a pat on her way back to the house, she found he was dead.

It was the gentlest of deaths, that peaceful and painless quietus beneath a summer sun – a final token of affection, perhaps. By expiring beside the rose bed in our garden,

Youyou seemed to have demonstrated that his real and ultimate home was with me.

There have been many other dogs in my life, but Youyou was my great canine love – a source of countless lessons about dogs in general, about their owners, about myself and my relations with clients and their animals.

5

The Fate of a Poodle

Youyou was not the first dog to cross my path or acquire importance in my life. When I was looking for a practice in Paris I had contacted a fellow vet with a view to taking over his practice. Tied up in one corner of his surgery was a little fox-terrier bitch. My colleague told me that she was covered with eczema and never stopped scratching and biting herself like a mad thing. This had finally become too much for her owners, who wanted to get rid of her. He had tried everything – tranquillizers, antipruritics, desensitizers and so on – but none of them did the trick.·

My colleague said he hated the idea of putting the animal down. I found her a fetching little creature. Rather than destroy her, I said, why not give her to me? He was only too glad to get her off his hands, so the terrier moved in with me that evening.

I was then sharing a studio apartment with the same girl-friend who had come to assist me when I operated on the cow at Souligné. She gave the funny little dog a warm welcome and we christened her Fafiotte.

What with one thing and another, I kept postponing Fafiotte's treatment from day to day. This is not to say I neglected her; in fact Fafiotte accompanied me everywhere. I took her to Saint Germain-des-Prés and let her gallivant around the café while I played cards with my friends. Any time she wasn't with me she spent with my girlfriend, whom she clearly adored.

Three weeks later Fafiotte was cured. We never gave her a pill or injection, just made a fuss of her. At the time, I found this a novel phenomenon. What had happened? I phoned the colleague who had bequeathed her to me and told him that the eczema had gone. The bitch was very quiet and had given up scratching and biting herself. He asked what the secret was. Just for fun, I played the mystery man. Before telling him, I said, I wanted the answers to a few questions.

Sure enough, I discovered that Fafiotte had belonged to a young couple, and that her troubles had started after the birth of their first child.

A lot of people were surprised at the idea that skin trouble in a dog could be associated with an emotional upset, but the diagnosis was inescapable. Fafiotte was the victim of her own jealousy. Although she had not been abandoned when the child was born, she had ceased to be number one – reason enough for her to start biting herself in such a demented fashion.

Her cure was the product of a contrary experience. With no children around Fafiotte became number one again. That was all she needed to be happy, and I now realized that unless she was happy she became ill.

Fafiotte had a frail emotional makeup. I found it highly instructive to note, as a newcomer to urban practice, that very little was needed to upset her and provoke a recurrence of her former troubles. On the very few occasions when I had to go out and leave Fafiotte behind, she promptly started to scratch and even relieved herself in the studio. I did not immediately spot the connection between abandonment and incontinence. I scolded her, telling myself she needed discipline, but soon grasped that the solution lay elsewhere. Before messing up the carpet, she staged another lengthy performance which gave me food for thought. She assumed a dejected air, lay down with her eyes shut and refused to budge when called. She appeared to be ill, but when I examined her I found nothing wrong. The truth was that she had intended to attract our attention and had got it. It was her form of protest against what she considered to be neglect.

One day Fafiotte taught me something else. She had made a mess on the carpet which could not have been a punishment for being abandoned. So what was it? I remembered her walking to the door a few minutes earlier. Had she been asking to go out? If so, she hadn't made her meaning very clear. She could have barked or scratched at the door to help us understand. On reflection, however, I realized that this would have been out of character. Fafiotte was quiet and discreet by nature. She hardly ever barked, and, like all fox-terriers, she

94

had the sort of poker face whose expression remains inscrutable to those who can't be bothered to pay attention. So that was it. She wanted me to be keenly attentive to her needs, physical as well as psychological. The attention she demanded was not vague and unsubtle but acute, refined and expressive of love.

This time, instead of giving her a smack, I petted her and delivered an affectionate little speech. 'Poor old girl, I'm the one who deserves a scolding, not you. You asked to go out and I didn't understand.'

Fafiotte never made another mess indoors, and I paid even closer attention to her comings and goings, as she had asked. I did not have to train her. It was she who trained me by intensifying my powers of observation.

To her dying day, Fafiotte was lucky enough to retain and enjoy the conditions essential to her health and happiness. When my girlfriend and I split up, not long afterwards, Fafiotte stayed with her mistress. Monique later married but did not have any children, so the little dog's status remained unchallenged. She never again felt any compulsion to scratch herself raw.

My own temperament and occupation did not permit me to be as exclusive as Fafiotte, who was the last lone animal to share my home. She was succeeded by a whole horde of dogs, cats and birds of various kinds, not to mention lions and tigers that dug holes in my garden and monkeys that mistook my curtains for jungle creepers.

Although they did not all live with me simultaneously, I never had fewer than three or four animals distributed between my home at Garches and my practice in Paris. When Pousse arrived on the scene I already had Youyou, a grey tom cat called Matou, Julot the monkey, and my birds. These were joined a few months later by Hirsute, one of Pousse's cousins.

Pousse was a bitch of the variety of wire-haired pointers known as Korthals. I had bought her from a breeder near Pithiviers, where I and a friend went to collect her as a puppy of two months. I found it enthralling to rear her in accordance with my own ideas and win her affection. The Korthal is a highly sensitive dog requiring firm but gentle treatment. The breed possesses great charm, and its present popularity is hardly surprising.

In the mornings, Pousse used to go with me to the Comète, a café, for a snack breakfast and a glass of white wine with

Rochette the grocer, Loulou the greengrocer, Kieffer the baker and Gineston, the proprietor. It was an enjoyable interlude. I would savour the pleasures of conversation until time caught up with me and I ended by jumping into my car, panic-stricken at the thought of all the clients who were waiting. I did not have to worry about Pousse. Alert to my every movement, she always jumped in after me.

Always, that is, until the day I reached my surgery and found the back seat empty. Anxiously, I phoned the Comète. Yes, they said, Pousse was there all right, but she was sitting on the pavement and flatly refused to come inside. As soon as my friends went near her she dodged them, then returned to her post in front of the café. They were keeping an eye on her through the window.

When I returned at the end of the morning, she hadn't budged. She was still sitting on the edge of the pavement at the spot where I had parked my car, as if confident that I would come and look for her where I had left her. Instinct or intelligence? I don't know, but it was certainly a well gauged course of action – one that would give us the best chance of finding each other again.

I lost Pousse on another occasion, this time at Courchevel. Her behaviour was just as admirable. She always tried to follow me around the ski slopes, so I had to shoo her back to the chalet. One day she pretended to obey me but followed just the same.

I took the Pralong ski lift. She followed me to the top, where I caught a glimpse of her, but halfway down I branched off towards the Biolley run. I did the Biolley, which is faster, and skied down to the cable car station. While waiting to climb aboard with some friends, I again caught sight of Pousse high up on the Biolley run near the ski lift. She was sniffing the snow and air in all directions. As we watched her, she set off towards us, unerringly following all the twists and turns that I myself had taken over an expanse of packed snow criss-crossed by the tracks of many other skiers. Since she refused to leave me, I decided to take her with us all the way up the Saulire.

Halfway down, we split up into two groups. The snow was soft. Pousse sank in and found it heavy going. I lost sight of her but did not worry. With her nose, she would easily find her way back to the chalet.

I myself got back at the end of the afternoon. No Pousse. Anxiously, I realized I had expected too much of her. She must have lost my scent in the snow. I called the police station to report her disappearance, afraid that someone might steal her; Pousse was a pedigree bitch, after all. I borrowed a loudspeaker van from the local cinema and combed the streets of Courchevel emitting the whistle I customarily used to call her and also broadcasting her personal particulars.

Night fell. I had to call off the search and resume it next morning. I telephoned Méribel, Moriond – everywhere. I reported the loss of my dog to the ski instructors and track wardens. Finally, one of the latter told me that Pousse had been seen at the *Panoramique* on top of the Saulire. I went there, only to be told that the ski instructors had sent her down by cable car. I skied down again, but there was still no sign of Pousse. I returned to the summit. This time I was informed that some friends of mine had *tried* to put her in the cable car, but that she had given them the slip.

It was nearly 2 p.m. by now, and I was starving and discouraged. I had just sat down outside the *Panoramique* to grab a snack before continuing the search when I gave a start of delighted surprise.

Jutting above the *Panoramique* was a steep and inaccessible cone of rock surmounted by a television aerial. There at the very summit, surveying the world around, sat Pousse. I called her. She saw me and came bounding down like a mountain goat, barking wildly, to hurl herself at me in an ecstasy of happiness.

I conducted a brief investigation. Despite the rash behaviour into which her craze for tracking had led her, Pousse had shown quite as much intelligence as she did the day she waited for me on the pavement. She had eventually lost me where the tracks diverged. Instead of pressing on regardless, no matter where, she retraced my route to its point of departure at the top of the Saulire, and there she resolved to wait for me in defiance of cold, hunger, darkness and the well-meant entreaties of those who wanted to shut her up for the night. To make quite sure nobody would catch her, she had taken refuge on an inaccessible rock, once again confident that I would return.

Just like Youyou, who had trained her, she understood everything. Together in Paris they would look for me in the café, trotting along shoulder to shoulder. Together they escorted me for evening strolls around Saint-Germain-des-Prés. I separated them only when Pousse was on heat, which was quite a business. Pousse was such an attentive pupil that I often used her as a canine demonstrator on television. It was she who helped me to show how a dog should be trained to wait for the red light, not cross the road without permission, obey calls of nature in the gutter, walk to heel off the lead, come when called, and so on. When I pointed to people and said 'Fetch!' she would take them gently by the dress or jacket and pull them towards me.

Pousse took advantage of her privileged position to play-act a little. She detested my cleaning her ears and would tremble and try to slink off when the dreaded moment came. However, she was well aware that I used a dummy for my televised demonstrations. Safe in this knowledge, she would leap on to the table with blithe alacrity, hunch her shoulders and strike the required pose as if she were awaiting my ministrations with the keenest of pleasure. She was mildly jealous whenever the cameras concentrated on another dog.

Pousse spent a long and extremely happy life in my company. Though more exclusively devoted to me than Youyou, her passion for me did not prevent her from having many other friends and enjoying great freedom of movement.

She was quite capable of going for long walks without me, either with her friend Youyou or on her own. Ever since puppyhood, she had preserved a remarkable affection for Marcel, the friend who had gone with me to collect her from the breeder and looked after the two-month-old puppy for a fortnight during her vaccination period. I believe that the first person to care for a puppy after it leaves its mother becomes permanently imprinted on its psyche. I should add that I have seldom known two people as conscientious, fair, consistent and gentle with their dogs as Marcel and Alice Delaporte. Pousse made such a fuss of Marcel during their sporadic reunions that I wondered if he was not even more her master than I was myself.

But, like Youyou, she reserved her death for me. One day I went off with my wife and children for a short break at Cabourg on the Channel coast, leaving Pousse in the care of some animal-loving neighbours. When we got back, the wife told us that something was wrong. She had heard Pousse howling strangely the night before and thought she might be pining away. I did not have time to examine her at once because there had been an emergency at Thoiry.

I returned at lunchtime to find Michèle looking worried. She told me to hurry: Pousse was in a bad way. I ran to look. Impelled by some mysterious instinct, Pousse had crawled into a little garden pool with a few inches of water at the bottom. I retrieved her just as she breathed her last. A brief examination disclosed a large tumour on her chest, which had developed during our few days away.

Pousse must have sensed the approach of death, hence the howls that had alarmed our neighbour, but she had held on until we returned because she wanted to die in our company. She was only twelve, but some breeds have a fairly short life-span.

I subjected Pousse to only one real tribulation in the course of her dog's life. She was forced to accept a companion whom she obviously found antipathetic despite her good relations with the parrot, the myna and the cats. This was Kid, a wild rabbit which I found in a ploughed field and stuck in my pocket. He couldn't have been more than a few days old. When I returned to Paris from the country, I fostered him on a client's cat which had just kittened. Kid burrowed in among her brood and attacked his adoptive mother's teat quite as vigorously as his foster brothers did. The cat made no attempt to reject Kid. He grew fast without arousing any noticeable hostility on her part. All I can say is that she sometimes gazed at him with a rather odd expression. Those two enormous ears . . . Still, I may have been imagining things.

Kid soon became a regular traveller by car. He happily commuted between the surgery and our two-room apartment, often in the company of Pousse and Youyou. They pretended to ignore him, but the bitch was a trifle jealous all the same. Being a gun dog, she sensed that Kid was a wild rabbit. She knew at the same time that he belonged to the household and must not be touched, but this did not stop her playing the occasional trick on him. She would sometimes confiscate Kid's carrot, a form of nourishment which held no interest for her, and bear it off to her kennel. Kid, who had no reason to feel intimidated, would go and retrieve his property from under her fearsome jaws.

This relationship between dog, cat and rabbit amused and

interested me. Although the public have since been familiarized with this type of experiment by a variety of books, films and television programmes, it was not common at the time. I even carried provocation to extremes by putting the rabbit on the bitch's back. Filled with embarrassment, she ostentatiously looked the other way but did not resist.

I do not, incidentally, believe that this behaviour was unique to Pousse. One day, a sportsman friend of mine came to see us with his Griffon Korthal. 'You'll see,' he said. 'My dog's got the hunting instinct; he'll gobble up your rabbit as soon as look at him.' But when the dog entered the house, whose occupants comprised – apart from my wife and son – Youyou, Pousse, Moumoune the Burmese cat and, last but not least, Kid, he took no immediate interest in the rabbit. He finally cornered him under the sofa. After sniffing him for a moment, however, he backed off and sat down beside his master without evincing the least agitation. It was just as I had thought. The dog was not in a hunting environment. To him, the rabbit was not a prospective quarry – not a rabbit at all. He formed part of a human group and, as such, was untouchable.

I am bound to add that human hunters were not always as tactful in their attitude towards our rabbit. One day my wife and I went off to spend a weekend at Sologne, taking Kid with us. To guard against any unfortunate mistakes Michèle tied a pink ribbon around his neck. By the time she came down to lunch, the restaurant was already crowded with hunters. She deposited Kid on the table, where he hopped around happily. The hunters promptly accepted this challenge and announced that they were going to draw a bead on her ridiculous animal after the meal. Confident of our protection, Kid toured the dining room. He ended by discovering the bread basket, made a raid on it and – as a crowning piece of impertinence – deposited a few bunny balls.

Under the control of human beings who, like me and my wife, loved and understood them and made their lives easier, all our animals lived on good terms, repressing their jealousy and their more or less predatory instincts. Natural violence sometimes regained the upper hand, however, and we were not immune from accidents such as Julot's killing of the dove.

Matou, a blue-grey tom cat which some clients had left with us after the birth of their first child, lived at peace with dogs and birds alike. For their part, Youyou and Pousse never touched the cat. They didn't play with him either, they just ignored him, so Matou serenely divided his time between my surgery and the street. He slipped out through the fanlight and re-entered by the main door of the building. Quite a remarkable animal in his own way, he learned to jump up and press the bell push of the outside door. Then he mewed and scratched at the door of the caretaker until she let him into my surgery.

Watching a dog's formidable jaws at work one can gauge the strength of the inhibitions that normally prevent it from using them as weapons and inflicting terrible wounds on those around them. Accidents demonstrate that there are circumstances under which these inhibitions cease to function, as this story shows.

Following my annual custom, I had paid an informative visit to London on the occasion of Cruft's, the world's largest and most widely attended dog show, with its eight thousand superb British-bred entries. A woman friend had asked me to find her a poodle, so I consulted a well-known breeder who specialized in poodles. At first he said he had nothing suitable. Then, on the eve of my departure, he offered me a puppy which a Swedish client had chosen but failed to collect – a marvellous little ball of grey fur endowed with a gaiety, liveliness and intelligence that struck me as quite exceptional. Once having seen and fondled it, I could not bring myself to hand it over.

It was hard luck on the lady who expected me to bring her back a poodle. Never mind, I told myself, I can always find her another in due course. She took offence, naturally, but I was quite within my rights. Besides, it was a present for Michèle, who also has a weakness for the breed.

We christened the little grey ball Poulbot, after the street urchins drawn by the artist of that name. It became instantly and passionately besotted with Michèle. Although I am on excellent terms with our family pets, just as I am with wild animals, I have to admit that they always show a certain preference for her. My touch is on the rough side. They seek my caresses but are fractionally afraid of them. Rinka, my big Alsatian bitch, tends to flatten her ears and lower her head when she comes up to show her affection, and is quick to whimper as though hurt when I pat her.

Michèle, on the other hand, is for all the animals an object of unalloyed love, and it came as no surprise that Poulbot fell for her at first sight. He became part of a family circle whose numbers were steadily increasing. Apart from the animals I have mentioned and my son Jean-François, a lot of space was now taken up by two recent arrivals of our own, the twins Florence and Isabelle. Nevertheless, Poulbot found himself a niche in this crowded *ménage* and was readily accepted by his contemporaries, human and canine. Six months later, when we all moved to a house with a garden, Poulbot was a handsome and healthy little poodle who raced madly around the rose beds and bounced exuberantly up and down in front of his mistress.

Our own animals were sometimes joined by clients' pets whom I kept under observation. Among these was a formidable Alsatian named Tarzan.

Tarzan had recently developed osteomyelitis as a result of a badly reduced fracture. After undergoing another operation, he demolished the surgery door with his teeth. His owner could not take him back right away. I had a feeling that he was afraid of Tarzan's temper, exacerbated as it must have been by pain, so we decided to keep the dog until his recovery was complete.

As soon as I introduced him to our household of dogs, cats and children, the holy terror underwent a transformation. I watched in vain for signs of ferocity. Tarzan was as quiet and happy as the rest. Like them he became infatuated with Michèle and obeyed her to the letter.

Arriving home from work one afternoon, Michèle opened the gate and started up the garden path. As usual, all the animals converged to welcome her: Tarzan, Poulbot, a new Burmese cat called Sottise, and Rinka the Alsatian, who had just come into our lives.

It was a contest for pride of place in which the mighty Tarzan yielded to no one. He stationed himself on Michèle's right, against her leg and within easy reach of her caresses. But Poulbot, too, wanted a place in the sun. He bounced up and down in front of Tarzan, seeking his beloved's hand. Michèle could not have been quick enough to bestow the joy he craved because he suddenly flew into a rage. All that stood between Poulbot and his mistress's hand was Tarzan, that gargantuan intruder and alienator of her affections. He flew at the Alsatian, hanging by his teeth from the corner of Tarzan's muzzle. The Alsatian responded with a jerk of the head and three swift bites.

Poulbot went into a coma. Tarzan's teeth had caught him in the throat and high up in the chest. His spinal column was fractured. Michèle rushed him to the surgery.

He was still breathing. I laid him out on the operating table, but his condition proved even more serious than my wife had suspected: extensive perforations and a crushed thorax. I patched up the torn lungs and flanks, but the injuries to the spinal column were beyond repair. Poulbot died. He was six, exactly the same age as our twin daughters.

6

Wotan Remembers

It was a little green monkey named Golotte who introduced me to lions and tigers and the novel range of problems they presented.

Golotte was brought to me just after I began practising in Paris. She came on the recommendation of my first veterinary nurse, having been a patient of her former employer. Golotte had grown crusty with advancing years and taken to biting her mistress, a journalist named Martine Beauvais, who adored her in spite of everything.

At the time, monkeys were quite new to me. Veterinary college had taught me how to look after horses and other domesticated animals, but there was nobody to tell me the proper course to adopt with a monkey that bit people, any more than there was later on, when I first came face to face with a bear half gutted by a slash of the paw or a lion dying of typhus.

There was, of course, a brutal but traditional expedient. Having trouble with your monkey? Simple: break its teeth. I found the method as barbarous as the castration box for cats. You took a pair of pliers and – crack! – snapped off the animal's canines. You also inflicted frightful pain, naturally, and exposed the animal to the inevitable danger of infection and abscess formation.

I had no intention of inflicting such agony on any animal, whatever its species. Instead I told Golotte's mistress that I would try a more humane form of dentistry. I would give the monkey a general anaesthetic, file down her four fangs, draw the nerves and fill them like human teeth. It was quite a straightforward idea, but nobody to my knowledge had yet taken it into his head that a monkey's teeth could be treated with such consideration.

There was only one snag: I was a vet, not a dentist. That left me no alternative but to make do, as I had with Mario's chickens. Besides, it so happened that dentistry was not entirely unfamiliar to me. I had a store of knowledge derived from the lectures on dental anatomy and pathology I had attended at veterinary school. What was more, I had often played in my uncle's surgery as a boy, messing around with his dental instruments, working his drill and mixing amalgams. He was fond of explaining how this or that was done – so much so that Golotte's problem seemed almost familiar. I would manage somehow, I was sure. As ever, I felt confident that a little initiative would work wonders.

Before operating on Golotte, I purchased a small range of dental equipment: bits, drills, abrasive discs, burrs and so on. I also needed a motor which would rotate these by means of a flexible drive. A dentist's chair was superfluous, of course. I did not sit my animal patients up, however great my consideration for them, but laid them flat on a table. This I improvised by securing a platform to the base of a hydraulic chair which could be raised and lowered by means of a pedal. I later rigged up an electric table with a stainless steel surface, which is still in use.

There was another little problem to solve. My surgery measured ten feet by twelve. These cramped quarters already housed my operating table, an instrument table, oxygen bottles and resuscitation equipment, a trolley, a small desk, my sterilizer, a chair for clients and heaven knows what else. I also needed room to get around the table, so how was I to install my motor, complete with flexible drive, in such a way as to enable me to work on the monkey's mouth?

I eventually procured a jointed arm and screwed it into the wall myself. To the end of the arm I attached a hook, and from this I hung my small electric motor. Thanks to three feet of flexible drive and the mobility afforded by my jointed arm, I now had the freedom of movement I needed. Although my inelegant contraption would have made a dentist blanch, it functioned quite satisfactorily.

The appointed day found me all set to go. The little monkey was brought into my surgery, fidgeting and trying to bite. The first step was to run the gauntlet of her fangs and administer a tranquillizer. I used one hand to clamp Golotte's arms behind her back so that she could not grab and bite me. With the other I injected the 'cocktail' into her thigh, which my nurse was holding steady.

Ten minutes later Mademoiselle Golotte was inert enough for me to find a vein at my leisure and inject pentothal, the anaesthetic proper. A small monkey's veins are fine and hard to locate under its comparatively thick, hirsute skin. The one I injected in the crook of Golotte's elbow was tiny. To penetrate it at all, I had had to obtain some very fine needles only three or four tenths of a millimetre thick.

The intravenous injection of a barbiturate must be perfectly executed because the slightest traces of such a drug in the surrounding tissue will cause phlebitis and severe necrosis. The intravenous use of barbiturates for anaesthetic purposes was still in its infancy. The commonest traditional anaesthetics were ether and chloroform, and many accidents resulted from pulmonary oedema.

The combination of a 'lytic cocktail' followed by an intravenous barbiturate was an attractive one, being both flexible and efficacious. Here again, however, I had to gauge the dose accurately or risk cardio-vascular and renal complications. I proceeded by guesswork in Golotte's case, having nothing to go on, but I did not fare too badly.

The rest was dentistry. I had two assistants, my nurse and a dental student who was interested in the operation and had brought me some extra instruments. I sawed the canines flush with the gum and rounded them off. Now came the tricky bit – denervation. What did a monkey's dental canals look like? Very different from ours: relatively much larger and expanding towards the base. The root did not end in a point, as it does with us, but was broad and flat. I embarked on a whole series of activities: nerve extraction, cleaning, coagulation, suction, and so on. Then, after disinfecting the canals and drying them, I had to fill them with dental cement and tamp it down with a plugger. As in the case of a human patient, I could not afford to leave the slightest bubble of air at the base of a canal or, sooner or later, an abscess would form. With care and dexterity, I succeeded.

One small problem remained. I had to fill Golotte's teeth so that she would not demolish all my work when she woke up. Even an allegedly rational human being tends to ferret around with his tongue or fingers when he feels a foreign body in his mouth. A monkey goes one better. If it gets the slightest purchase on a suture, for example, it will make every effort to rip open a wound that has been hermetically sealed and pull out everything its fingers can grip, guts included.

I embedded the fillings firmly by drilling inverted cones in the normal manner. Then I buffed and rounded them thoroughly so as to leave no purchase for the monkey's nails.

I soon got the hang of things. Within an hour, the four canines were cut, rounded, denervated and filled. To denervate and fill four teeth in an hour may strike some people as slapdash, but I worked with care and precision. Good assistants and thorough spadework make for speed of execution.

Once the job was done, I wrapped Golotte's inert little body in a blanket and took her round to see a local dentist recommended by a friend of mine. I wanted to be certain that the canals had been perfectly stopped. This time Golotte was privileged to sit in a dentist's chair like any lady patient, and each of her canines was duly x-rayed. The plates, which were developed on the spot, revealed that all was in order.

Golotte came around slowly, thanks to the tranquillizers, and did not fully recover her spirits for twenty-four hours. As I had expected, she searched everywhere for the missing teeth with her tongue and fingers, pulling all kinds of faces in an effort to locate them. She finally gave up, but her loss was also her gain. Deprived of her fangs, she acquired a new freedom. Having spent most of the time in confinement when her bite was dangerous, she now regained the right to run around freely, and her character, which had turned morose, underwent a change for the better. She enjoyed many more years of life in her owner's company. Although I treated her on subsequent occasions, we never had any trouble with her teeth.

The same quirk of fate that had brought the first monkey to my operating table renewed my links with a retired animal-trainer and handler who introduced me to some animals of a far more impressive kind. Although I had known Teddy Michaux for years, he only now began to consult me about his charges, and it was partly his doing that I really discovered an affinity with wild animals. I should emphasize that, to begin with, it was I who consulted him rather than the other way around. I kept my eyes and ears open in the presence of this exceptionally knowledgeable man, whose experience of animals was almost unlimited.

I had seen Teddy's animal acts as a child, so his fascination for me was of long standing. A tall, heavily built man with thick lips, he always had a thousand-and-one tales to tell.

The old trainer's base was a sort of ruined and overgrown manor house near Villeparisis. This was the 'Jungle' to which I often retired at weekends for the pleasure of seeing Teddy and lending a hand with his animals. Rain poured through holes in the roof and most of the doors were smashed. Two tigers occupied the main drawing room. There was a fox tethered in the courtyard and a donkey which used to stroll casually into the house, looking for bread in the kitchen and opening the cupboard to browse on anything it could find there. I also had a soft spot for Romeo the drake, who was trained like the rest. Romeo said thank you with a special series of rhythmical quacks when you threw him pellets of bread, which he caught in the air like a juggler. Teddy's passion for schooling animals was such that he had actually trained a trout. There was a stream not far from the house, at that time still stocked. Teddy dug a ten-yard diversion and enclosed it with gratings at either end. When he knelt on the bank, the trout would emerge from its lair to be fed by hand with titbits.

My friend the crow was another resident of the 'Jungle'. All those doorless rooms, many of them open to the elements, were a bird's paradise. The crow would rap on the window with his beak in the morning to claim his breakfast, cawing the French equivalent of 'Rise and shine!' He could enunciate quite clearly, because I had made a slight adjustment to his tongue. This minor operation, for which he was none the worse and never bore me a grudge, endowed him with the linguistic aptitude of a parrot or myna. His remarks were quite spontaneous and to the point.

It was at Teddy's place that I first came to cudgel my brains over a lion with chronic catarrh. I began by administering some antibiotic and aromatic injections. They did not seem adequate so I decided to try inhalations. I had previously brought an atomizer designed for human beings and used it for treating cats, but would it work on a lion? Anyway, how to go about it? There was no question of putting the nozzle under his nose and asking him to breathe in like a good boy. Teddy was intrigued by my final solution, which was really quite simple. I draped an airtight tarpaulin over the entire cage, inserted the nozzle through a hole and switched on. The problem was how to fill such a relatively large space with the aid of a gadget designed to dispense a small volume of aerosols, so I had to push the atomizer well beyond its specified capacity. The lion growled, coughed and sneezed under its tarpaulin, but it certainly inhaled a good dose of my antiseptic mixture. After I had repeated the process several days running, there were marked signs of improvement.

One day a small circus visited the local town. Teddy went to see the animals and found that two of the lions had coughs and runny noses. He asked me to come along with my atomizer and whatever was needed to administer injections. I treated the animals in the middle of the town square, surrounded by interested spectators.

It was with Teddy, too, that I rigged up various makeshift contraptions which added to my knowledge of animal behaviour. His slender resources would not run to a properly constructed restraint cage in which wild animals could be pinned between one fixed and one mobile wall, so we jointly devised an adjustable grill that performed much the same function.

All these odd jobs, which were done during my weekends with Teddy, helped me to interpret and understand the movements, reactions, fears and responses of wild animals. I learned to talk to them, handle and soothe them.

The day came when Teddy's menagerie dwindled to a mere handful of animals. These he kept, not as a source of income but because he could not have borne to live without them. His last tiger, which he was training on behalf of a circus, roamed mournfully between the drawing room and dining room that were reserved for its more or less exclusive use. Teddy had a wife named Malika, who shared his way of life. Animals were occasionally boarded out with him for a modest fee which supplemented his basic income, a war pension. Sometimes a minor miracle gave him an illusion of prosperity. One day, for instance, his 'Jungle' was rented as a set for the film *Trapeze*, starring Gina Lollobrigida. Teddy promptly treated us all to champagne. But, broke as he was, he always managed to feed his animals.

I soon became attached to zoo and circus animals, different though they were from the dogs, cats and birds that were gradually accumulating at my home throughout this period, and both categories enabled me to make some interesting psychological observations.

I had been a frequenter of fairs and circuses well before going into practice on my own. I had also made the acquaintance of animal trainers like Jim Frey, Marfa la Corse and even Jeannette MacDonald, formerly a celebrated actress.

One day, during an international circus festival at Porte de Versailles in 1957, Jim Frey called me in to treat a brown bear named Charlot which had been disembowelled by the claws of another bear.

This was a tall order. I gauged the extent of the trouble as soon as I saw the animal in its cage. Charlot was lying in one corner, growling. Now and then he rose and trailed his intestines to and fro in an attempt to relieve the pain. The very sight of him made me feel like giving up. The problem he presented was as novel as Golotte's canines but far more intimidating. I had to approach those immense jaws and paws, retrieve the errant organs, cut, disinfect and sew up the wound. Charlot was a rather difficult customer, they told me. How was I to tackle the job? Once again, I had no precedents to help me and nobody to consult. Had anyone sewn up a disembowelled bear before? Quite possibly, but not to my knowledge. If so, the operation would probably have been performed 'under restraint' and without anaesthetic on an animal firmly secured by ropes. What was more, phenobarbitone would have had to be administered in its food. But would a disembowelled animal feel like eating? How had they managed it? Had the bear survived? No information.

It was my asset and good fortune to have begun to acquire a thorough knowledge of the techniques of anaesthesia and resuscitation. Largactil had been developed by Laborit a few years earlier (in 1952). 'Lytic cocktails' consisting of blended tranquillizers had recently made their appearance, and intravenous barbiturates were just coming into use in human and animal medicine. The first step was to get some tranquillizers into my disembowelled bear and anaesthetize that great mass of muscle.

Charlot must have been in poor shape, but he struggled fiercely. One swipe of his paw could have torn off my arm or my head. After much manoeuvring, we managed to haul one of his paws through the bars. But that was only the start. I now had to locate the confounded vein beneath his thick skin, with its shaggy fur and layers of subcutaneous fat. The ordinary tourniquet was insufficient to distend it properly,

so I reinforced it with a rope. Even then the ⸱
protrude. It was all I could do to feel it, yet r
be perfect.

Next, the agitated colossus had to stop flexⁱ
straining at the ropes that were supposed to ⸱⸱
at least for a second or two, so that I could insert the ⸱⸱
We redoubled our reassuring remarks. At long last, Charlot
relaxed and I was able to proceed.

The bear lay slumped in one corner of the cage. He was too
heavy to remove, so the attendants raised him a little and
propped his back against the bars. Once his paws were lashed,
I climbed into the cage and squatted down between his out-
spread limbs. Nobody looked very sanguine. What if he came
round?

A layman's natural reaction would have been to wonder if
the dose was sufficient. What if the ropes snapped? Think of
that monstrous embrace – think of one's frail human body
crushed to a pulp against that mighty chest! Fortunately, no
such visions haunted me while I was at work. I knew the ropes
were strong and the knots securely tied. I also knew that the
barbiturate had been properly dosed. To repeat, fear means
nothing to me – at least on occasions like these. I claim no
credit for the fact. It is simply a natural attribute, like having
fair hair or dark.

The wound was an enormous zigzag rent. I cleaned it,
bathed it with antiseptic solutions, painted and powdered it
and replaced the intestines in the abdomen. The next step
was needlework, which posed a problem. What needles were
suitable for sewing up a bear? After rummaging through my
do-it-yourself kit, I had settled on some large needles designed
for stitching hessian. Using these, which proved to be ideal,
I soon had the wound safely closed.

Charlot survived the night. I gave him a course of antibiotic
injections over the next few days. It was a real battle of wits
each time. I had to insert the needle at precisely the right
moment while Jim Frey distracted my patient's attention.
Another few days and the injured bear was definitely out of
danger.

So much for my first major operation on a wild animal. I
passed the test with flying colours, and my stock in the circus
world rose considerably. I had shown dexterity, the cardinal
requirement in circus work. I had got by. More than that, I

nad established contact with wild animals.

Like the monkey's fangs and Youyou's osteomyelitis, my abdominal operation on the bear brought it home to me that innovation and discovery were my forte. I was no more suited to routine than routine suited me, though every profession has its share. I have treated spaniels with ear complaints innumerable times, for example, but there is novelty even in the commonplace. No one condition exactly resembles another, and you always have to spot the difference between this case and the last.

The first time I encountered a sick elephant, however, I felt I was tackling a novelty of totally different dimensions. This particular beast belonged to the famous Cirque Bouglione. I had treated horses and cows, which are sizeable enough. I had worked on a bear and had dealings with lions, but the spectacle of this mountainous pachyderm with the swaying head and woebegone air made me realize that I would have to rack my brains afresh – that it was futile to go looking for help because I wouldn't find any. Besides, something had to be done right away.

What was the matter with the animal? It was a big she-elephant – there are never any males in circuses and very few in zoos because they are considered too dangerous. She wasn't eating, she looked dejected. Her trunk was flabby. She was too weak to mount her pedestal during the show; she even had trouble standing.

The mahout drew my attention to her right ear. Sure enough, it was suppurating badly. How to look inside? A spaniel's ear presents no difficulty, but how was I to deal with this enormous leaflike appendage which never stopped flapping – with a head that wagged to and fro as though forbidding me to approach?

I sent for a pair of steps, but the animal nudged me with her shoulder and almost sent me flying. The mahout urged her to kneel, which she finally and rather reluctantly consented to do. More feats of tact and diplomacy were required before I managed to get a look at the auditory canal. It took flattery and many caresses. She loved being stroked on the eye and was crazy about having her teats fondled. It not only tickled her but excited her sexually, so you had to take care not to overdo things. Too much titillation might prompt her to clamp your elbow against her chest, crushing your arm and fracturing it – if nothing worse.

Everyone joined in. Her mahout coaxed her by putting lumps of sugar on her tongue, but a third man stood by with a goad to enforce obedience if she became refractory. Here again, however, one had to steer a middle course and not push her too far – in other words, provoke her into crushing the three of us like flies.

She was suffering from catarrh of the ear. Very well, so my diagnosis had been correct, but what was the cause of the discharge? Had a grass spike become lodged in her ear while she was strewing her back with hay, as sometimes happens with dogs? If so, how was I going to locate it when she was growing less and less docile?

I sent for a bucket of lukewarm water containing a mild detergent and tried to bathe her with a sponge. Given a little luck, I might dislodge the foreign body – if there was one – and disinfect her ear at the same time. Once again, however, she resisted by shaking her head and prevented me from accomplishing very much.

Things would go better, I thought, if we could gently but thoroughly wash out the ear with a jet of lukewarm water, but how? What about trying a douche? I could hardly remember what this gadget looked like but seemed to recall that it incorporated a small nozzle which allowed one to regulate the flow. Just what I needed.

But where to find a douche in a circus at night? Fortunately, circus folk are ultra-resourceful. I wanted a douche. Fifteen minutes later they brought me one. Never mind where they had unearthed the thing; it was a proper one and the regulator worked. All that remained was to persuade my patient to accept her ear wash.

She seemed to find the treatment rather agreeable. I repeated it several times, adding an antibiotic.

Although all went well on this occasion, elephants with objects lodged in their ears have been known to become frantic. One of my friends told me that this tendency has sometimes been exploited in a cruel way. A specially fashioned lead pellet slipped into an elephant's ear will guarantee you a terrible revenge on any mahout or circus boss who happens to have offended you. The animal will break loose and smash everything in sight, and few walls are capable of withstanding such an onslaught.

As a matter of fact, I did get a scare that night at the Cirque d'Hiver (where the Cirque Bouglione performed) after my first brush with an elephant. But not from an animal: human beings can be far more alarming. It was late, the show was over and I was having a drink at the circus bar with the elephant handler when Michèle burst in, looking very perturbed. Hot on her heels came two men – sinister-looking types, or so it seemed to me. Michèle, who was then not yet married to me, pointed at them with childlike terror and finally said, in a choking voice: 'They tried to kidnap me.' She paused, struggling for words, then added, 'They were going to kill Youyou and Pousse.'

I bristled, ready to do battle. The two intruders must be crazy. I was on home ground and could summon reinforcements, be they only the mahout and his goad. But all the men did, rather grimly, was ask to see my papers.

I finally grasped that they were Vice Squad detectives who had spotted Michèle and the two dogs waiting for me outside in the car. I was a long time, as usual, and the two plainclothes men had taken it into their heads that she was a carborne prostitute. She, in her turn, mistook them for a pair of crooks – not surprisingly, in view of their manner, physiognomy and dress. They demanded to see her papers, but she didn't have them on her. Although she explained that she was waiting for someone from the circus, they didn't believe her story and tried to take her in.

This sent the two dogs wild. The plain-clothes men released their hold on Michèle and told her to order them back into the car or they would shoot them. Michèle did so but flatly refused to be taken down to the station. She took to her heels and made a dash for the circus with the two men in hot pursuit.

The detectives were highly annoyed. It so happened that I wasn't carrying my papers either. I volubly insisted that I was the circus vet, but it was no use. The two leather-coated myrmidons proposed to take me in too. In the end I lost my temper at their complete lack of psychological discernment. I would happily have set the inmates of the circus on them – the elephant I had just treated plus a couple of tigers. Fortunately, one of the Bouglione family arrived in time to pour oil on troubled waters, and our friends from the Vice Squad left empty handed. We rejoined Youyou and Pousse, who needed a lot of calming down.

I soon had to deal with a lion in far worse condition than the disembowelled bear. Once again I was faced with an unfamiliar problem made even more difficult by its urgency. Everything had to be improvised, but right away. Death was already imminent.

Wotan was a magnificent creature – Jim Frey's handsomest lion and his pride and joy. He was two years old at the time, but when I arrived at the Château des Forgets, Jim's current base of operations north of Paris, he was sprawled on his side like a limp rag, and weltering in his own bloodstained excrement.

It was feline paraleucopoenia. Wotan was voiding the contents of his body at both ends in great red spurts. He hadn't long to live. If I were going to try something, I should have to do so at once and without taking the usual precautions.

The first step was to enter his cage. Jim Frey, being a prudent trainer and handler, lodged a formal protest. Although the lion seemed to be at his last gasp, you never could tell. One last paroxysm at the approach of a stranger and I would be torn to shreds. On the other hand, there was no question of forcing an animal in Wotan's condition into a corner and tying him up; he would die first. No question, either, of anaesthetizing him, so I would just have to go in. My sixth sense told me that I could afford to take a gamble.

I slipped into Wotan's cage through the trap that gave access to his training cage. I had to bend double to negotiate it. It was the first time I had entered a lion's cage, and I did so in a rather unimpressive, rather 'inhuman' way. To animals, man is an erect creature. My own posture was less likely to induce submission than to arouse the hunting instinct by marking me out as a quarry on which it was legitimate to pounce, but there was no door the height of a man. Besides, just as I expected, the sick lion did not even seem to notice me entering his domain.

Laden with a full set of equipment, I made my way towards Wotan across the filthy floor of his cage. Still no reaction. I took the skin of his back between my fingers, it was dry and unresilient – the skin of a dying animal. Wotan was completely dehydrated. My first task was to rehydrate him fast.

I injected a large dose of antibiotics and antihaemorrhagics directly into the peritoneum, the membrane lining the abdominal cavity. Then I gave him three simultaneous drips, one into each of two veins in his paws and a third into the peritoneum. Every minute counted, so my infusions were not the usual slow drips but a continuous flow. I had to get the maximum amount of fluid into him in the minimum amount of time. Under a normal drip he might have revived a little and compelled me to leave the cage before receiving a sufficient dose. By forcing the pace, I should at least maintain the fullest possible flow until the time came to leave in a hurry. Besides, a slow drip would certainly not have been enough to save him. I attached my bottles to the bars of the cage with wire. Rehydration at this breakneck speed was extreme unction with a vengeance. I got over a gallon of serum into Wotan inside two hours. For purposes of comparison, it would take thirty-six hours to inject the same volume into a human being weighing 150 pounds.

While the serum was steadily flowing into Wotan's veins, I moved around him. I felt and pinched his coat, checked his heartbeat, respiration and pulse, listened to his chest with my stethoscope. Was he sinking? No, holding his own. Even his coat felt more supple. The haemorrhage dwindled, then stopped. The lion made a few feeble movements with his paws. If only he pulled through . . .

Meanwhile, night had fallen. There was no electricity in the shed which housed the lion's cage, so Jim Frey and his assistants brought torches and a storm lantern. But Wotan was not out of the woods yet. He had stopped vomiting, but he might still die at any moment. Although he occasionally stirred a little, he remained inert most of the time. I continued to watch him from inside the cage. I gave him some more intramuscular antihaemorrhagic injections and administered some cardiac stimulants, ready at all times to beat a hasty retreat if life and strength returned to his limbs in a flash. But he never gave me any unpleasant surprises of that kind. By midnight, I felt I had done all I could for him, so I gathered up my equipment and left.

I telephoned the next morning. Was he dead? No, still holding his own. There had been no recurrence of the severe diarrhoea and vomiting. He had even shifted his position slightly. I returned to the château as soon as I could, anxious to continue treatment.

But a problem awaited me. Wotan was considerably more

116

alert now. He even struggled into a sitting position before slumping back on his side. I could tell he was better from his coat, his eyes, his general appearance. How could I put him through the whole performance again? I knew I had to persevere with the treatment somehow. The outward signs of haemorrhage had ceased, but it would certainly be continuing internally. A severe attack of typhus affects the entire digestive tract from the stomach to the anus, causing general bleeding and congestion. Besides, I knew that Wotan would die without further treatment in spite of his markedly improved condition. The flames had been quenched but the fire was still smouldering beneath. I had to extinguish it completely.

Wotan was still too weak for me to risk manhandling him and tying him up. I did not possess a gun designed to immobilize or anaesthetize animals from a distance. That left me with no choice but to enter the cage, even though the risk was greater than it had been the night before. Jim Frey lodged another objection in the name of prudence, but once again something told me that I could approach the beast with impunity.

I climbed inside. Wotan had sat up again. I stood a little to one side, just out of paw range. He stared at me but didn't growl. As for me, I refrained from looking him in the eye. Lions tend to take offence at a steady gaze. Far from inspiring confidence, it strikes them as a threat – even as an assault on their dignity – and may prompt them to attack. You have to become a lion's intimate before he will tolerate your gaze, but something told me that I was already acquiring that status. Wotan greeted me with no sign of misgiving. I talked to him and he listened. Feeling a sort of current flow between us, I risked a quick look in his eye. The current seemed to flow even better: I was sure he had accepted me. I laid my hand on his flank and felt his skin. It seemed more supple than before. No hostile reaction. Still talking, I fondled his head. This can be a very dangerous thing to do, but Wotan made no attempt to bite my hand. Wearily, he raised his great head and licked my arm above the wrist.

I had won. Exhausted by this effort, Wotan fell back on his side. He was still very weak and still in danger. I would have to hurry. Without ropes or restraints of any kind, I went through the whole performance again: intravenous drips, intramuscular and intraperitoneal injections. Not a sign of protest, not even a growl to warn me that he had had enough. Although the lion was still so weak that he would hardly have had the strength to turn on me, I was sure he sensed that I wished him well and was doing him good.

I continued to administer the same treatment for another two days, always with my patient's acquiescence. On the fourth day Wotan was standing in his cage. This time Jim Frey flatly refused to let me go inside. The animal was now strong enough to be put under gentle restraint. Somebody caught hold of his tail through the bars and pulled him towards them so that I could give him an injection without venturing inside. I am sure he understood, because he offered virtually no resistance. Although he might well have tolerated an injection from me inside the cage, the risk was considerable. His limbs must have been tender, and a lion's paw moves at lightning speed.

Wotan made a complete recovery. Some time afterwards, Jim Frey left the Château des Forgets and moved to Marseilles. Thirteen years later, in 1973, I paid my first visit to his new establishment. I asked about Wotan. Jim told me that he was still flourishing and invited me to come and see him. Wotan, who had been a handsome young male when I treated him, had become a true *grand seigneur*, mighty of limb and serene of temperament. He ambled slowly over when he saw us. I spoke to him. He listened with obvious attention. Then, as lions will, he started to speak in his turn. I put my hand through the bars and he licked me as he had done thirteen years before, when he was fighting for his life. He recognized me; his mode of self-expression spoke volumes. Everyone agreed that it was so. To me it was a certainty.

Jim Frey mischievously took advantage of Wotan's amicable reception to involve me in an ordeal which was wholly unrelated to my profession. He was putting on a display of animal training after lunch the same day. I was seated beside him near the circular cage, which the lions – Wotan among them – had already entered, when I suddenly heard a public announcement: 'Dr Klein, the veterinarian who . . .' To cut a long story short, said Jim Frey, *I* was going to put the animals through their paces. I threw up my hands and laughingly protested, but he told me not to worry; he would act as my prompter.

I entered the cage. There were seven or eight lions inside. I knew they were good animals which had been carefully selected and trained by Jim Frey himself, who never took unnecessary risks. They had worked together for so long that their act was almost second nature. I also enjoyed the good will of Wotan, their unofficial team leader, but it was a daunting prospect all the same. I did not have to be a trainer or handler to know that every lion act is a ritual which must preserve a strictly identical sequence every time. The slightest deviation from routine will upset the performers and expose one to the risk of disobedience or aggression. How could I possibly manage without any idea of how the show should proceed?

But Jim Frey knew what he was doing. His act went like clockwork. He dictated the preordained commands and gestures, and the goodnatured animals obeyed me without question. For all that, I took good care not to misunderstand my prompter. Little by little I grew bolder. There is something of the would-be lion tamer in everyone, I suppose. At the end of the act the lions stood up with their forepaws resting on a metal bar and were each rewarded with a piece of meat. The rule was to deposit the meat on the rail, but when I came to Wotan I could not resist offering it to him on the flat of my hand. I saw Jim clutch his forehead. My impromptu departure from ritual was highly imprudent, but Wotan refrained from devouring my hand as well as his lump of steak. Once again, I had sensed that I could trust him.

The current flowed with a lioness, too. At the same time as Wotan's illness at the Château des Forgets I had to treat a young lioness whose tibia had been fractured close to the hock. I anaesthetized her – not, I repeat, a very common practice at this time – and finished off my work with a nice neat plaster.

Jim Frey and his circus friends laughed. 'She'll chew your plaster to ribbons,' they told me. According to them, she would have it off within twenty-four hours. I let them have their say, convinced that they were wrong. She was a good girl. Although the plaster undoubtedly annoyed her, she must have sensed that it served a useful purpose. Not only had she refrained from touching it after forty-eight hours but it was still there six months later, almost intact. I only had to reinforce it once, after she had given it a bit of a hammering. This meant anaesthetizing her again, so I took the opportunity to x-ray the fractured leg with portable equipment.

I removed the plaster in public, in the big circular cage. The television cameras were there too, but the lioness was used to an audience and felt quite at home. Jim Frey entered the cage with me and distracted her while I surreptitiously gave her a tranquillizing injection. She tried to swing around, but the plaster on her hindleg hampered her movements. I then anaesthetized her completely, and the rest of the operation passed off without incident. The leg healed.

But the current doesn't flow with all animals: for instance, I forged no psychical links with the disembowelled bear. Communication with my dogs has always been deep and immediate, but dogs are domesticated animals and communication with man doubtless comes naturally to them. Although it is not automatic with wild animals, Wotan, the lioness and others proved that its establishment is possible. As a man and a vet, I rejoiced that the bond between us had not been forgotten.

7

Ocelots in Love

The friendliest of all big cats and the one that most clearly sensed what I expected of her was Zora, Jean Richard's favourite tigress. She belonged to a group of five or six tigers which he kept at Ermenonville.

Jean phoned me one day to report that Zora had developed a large swelling on her left forepaw. I stood outside her cage, debating the nature of her trouble. The head of the zoo, Jo Clavel, kept her occupied by talking gently to her. She fluttered her lips in a friendly way, grunted affectionately and raised her bad paw as though showing it off. 'Do something,' she seemed to be saying. I was standing alongside. The affected paw was within reach of my hand. I looked at the swelling again and came to an immediate decision.

I took a lancet blade, put my hand between the bars as if I were going to fondle her paw, and laid it open at a single stroke. The cut I made was just over an inch long and aimed at the base of the swelling. The vein was dangerously close, but I had gauged my stroke well and limited its depth by holding the blade between two fingers. The pus began oozing at once.

Taken unawares, the tigress turned her head in my direction. I knew, however, that I could not have hurt her. The pain of her abscess would completely have overridden any sensation resulting from the lancet stroke, and a lancet never causes pain as long as it is sharp and wielded cleanly. Zora did not make a sound. She certainly experienced immediate relief. At once, she did the best possible thing: licked the wound and helped to clear it of pus.

Seeing her so well disposed and friendly, and confident once again that the current was flowing between her and me, I put my hand through the bars and helped her. I squeezed the abscess gently with my fingers, working downwards, to drain it thoroughly. My hand was right up against Zora's muzzle. I could feel her whiskers brushing my fingers and her breath fanning my knuckles. If she turned irritable, or if I hurt her, one bite would dispose of my hand for good. But I felt confident. While I exerted gentle pressure on the swelling, she licked me with her big rough tongue as if to say 'Go on, friend, you're doing me good.'

I was able to complete this process without her showing any sign of annoyance. Then I washed out the abscess with a syringe and, still through the bars, gave her an antibiotic injection. She continued to purr and grunt in a friendly manner.

Zora didn't forget me either. One night when I was dining with Jean Richard at Ermenonville, we went on talking animal shop until the small hours. At about 2 a.m. we made a tour of the animals' quarters. Zora extricated herself from a huddle of dozing tigers and walked over to us. She rubbed against the bars of her cage, purring and licking our hands.

I treated Zora again. She had a fistula on her throat. She was also losing weight and looking off colour. One of the other tigers must have clawed her. Infection had set in, causing the fistula to suppurate, so it was essential to discover the source of the trouble.

I had brought along my portable x-ray equipment, intending to outline and trace the course of the fistula. I had also armed myself with some oxygen bottles and a home-made foot pump in case it became necessary to revive the patient. I was going to have to use a general anaesthetic, not only for x-ray purposes but to enable me to operate at once if necessary.

I developed the plate on the spot. It looked bad. The fistula ran up and disappeared beneath the shoulder blade, which had been attacked by osteomyelitis. The tigress must, in fact, have been clawed to the bone. The wound healed quickly and became invisible, but the infection had persisted beneath her shoulder blade.

But how to get at it? I should have had to lift the shoulder blade and work in close proximity to a delicate neuromuscular junction. The risks were too great. An operation might have compelled me to amputate. If so, what was the use? I shrank from the prospect; you can't win them all.

Zora lived with her fistula for another three years. I treated her from time to time and obtained periods of remission, but she continued to lose weight and go downhill.

The poor animal's death saddened us all. I shall never forget the sensation of her rough tongue rasping against my fingers as she licked the pus from her abscess. She had a heart of gold and a nature more gentle and human, or so it seemed to me, than the best of men. I think she left quite as indelible an impression on Jean Richard as she did on me.

Though considerably less docile, two other tigers confirmed my belief in the wild animal's capacity for self-restraint under certain circumstances. They also demonstrated the power of gentleness when the current is flowing – and gentleness is the prime essential.

The first of them, Clan, a huge beast belonging to the Cirque Bouglione, had once ripped open the chest of its trainer, Joseph Van Bem. Though mauled so terribly that his heart was exposed, Van Bem survived thanks to the courageous intervention of another trainer.

The hero who had subdued the tiger was a scrawny, bent old man with a bad heart. Despite his age and state of health, Michel Matarassof continued to share in the life of the circus by working as an animal minder. More than that, he still retained his amazing mastery over wild animals. He had, for example, bottle-reared a tigress and could do anything he liked with her. I was called in to see her one day because she had given birth to some cubs but was having trouble feeding them. A tigress with a new litter tends to be extremely fierce and irritable, so I was rather taken aback when Matarassof invited me to enter the cage with him. I followed him in feeling less than reassured, but he made the tigress lie down like a tabby cat to show me her teats. Then he quietly removed the cubs so they wouldn't get in my way. The mother made no move although she ought by rights to have torn us limb from limb. It was a remarkable performance.

The old man genuinely communicated with his charges, which he controlled by voice alone. That was how he saved Van Bem – by saying the right things. Bent double, he entered the cage where Clan stood growling with his teeth sunk deep in his trainer's chest. Matarassof approached him, talking all the time, and calmly prised open his great jaws barehanded. Instead of resisting, Clan released his victim and let the old man coax him back to the tunnel which led to his cage.

Clan could reasonably be considered dangerous despite old

Matarassof's demonstration that he was amenable to gentle discipline. One day, a well-meaning young keeper decided to cut his claws. He put Clan under restraint, took a pair of pliers and simply clipped the claws like so many pieces of wire. Predictably enough, he cut through the matrices inside them. Infection set in, and three toes were suppurating by the time I was summoned. The infection had begun to travel up the leg and there were obvious signs of gangrene in the joints.

I had to operate, following the usual procedure and coping with all the familiar problems: tranquillizer cocktail, paw through the bars, intravenous injection. Everything was in readiness outside the cage. An operating table had been set up on bales of straw just in front of it and a neighbouring table held my sterile equipment, surgical gloves and operating towels. My problem was how to carry out bone surgery in conditions aseptic enough to prevent a recurrence of infection.

Joseph Bouglione looked apprehensive. Although he could see Clan lying limp on the floor of his cage, he was only too aware that the huge tiger had nearly killed Van Bem. He was asking me to work inside the cage. What if the tiger came round more quickly than I expected?

There was, of course, no question of my operating on all fours inside the dirty cage. As for the duration of anaesthesia, I reassuringly told him that he had nothing to fear: I could prolong it at will. I found out later that Joseph could not have been as reassured as all that. He had notified the police and, for good measure, instructed his son Emilien to carry a gun. Better safe than sorry . . .

We carried the strapping great creature out of his cage and deposited him on the operating table. There followed a delicate cutting and cleaning operation which lasted three hours. I opened the upper side of the toes and cut away everything that was gangrenous. Then I removed three terminal joints, retaining the pads, and neatly sewed up the ends. No sign of the operation would be visible after they had healed. Only when Clan put his claws out would it become apparent that three of them were missing.

Like the plaster on the lioness's broken leg, my finishing touch earned me one or two complimentary remarks. I put a dressing on Clan's paw and swathed it in bandages. More derisive laughter from the experts. 'A dressing on a tiger's paw? He'll rip it off with his teeth as soon as he comes round!'

But he didn't. Somehow or other, Clan sensed that it was there for his own good. He sniffed and licked it a little but made no attempt to chew it. The dressing was still there four days later, when we had to remove it as best we could. This entailed momentarily trapping his paw and unwinding the bandage by degrees. He offered no real resistance. Potential man-eater or no, I honestly believe he knew what was being done to him. He not only recognized me but welcomed me with friendly growls – licks too, when I risked putting my hand near the bars – even though I had meanwhile given him some antibiotic injections which he could scarcely have enjoyed.

Even more surprising was the behaviour of Vichnou, an exceptionally large specimen belonging to a group of nine huge Siberian tigers owned by the Bougliones. Vichnou had suddenly developed a limp. If circus folk sent for the vet it meant that they had already tried everything, examined the animal from every angle and found nothing. Such was the lot of my profession; I had no illusions about that. Only the worst was good enough for me.

I turned up at about nine o'clock in the evening. Catherine Blanckaert, one of the Bouglione trainers, led me to an enormous wheeled cage where the nine Siberians were pacing to and fro. She was a sturdy but extremely gentle and feminine young woman. The tigers crowded against the bars and plied her with civilities. I could see that they adored her.

Vichnou was a magnificent creature. Catherine persuaded him to walk past us. He was obviously lame in the right fore-leg. Examining him closely, I gained the impression that there was something wrong with his paw. I told Catherine we would isolate him from the others, coax him into a corner and try for a closer look. Together, we inserted the heavy mobile partitions that enabled the cage to be divided into several compartments.

We were joined by Roland Prin, Catherine's immediate boss. He was angry. Why bother to call in the vet if it meant starting all over again from square one? There was no time to lose. The animal must be anaesthetized at once. That was the only way to conduct a proper examination.

Because he insisted, I got my dart gun ready – this was in 1972, by which time projectile syringes were in common use. The trouble was that if I anaesthetized the tiger tonight and had to repeat the process tomorrow for surgical purposes, the animal's life might be endangered. I explained this to Roland, who calmed down, and asked him to let me try something else. If I failed, I could always fall back on the anaesthetic. 'Okay,' he said, 'but you won't find anything.'

Catherine and I resumed our manoeuvres and finally managed to isolate Vichnou. Meanwhile, a dozen or more interested spectators had gathered behind the barriers enclosing the cage. Catherine kept up a stream of patter throughout the operation, and the animals responded affectionately. As soon as Vichnou was isolated, she devoted her soothing words to him alone. He listened, fluttering his lips, and rubbed against the bars. I joined Catherine in a sort of duet so as to share in his affection for her. He sensed that Catherine and I were friends and that our mutual understanding was to his advantage.

Calmed, soothed and mellowed by all this talk, Vichnou soon accepted our invitation to come and sit in a corner facing Catherine, who kept him entertained. He was sideways-on to me with his flank against the bar, but his right forepaw – the injured one – was on the far side. That left me with the problem of how to reach it without putting him to sleep.

Right beside me was the trap through which food bowls were pushed into the cage. It was just wide enough for a man to insert his hand and arm but too small to admit a tiger's massive paw. I obeyed my instinct without weighing the odds. In a natural, irrational way, I acted as spontaneously as an animal might have done. I had no feeling of man-beast ascendancy. I was on equal terms with Vichnou, and it may have been the lack of condescension in my approach that helped me to read his mind so well.

I put my bare hand through the hatch, slipped it behind the tiger's nearer leg and finally – with my arm fully extended – reached the right paw. Vichnou, who was still chatting to Catherine, affected not to notice. He could, of course, have bent down and fastened his jaws on the importunate pink snake that was gliding between his legs, but the thought never occurred to him.

I took the suspect foot in my hand – a great furry paw eight inches across – and gently pulled it towards me behind the left leg. Vichnou not only kept his claws in, but I could have sworn that his paw was more than usually relaxed, as if he were trying to make things easier for me. I put both hands

126

through the hatch and felt the big, unresisting foot. I examined one toe, then another, then the rest. Then I started with the claws, which I extruded in turn. At last I spotted a small wound on the median. I pressed it, and this time I felt something crack. That was it.

Vichnou did not withdraw his paw even though I must have hurt him a little by cracking his toe. I called Roland Prin. 'You see,' I told him, 'it wasn't worth putting him out. That's the trouble, a broken toe – a slight fracture of the median.' To demonstrate, I got Roland to put his finger on the bone and cracked it again.

Still no objection from Vichnou. What now? Should I run the risks attendant on any operation, just for a minor fracture? The cure might prove worse then the original condition. There was every chance that the trouble would right itself, so I decided to disinfect the place thoroughly and leave the rest to nature.

I had meanwhile released Vichnou's paw. To bathe the wound I would have to retrieve it. Once again I slipped my hand behind the tiger's left leg, and once again he amiably surrendered his paw. I had previously sent for a bucket of warm water, added some antiseptic and fetched a new sponge from my car. I bathed the injured foot for quite a while. Vichnou closed his eyes and fluttered his lips, listening to my continuous flow of soothing patter and abandoning himself to the pleasurable warmth of the water. I even managed to inject a dose of antibiotic without having to pin him against the bars with a mobile partition.

The little jobs I had done in my dentist uncle's surgery not only equipped me to tackle the diminutive canines of a monkey but emboldened me to pit myself against a tiger's fangs. This, I might add, is work of quite another order, and one which calls for a sculptor's touch as much as a dentist's skill. Going one stage further, a vet looking into the jaws of a hippopotamus or elephant may be forgiven for wondering if he is dealing with teeth at all. Nevertheless, circumstances conspired to make the mouths of wild animals one of my frequent fields of activity.

Confronted for the first time by that awe-inspiring item of natural equipment, a tiger's fangs, I was again forced to ask questions and answer them myself.

The tiger, another Bouglione animal, had one eye closed and a swollen cheek. I persuaded it to open its mouth and saw

127

that it had snapped off the point of one of its canines. Although this is not uncommon, the canal had become infected and there was an apical abscess round the root.

Theoretically, I could have fenestrated the jawbone to reach the site of infection, but this would have meant cutting across the sinus – a risky procedure. In practice, the only solution was to extract the tooth altogether.

But a tiger's canine is a sizeable object, six inches long from tip to tip and three quarters of an inch across at its thickest point. It consists of two inverted cones joined at the base. Mechanically speaking, this conformation invests it with immense strength.

But how to get at it? In theory, you pull a tooth by introducing a pair of dental forceps into the socket and cutting the ligaments that retain it. I had a whole collection of forceps at my surgery, as well as other dental instruments, but would they work on a tiger?

Needless to say, the operation had to be performed under general anaesthetic. When the day came, I set up my makeshift operating table on bales of straw between two rows of tethered horses in the Cirque d'Hiver stables. It was wintertime. The stables were more convenient than the tiger's own quarters, and the anaesthetized animal would run less risk of catching cold.

After administering an anaesthetic in the cage, as usual, I had the big limp body carried to the stable. The horses fidgeted a little, but not for long. The tiger lay supine. Its four paws were attached by ropes to ring bolts to keep its head back and prevent its body, which was inclined, from sliding off the table. Everything was in order. The syringe containing barbiturate was taped to one paw with the needle in the vein so that anaesthesia could be prolonged as required. I could go to work.

I took my nice little forceps – designed for human teeth, but the biggest obtainable – and my dental mallet. I broke one instrument, then another. I had to dig down a good two inches, but it proved impossible to penetrate more than a quarter of the required depth. Improvisation was the only answer.

Then I had a crude but effective idea. What about a chisel? I asked for a chisel, a full-sized hammer and a grindstone to whet the edge.

I had once bathed an elephant's ear with a douche unearthed

128

by some enterprising soul. My patient was already anaesthetized, so this was even more of an emergency. You want a chisel and a grindstone? No problem – here you are. Circus folk are like that. Ten minutes later I had all I needed. Quickly I proceeded to sharpen my instrument and make the shaft slightly concave, so that it more or less matched the curve of the tiger's canine.

With the tooth almost detached, I found I could not extract it. Even a pair of men hauling two-handed would have failed to dislodge the thing. It was too firmly embedded in the jaw.

I had no alternative but to demolish it – quite a business, given that the tooth was extremely hard and healthy down to the very tip of the root. I hammered away, splitting the dentine and removing it piece by piece. It was an exhausting rather than a delicate operation. The only real difficulty consisted in forcing myself to do a thorough job and resisting the temptation to leave stubborn little fragments behind. I had to remove every last one, although it was growing late and I itched to get home. I could not even allow myself to flirt with the layman's notion that the tiger was 'only an animal', and that I had already done more than enough. It was a test of perseverance.

After much exertion, the pus found an outlet and started to flow. My work was far from done, however. I still had plenty of debris to remove. Even when I could see no more, there remained the bone to be cleaned. The infection had pitted it, so I had to scrape away patiently with a curette to remove any diseased portions.

The job was done at long last. One more rinse, some penicillin powder at the base of the socket, and, finally, a temporary dressing complete with plug and drain. The tiger did not come round for several hours, having received a fair dose of anaesthetic in the course of the operation. It was a dangerous ordeal from his point of view, and I had to restore his strength with a drip. Meanwhile, he had been carried back to his cage. Another good hour's supervision and I could finally go home to lunch, almost as exhausted as my patient.

Next day came some postoperative treatment in the shape of a mouthwash. The tiger needed little inducement to open his mouth and let me rinse the gum and socket through the bars. He was so quiet and long-suffering that I was also able to give him an antibiotic injection without immobilizing him. We tricked him into this. A keeper caught him by the tail and tugged gently. The tiger gave ground, and I soon had his thigh within range of my syringe.

Carrying out dental work on a hippopotamus has its problems. You cannot tie the animal down on his back, turn him over or carry him around as you can an anaesthetized tiger. A hippo is so bulky that you can only work on his mouth in the position he dictates, not at your own convenience. Luckily, his mouth is so big that you have plenty of room to insert your hands and manipulate your instruments – all the more so because he opens it very readily.

Bengali, the hippo belonging to the Cirque Bouglione, presented a dental problem which was not very complicated in itself. The difficulty lay in manhandling the enormous creature and getting near enough to his two tons of bone and muscle without being crushed to death. Though outwardly sluggish and somnolent, Bengali could move with the speed of a panther when he chose. On one occasion, he seemed to be dozing on his feet at the rear of the heavy trailer used for transporting his bulk around. His handler was busy doing something just in front when, quite suddenly and for no apparent reason, Bengali attacked. Always on his guard, the man leaped over the rail and clung to the cab of the truck to which the trailer was hitched, but the hippo still had time to bite him in the buttocks. He spent some time lying face down on a hospital bed before he returned to work.

The hippopotamus, which is related to the pig, has two tusks like a boar. These grow outside the body and normally give no trouble. In Bengali's case, however, the left tusk had slightly penetrated the upper lip, perforating it and causing an abscess. The answer was to shorten both tusks for the sake of physical and aesthetic symmetry.

I armed myself with a blowpipe which could put Bengali to sleep at long range if I had trouble getting near him, but he seemed to be in a benevolent mood. He raised his head several times to admire the chestnut trees in the Jardin-des-Tuileries, where the Cirque Bouglione was pitched. It was a summer morning, fine but not too hot. The gardens were on the dusty side, so Bengali was given an occasional shower with a hosepipe. He opened his mouth in a continuous yawn as though inviting me into his jaws.

I scrambled up the side of the wagon and leaned against the rail. 'What are you going to do?' asked Emilien Bouglione.

'Immobilize him or put him to sleep?' Bengali edged closer. Quick as a flash, I buried my needle in a chest muscle. A little blood seeped back through the head. All appearances to the contrary, the hippopotamus has a delicate and fragile epidermis. Bengali winced, but nothing more, and I soon returned with my syringeful of anaesthetic. He let me fit the barrel of the syringe to the head of the needle and inject him.

The product I used was not exactly what I would have chosen, but it was the only one available. Special preparations are always hard to obtain.

To put Bengali and his two-ton frame to sleep, I had to take account of the peculiarities of his species: general conformation, bulky digestive tract resting on diaphragm, consequent risk to heart and respiration and so on. I did not require the deep anaesthesia proper to major surgery. Relative immobilization would be quite enough for my purposes, and it would be safer to get the animal back on its feet as soon as possible. Apart from anything else, I had no wish to kill a patient in front of the crowd that had gathered around us!

But I soon saw that the first dose was insufficient. Bengali resisted its effects. His lower lip trembled and he looked uneasy. Still fighting the drug, he sat down. He raised his head and yawned hugely, displaying his blood-red gums, but did not collapse.

I administered a second injection. Still he sat there on his hindquarters, with their pudgy, abbreviated legs. This time we decided to give him a little help. He was past attacking, so we put a rope around his chest and tried to pull him over sideways so that I could work on him. Four or five men heaved on the rope. Before long, pink weals appeared among the black flecks that dotted Bengali's delicate skin, which was oozing sweat. We were chafing him slightly, but not enough to matter. 'Poor little thing,' said Catherine, the trainer we met earlier in this chapter, 'I'll give him a nice bowl of stewed apple when it's all over.' Bengali loved apple and Catherine was a kindhearted girl.

He lay down at last, but not – needless to say – on the side I wanted. Too bad, I would have to make do. Suddenly Bengali righted himself. I froze, but he wasn't going any-where. He remained flat on his belly with his hindlegs straight out behind him and his forelegs flexed like those of a pussycat. Again he yawned, head erect now, conveniently presenting his jaws for my inspection. They were held open with a gag, and all I had to do was saw.

Unlike a tiger's canine, the exposed portion of a hippo's tusk is not supplied with nerves, so I could trim it without having to devitalize the rest. I had brought along my dentist's drill, but this time I was dealing with a tooth well over an inch in diameter. Bengali was not as inert as I would have wished. He moved slightly, breaking five or six abrasive discs in succession. Eventually I asked for a hacksaw. It was a long, strenuous job, and the sun was gaining strength. I finished up sweating as hard as my patient. One last tap with a hammer and Bengali's troubles were over.

My discs proved inadequate for rounding off the edges, so I finally buffed the extremities with a powerful electric drill rotating at 3000 r.p.m. All that remained was to cut the other tusk, round it off and disinfect Bengali's wounds. He had thoroughly earned his bowl of stewed apple.

From time to time, new animals entered my orbit and presented me with unfamiliar problems to solve. One such was an ocelot belonging to Michèle and Philippe de Broca: an animal which – even more than any other – put me on my mettle and provided the occasion for an unusually dramatic display of veterinary treatment.

The de Brocas had brought three of these so-called 'tiger cats' back from Brazil, where they had been shooting *That Man from Rio* with Jean-Paul Belmondo. One of them was for Gil Delamarre, the stunt man who appeared in the film. Of the other two, one soon died of poisoning induced by anti-parasitic powder. That left Charly, a handsome but timid and delicate creature with a rather melancholy disposition which all Michèle de Broca's loving kindness failed to cure.

The ocelot is a marvellous feline with a coat the same colour as a panther's, except that it is marked with numerous elongated fawn spots, edged with metallic black, which merge to form longitudinal bars. Its luxuriant fur is gold on the head and silver on the flanks, and its size ranges from that of a large domestic cat to that of a small panther.

One New Year's Eve, just as I was getting ready to go home and celebrate, the phone rang. It was Michèle de Broca: 'Charly looks very sick. Can you see him?'

She put her ocelot in the car and raced to my surgery from

Carrières-sur-Seine. Gil Delamarre also turned up to lend a hand. They carried the animal inside. I saw at once that the situation was very grave. Charly was already comatose. He collapsed when I set him on his feet and pitched forwards when I sat him down. His eyes were quite dry, like his skin, which had lost all resilience.

I immediately took a sample and did a blood count: 300 white cells when there should have been 6000–8000; 1.2 million red cells compared with a normal count of 6 million. It was infectious leucopoenia, a typhoid condition found in felines. Using an auto-analyser, I ascertained that the blood electrolytes were grossly disturbed. Cellular exchange had ceased. Charly was in a toxaemic state and completely dehydrated – at death's door, in fact.

The first step was to rehydrate him as much as possible with the aid of a drip. He revived a little. There might still be a chance, but this was where our real difficulties began.

The ocelot is an extremely frail and sensitive creature. It is also a masterpiece of strength and grace but, like many felines, very emotional. As people in the trade say, it has a 'heart of glass'. Sudden and excessive fear quite often has fatal consequences.

Treating Charly called for the utmost care and a minimum of physical restraint. We would have to be unremittingly gentle if we did not want him to die on us before the infection carried him off. The fact that he had revived slightly made my work even more difficult. Though docile enough while comatose, he squandered his last reserves of strength on a futile effort to escape my attentions.

As I saw it, a transfusion was our only chance of saving him. We needed the blood of another ocelot, but which? Gil Delamarre's was down in the Pyrenees. The only other ocelot within reach belonged to Jean Richard and lived at Ermenonville. I would have to go and take some blood down there, bring it back to Paris and administer a transfusion.

I telephoned Ermenonville. Jean Richard was at a New Year's Eve party in Lyon. I called Lyon. As ever, Jean generously expressed his faith in me and told me to act for the best.

Meanwhile, Michèle de Broca and Gil Delamarre were taking it in turns to cajole, comfort and talk to Charly. They had held and soothed the ocelot throughout his treatment, never leaving him for a moment. We now put him in a large basket and set off for Ermenonville in two cars, hoping he would still be alive by the time we got there.

Paris was thick with New Year's Eve traffic, but we drove like maniacs as soon as we cleared the outskirts. At Ermenonville we found Jo Clavel, the zoo director, preparing to see the New Year in with his staff. We felt like terrible spoilsports, but they all put a good face on it and readily agreed to sacrifice part of their evening.

This time we were dealing with a large ocelot in full possession of its strength, not a moribund animal, but its heart was just as frail. Although Jo Clavel and his men were there to soothe it, our sudden incursion alarmed it nonetheless. Anaesthetizing it was a laborious and time-consuming business, but we finally got it out of its cage and into the passage. Working by the light of torches and inspection lamps, I took the blood from its femoral artery. The animal was in good condition, so I drew off about a hundred cubic centimetres. We waited for it to come round. All went well. We left Jo Clavel and his team to enjoy their party – or what remained of it – and plunged back into the fog.

It was about midnight when we got back. Charly looked very bad. Would the donor's blood suit him? I had no information about blood groups relating to his species. All I could do was try a quick cross match by putting a drop of blood from each animal on a slide and examining them under a microscope to check that they did not agglutinate or precipitate, and that no perceptible physical phenomenon occurred which would cause a fatal anaphylactic shock.

The two samples seemed to marry well, so the transfusion could go ahead. Next came the problem of finding a vein. In spite of the tourniquet, there was no way of locating it. I had to shave the jugular and insert the needle there. Once again, Charly summoned up his remaining strength and struggled. Michèle de Broca and Gil Delamarre had to hold and stroke him throughout the transfusion.

It was about 2 a.m. by the time we completed the process. Charly's various treatments had put as much blood and fluid into his body as it could tolerate. We wrapped him up in a blanket and the two cars headed for Carrières-sur-Seine. He was still alive and kicking when we got there. So were we – just. The New Year was well under way by then, and my one thought was to grab some sleep.

I wasn't dissatisfied; in fact I felt I had brought off something of a *tour de force*. I had no cause for self-reproach, clinically, analytically or therapeutically. Looking back on that New Year's Eve, I could happily claim to have performed a medical feat of considerable magnitude.

Charly received additional treatment next day. A week later his recovery was complete, but I hadn't seen the last of him.

The de Brocas let Charly roam at will, and he sometimes abused his freedom by raiding the local henhouses. One day he sustained a gunshot wound. Ten or more pellets were lodged in his head, one of them behind his left eye, but he again recovered after treatment.

Next he broke a leg – the humerus, to be precise. While repairing it, I discovered why Charly was not as lively and contented as he should have been. He was handicapped by a congenital diaphragmatic hernia, a defect which causes some of the abdominal organs to protrude into the thoracic cavity and embarrass the lungs.

Charly thanked me for all my trouble in his own way. Much as he adored his mistress, he had gathered that I was also a friend and used to come and rub against my legs, purring. One summer he did better still. I had just turned up at the de Brocas' Saint-Tropez abode during a game of *pétanque* when a purring mass descended on my back. It was Charly expressing his affection. He leaped so nimbly that he managed to preserve his balance on landing, but not without driving his claws into my shoulder. I suppose I should have been thankful that he was in possession of all his physical resources.

8

Blind Baby Gorillas

Are they unhappy, these lions, tigers, monkeys and other wild animals – most of them circus inmates – which I have gradually come to know and tended to the best of my ability? And what of the trainers, those showmen who display them illuminated by caricatures of the sun in cages and sawdust rings that seem an affront to freedom? Are they enemies of nature and the animal world? Should they be condemned, should their charges be taken away from them and returned to the bush or jungle; should they be permanently banned, out of respect for our fellow creatures, from exhibiting them and putting them through their paces in public? I have seen both sides of the coin.

During an information-gathering trip to Cologne, I made the acquaintance of a remarkable troupe of chimpanzees owned by Werner Muller, a former figure-skating champion who was contributing a number to the celebrated revue *Holiday on Ice*. Werner and I became friendly, so he offered to show me his six chimps and the way he worked them.

From my point of view, the most impressive part of the performance took place in his dressing room. Werner and his wife were getting ready to go on stage with their chimpanzees. The general impression was that of a genuine family. 'Mother' dressed her children in rubber pilches, jeans and pullovers. Werner was every inch the 'father'. Whenever he proffered a sweet to one of his chimpanzees as a reward during training, he would ask '*Was sagt man zu Papa?*' and the animal promptly hugged him. An acquired behaviour pattern? Certainly, but the first thing that sprang to the eye was great mutual affection. Werner's troupe was more than a family – it was a united family. Shameful? A horrible parody enacted by a pair of abnormal people? Not at all: a perfectly harmonious and balanced relationship between human beings and animals. Werner and his wife had a young son who adored his parents' chimpanzees and got on very well with them.

Watching that man and his apes working in public, did I sense domination and contempt on the one hand, fear and subservience on the other? Anything but. The Mullers were skaters who had taught their charges an activity of which they themselves were fond, and the chimpanzees had grown to like it too. They enjoyed themselves on skates as much as any children, were proud of their accomplishments and revelled in applause. They certainly made an exhibition of themselves, but not in the humiliating sense and no more so than the artistes who were their 'parents'. The Mullers never cracked a whip. They relied on kind words and caresses alone. In order to stage their act at all, they had to be fully assured of their chimpanzees' sociability and good will. Little or nothing separated the powerful animals from their audience. Aggressive reactions could have had dire results, but there was no risk of that. The chimpanzees were not 'vicious' because they were not afraid, because they had been loved and well treated, because they received the satisfaction they needed, because – if I may venture to say so – they were happy.

Happy? Happy when they had been snatched from their native forest? Happy when, however well treated, they spent most of their time in a cage? I am simply stating the facts. Those chimpanzees were good-natured and in excellent health. They loved and were loved by their 'parents'. Call it what you like, but the word happiness springs to mind and I think it fits the case. Of course they were captives, in a sense. Of course they were 'exploited', if you insist, but they were well fed, well treated and well loved.

Let us reflect for a moment. Were those apes worse off than millions of human beings who are also prisoners in one way or another, some of totalitarian and authoritarian regimes, others of hunger, others again of a trammelled existence, inadequate housing and the boredom induced by a monotonous job? Far better off, surely.

As for the exploitation to which these people, like others, subjected their chimpanzees, let us be reasonable. Human beings have always exploited animals. They feed on them and make use of them. What is more, they dominate them. This is a characteristic feature of the human race. There is no point in condemning it. What matters, on the other hand, is to condemn *excesses* of exploitation and domination. We may kill cattle in slaughterhouses but it is unpardonable to make them suffer. Is it abnormal of us to school saddle-horses or train guard- and gun-dogs?

We cannot and should not renounce our domination of nature and the animal world. The absolute duty we do have is to control that dominance and so prevent it from leading to the misfortune and destruction of other species. As I watched Werner Muller's chimpanzees skating, it seemed to me that the relationship established between man and beast in this case was beneficial and advantageous to both, given their respective natures.

Exhibiting animals in public is not a human vice or perversion. It has always been, and still is, one of the major aspects of the relationship between man and beast. The sight of animals has helped man to reflect on himself, to develop his humanity, his artistic and cultural achievements. It was the exhibitors and trainers of animals who first gained an intimate knowledge of them, and it was from their experience and observations that the study and investigation of animal behaviour first derived.

Haven't times changed? Don't we now have other ways of establishing contact with animals than through the medium of a public spectacle? Yes, we do, but the exhibition of an animal in a circus ring serves a useful purpose. After his own fashion, the gaily skating chimpanzee conveys a whole range of messages. 'Look at me,' he says. 'I may be an animal but I can do all sorts of things. I too am intelligent in my own way. I'm sensitive and affectionate and not without my own kind of dignity. What is more, I'm very much your friend when you are mine.' Even before we applaud, he has pleaded his case and that of the animal world. His beauty and agility claim our attention. The very fact of his captivity does likewise because it gives us food for thought. If he is unhappy, maltreated and sick, his appeal to our better nature is even stronger. He thus renders a service, both to man and himself.

I have, it is true, known trainers who were hard on their animals. A member of this rare breed once called me in to treat one of his chimpanzees. He had struck it with a poker, point first, and made a hole in its calf. The trainer was a morose man who got on badly with his wife-cum-partner. On this occasion he had quarrelled with her. The chimpanzee had started to squall and make a fuss like a child upset by a row between its parents, so he lashed out at it.

He had done little more than some parents do to their children. The difference, obviously, was that they risk imprisonment whereas he risked nothing but a baleful look from the vet. French law merely prohibits the public and gratuitous maltreatment of animals. It also prohibits acts of cruelty against them, but was the blow with the poker an act of cruelty in that sense? Not really. It was less a sadistic attack on a virtually defenceless animal than a temperamental outburst on the part of a rough and insensitive man who might have done the same to anyone around him. He went too far, of course, but the injured chimpanzee can hardly be cited as an example of the torments inflicted on circus animals. The trainer did not treat it badly as a rule, and certainly no more so than his other animals. If he had not regretted his impulsive act, he would never have summoned a vet in the first place.

For many years, people liked their animal shows – among other spectacles – to create an impression of savagery. To satisfy them, trainers strove to spice their acts with violence and emphasize the awesome side of an animal's nature. In circus parlance, this is called working *en férocité*. By goading and teasing his charges, the trainer highlights the ascendancy of man over beast. But even in this traditional situation, which some find distasteful, man and beast develop a close relationship. It is not love, but neither is it hatred or terror. Besides, the genuine and dangerous violence that finds expression between them is diluted with the mock ferocity characteristic of a televised wrestling match. All this was evident in the relations between the aforesaid trainer and his chimpanzees. The latter behaved quite differently from those of Werner Muller. They were anything but gentle creatures, and their trainer worked them in a big circular cage, not in direct contact with the audience. They showed what they could become when provoked: aggressive, spiteful, clamorous creatures endowed with fearsome physical strength and a natural fighting instinct. By exhibiting them, their trainer was demonstrating one aspect of animal nature and the man-beast relationship rather than his personal spite and the cruelty of mankind in general.

Today, the same spectators who dote on violence in the

139

cinema have lost their taste for it at the circus. They would never tolerate the gladiatorial spectacles popular in the last century – for example, a duel between a lion and a bull. Trainers have conformed to this trend. Their acts are ferocious no longer. The proof of their skill and success lies in coaxing performances out of animals by affection and emphasizing the friendship between man and beast rather than the domination of one by the other. In this context, it is interesting to note that the uneasiness which animal shows sometimes evoke today, and the campaigns to which they give rise, are products of an age in which the vast majority of circus animals have never been treated with greater consideration.

But the animal teaches us yet another lesson. It discloses the limitations of harsh as well as gentle treatment. The poker-wielding trainer who worked his chimpanzees *en férocité* was well aware, like all trainers, that he could not do anything he liked with them. Whether rehearsing behind the scenes or performing in the ring, he was constantly menaced by the terrible penalty of rebellion. This is an ever-present possibility. What can a trainer do if an adult chimpanzee becomes over-wrought and grabs him? He will be transformed into a limp and bloody rag in a moment.

Kindness can also prove ineffective in certain circumstances. The Mullers were models of gentle efficiency with their skating chimpanzees. Well though the troupe reacted to such a benevolent atmosphere, they nevertheless were as subject to sporadic fits of ill temper and rebellious impulses as any human being. There was no question of letting them get away with it. Slaps, ear pulling and sometimes, even, a touch of the stick had to be administered as a reminder that the Mullers were *in loco parentis* and that children are children.

But experience proves that this harshness is a precondition of love as well as obedience. Once you forfeit a chimpanzee's respect, you also forfeit its affection. Fear and love are inseparable from the relations between man and ape. I found still further confirmation of this in the case of Charlotte, the little female chimpanzee we reared at home. She adored and never tried to bite my wife, who treated her firmly, whereas she was suspicious of, and often aggressive towards, those of our acquaintances who were over-indulgent with her.

That said, I am entitled by over fifteen years' contact with circus animals, their trainers and those who put them through their paces to assert that cruelty is infinitely rarer than kindness and that animals are far more often petted than struck.

One of the most brilliant members of Werner Muller's troupe and the star of his skating act was Johnny, a big chimp aged fourteen and weighing nearly a hundred pounds. One day Johnny slipped on the ice and cracked a central incisor. The same thing had happened to me at twelve. Later on, a combination of bad luck and poor dentistry caused me to lose that tooth and several others without anyone thinking me a victim of child cruelty. Johnny, I am sure, was just as little inclined to attribute his fall to maltreatment. He didn't seem to notice a thing, but his master was worried about him.

Contacting me from Cologne, Werner asked me to examine him. I fixed Johnny an appointment in Paris, where the 'family' would be performing at the Palais des Sports. I proposed to make him a 'jacket' or porcelain crown – from my point of view, an interesting exercise in dentistry.

Johnny arrived at the surgery punctually on the allotted day, with his hand in that of his 'Papa'. The family had given three performances the day before, so everyone was tired. A nice restful Monday would have been very pleasant, but there were two obligations to meet: Johnny needed treatment and the show must go on. That left me very short of time. I had undertaken to crown the tooth in a single day. There was no question of granting Johnny the leisurely delights of half a dozen appointments like a fortunate human patient.

So Werner walked into my surgery holding a rather uneasy Johnny by the hand. The operation was to be carried out under a general anaesthetic, but first came the little problem of administering a tranquillizer. Johnny was not a lion to be penned up in a restraint cage. He was free in my surgery, so he had to cooperate. If he lost his temper he would smash the place up and might even swat the two of us like flies.

The most convenient way to inject Johnny would have been to sit him on the table, but that was an unaccustomed position which might have scared him all the more. Instead, his master invited him to sit down in the armchair reserved for clients. Being used to chairs, Johnny sat. Very quietly Werner proceeded to explain the situation in German: 'You see, he's going to give you a little injection just there – it won't hurt at all. It's only so he can give you a nice new tooth and make you handsomer than ever. You're going to be a good boy and sit still . . .' Still talking, Werner stroked the place on Johnny's thigh where the needle would be planted. At my request he gently pinched the skin, took the chimpanzee's hand and placed it over the site of the injection. After a while, I joined in this little game, gently stroking and pinching the skin of the thigh to an accompaniment of soothing remarks in German. Johnny put out his lips and said 'Uh-uh', gazing with interest from his 'Papa' to his thigh. He hardly winced at all when I inserted the needle.

Johnny soon became drowsy and made no fuss when I injected the barbiturate into a vein in his arm. The next step was to draw the nerve. I had arranged for a dental mechanic to be in attendance. After trimming the stump, I took impressions of all the teeth. The dental mechanic had to fashion a tooth of the right shape and colour. He made a mould, cast the porcelain and started baking. We needed something really tough and well adapted to the conformation of the chimpanzee's mouth so that the crown would not be subjected to permanent strain. Johnny's jaws were so powerful that they would test our handiwork to the limit. The baking process took four hours. I let my patient come round a little during this time, then put him to sleep again before fitting the crown and cementing it in place.

Johnny performed as usual on Tuesday afternoon and went through his skating routine without incident. I regularly received news of him after that. One year I would get a post-card from Las Vegas or San Francisco, the next from Rome or Pretoria. All was well. Johnny still had fine teeth and his crown hadn't budged.

Why did Werner Muller go to so much trouble for the sake of an ape? Self-interest, cynics may say – a gap-toothed chimpanzee would have made a bad impression. They would be wrong. Repairing Johnny's incisor was a dead loss from the show business angle. One missing tooth in the jaw of an ape circling the ice would never have been noticed, especially since a chimpanzee's teeth are usually masked by its protruding lips. No, if Johnny's owners had a nice porcelain crown made for him, they did so out of care and affection.

These former skating champions had become exhibitors of animals because they were, in the first place, lovers of animals – in this case, chimpanzees. By combining talent with affection, they made a living which enabled them to fulfil that affection. Many of the trainers and showmen I have known fall into the same category. They are exceptional performers in their own right and animal lovers as well – more interested in their charges, more responsive to their joys, sorrows and problems than the bulk of those who commiserate or condemn without personal knowledge. But they are also devoid of spurious sentimentality because they know that animals are animals, because they live with them, and in most cases, love them in a responsible manner. I have known many broke circus artists, but few instances of abandonment. When times are hard a trainer feeds his animal before himself. This may be in his own interest, but it is also a duty of the sort owed by parents to their children.

I have found this interest and affection at the humblest level. A 'beast-man' who slept beside his charges and earned next to nothing – once showed me a fine new book on horse doctoring. It had only just come out. 'That must have set you back at least three hundred francs,' I said. 'Four hundred,' he proudly replied.

I would go so far as to say that even the hard-handed trainer has a soft spot for his animals. The fact that he works them *en férocité* does not necessarily imply unkindness. He makes them roar or lash out to highlight or exaggerate the attendant risks for entertainment's sake. Behind the scenes, he will often fondle and caress them. He is certainly worth more than the sensitive souls who take dogs or cats home because they fancy themselves as animal lovers, only to abandon the creatures in a wood or badger a vet into destroying them at the first hint of a mess on the wall-to-wall carpet.

Some years ago, the press splashed the story of a celebrated French pop singer and his troublesome chimpanzees. He had loudly denounced the imprisonment of chimpanzees in circuses and thought it abominable to put them on show. Little by little, to deliver them from this servitude, he assembled a colony of four or five chimpanzees at his home. He was genuinely fond of the animals and allowed them to live like members of the household, but it was not long before they started ruling the roost. One day, upset by an emotional crisis, he dropped everything and walked out. The chimpanzees stayed behind with his wife. Having already started to play up when their master was at home, they became a pest and a danger in his absence. They broke out, scaled the roof and wrenched off tiles and guttering. The woman summoned help. What was to be done with the animals? Could they be anaesthetized and recaptured? Should they be destroyed?

At this stage my advice was sought. My assistant went off to reconnoitre under strict instructions not to kill the chimps. Meanwhile, however, one of them had headed for the nearest village, where it committed a variety of misdemeanours and terrorized the local population. The gendarme shot it, but the others were spared for a return to life in captivity. One of them found a new master who reintroduced it to the pleasures and constraints of show business. The other two went to a zoo.

Far be it from me to cast stones at anyone. I would only say that, from the animal's point of view, it is not always easy to distinguish friend from foe.

Some time after my visit to the Mullers, a woman animal-trainer asked me to treat her dogs. She was presenting her act at the Folies-Bergère in Paris, and her affection for her dogs was obvious. Madame Hans turned up in my consulting room, accompanied by all fifteen of her poodles. She was a good-looking woman in her mid-thirties, with a gentle and serene manner. I was immediately struck by the relationship between her and her dogs. Total obedience, no barking, no shouting. Peace and friendship reigned, yet the animals were all males. Trainers seldom use females because experience has shown that males work better. Bitches in heat not only become inattentive but upset the males, distracting them and making them lazy. However, Madame Hans had added a sixteenth dog to her troupe of fifteen poodles. This was an Alsatian which had followed her home one night at Argenteuil, near Paris, when she was returning from the Folies-Bergère. He had sneaked into the small garden of her suburban villa the moment she opened the gate. The other dogs, led by the stalwart of the troupe, a giant poodle of exceptional size, tried to repel the intruder, but the Alsatian refused to be intimidated even though he was not on his own territory. It was as if he sensed that the real pack leader – in this case the dogs' mistress – would not drive him away. She did not, in fact, have the heart to do so and persuaded the others to accept the newcomer.

The Alsatian tactfully spent the night outside while the fifteen poodles retired to their usual quarters in the two rooms reserved for them. Next day, Madame Hans made inquiries in the neighbourhood and called at the police station. The dog must have belonged to someone but nobody recognized or claimed him. He remained in the little garden at Argenteuil for another two days, attentive to every word or gesture of the woman he already regarded as his new mistress.

Before long, his integration in the family was complete. Although he was extremely jealous and would not let anyone near his mistress, there was no trouble with the fifteen poodles. They too were jealous, particularly the strongest one, who could have held his own against the Alsatian. In accordance with the instincts of his breed, however, the latter constituted himself the guardian of the troupe. He guarded them like sheep, rounded them up when it was time to go out, and generally behaved as if he were the bearer of special authority delegated by his mistress.

The dogs were the tools of Madame Hans's trade, but they meant far more to her than that. As if she did not have enough to cope with already, she had gone to a kennels and acquired yet another dog – the unhappiest-looking of the bunch. This she had brought to see me because of the sores on its body. She thought they were wounds inflicted by blows or bites. In reality, they were a skin complaint caused by a highly contagious fungus which could not fail to contaminate the whole troupe. 'You too,' I told her. 'Are you sure you don't have an itch somewhere?' She was already infected, of course. I had to treat the entire family from the tiniest miniature poodle to the Alsatian. That included Madame Hans's son, a ten-year-old boy who was also on the best of terms with his mother's dogs and assisted her during training sessions.

It was more than affection: it was genuine devotion. Another woman confronted by this ailment and the risks to which it exposed her troupe would have got rid of the offender by leaving him with me, but Madame Hans's love for her animals was heartfelt. She later consulted me about the star of her act, a grey poodle. He had developed a growth. An exploratory operation revealed that he was suffering from disseminated and inoperable cancer. His mistress's tears were genuine. She was not mourning her star turn but a dog she loved.

I would put Annick Richard's attitude towards her baby gorilla on an equally exalted plane – one characterized far more by moral and humane considerations than professional.

Annick is the wife of Jean Richard, whose circuses and zoos are widely known in France. At home in her converted mill at Ermenonville she lives surrounded by animals – pet animals unconnected with the zoo. She has a parrot, a wool-monkey, a cocker, a mastiff, two poodles and several cats. One day she called me about a baby gorilla which appeared to be dying. She drove it straight to my surgery, where I joined her.

I deposited the wretched little creature on my table. Less than a foot long and weighing 28 ounces, it had just arrived from Africa. A tourist had bought it in a village, much as he might have bought a puppy. It finally dawned on him, when he returned to Europe a few days later, that the animal was unwell. How could it have been anything else? A gorilla of that tender age cannot survive without intensive care if separated from its mother. The tourist, who might easily have consigned the poor little thing to a trash can, showed at least some sense of responsibility by consulting Jean Richard's zoo. Annick had taken it in without a moment's hesitation.

Now it lay stretched out on my table, only just breathing. Every feeble cough that racked its little body threatened to be the last. Diagnosis: pneumonia. It was dying of asphyxia. I immediately gave it oxygen and an antibiotic drip. We cleared the encrustations of mucus from its nostrils. It began to breathe more easily and revived a little. We persevered. We also administered aerosol inhalations. Several days went by, and still it clung to life.

But the baby gorilla would never have pulled through, for all the care that was lavished upon it, if Annick had not taken charge of it like a mother. I knew what that entailed, having experienced similar problems at home with Charlotte the chimpanzee: six to eight bottles every twenty-four hours, one change of diapers per bottle, and an acceptance of permanent physical contact. A newborn baby consents to sleep in its cot between feeds, but a baby gorilla or chimpanzee is far more demanding. It has to be in contact – close and clinging contact – with its mother night and day. The same applies if a woman takes its mother's place. The baby is there, clasping your leg, when you go to the lavatory. It is there when you take a bath – not in the water but craning over the edge and bawling with resentment at being separated from you and deprived, even for a moment, of the touch of your hand. It is also there at night, refusing to sleep outside the radius of your body warmth. It can, at a pinch, be dissuaded from creeping beneath the bedclothes, but it must at least have your hand resting on its head or arm or clasping its hand. This total servitude lasts for months, then eases a little. Your reward is to watch the baby grow into a healthy bundle of mischief. And afterwards? You have a problem on your hands. What to do with a creature which, however good-natured it seems, is considered a hazard to its human and animal companions? Sooner or later you have to put it in a zoo, and even the best zoos keep their gorillas behind bars.

It isn't an ideal solution, but what else can you do? What other more satisfying life awaits an animal of this sort? It could have been left to die, and some would call that the best policy. Better still, it could have been left to live peacefully in its native forest among its own kind. The fact is that it wasn't: its mother had been killed. Why? So as to capture the baby and exhibit it in a circus or a zoo? The uninitiated might think this the obvious answer, but they would be wrong. The real situation is altogether different.

I know a restaurant in Africa where the menu lists a portion of chicken at five francs eighty and, on the next line, a portion of gorilla at three francs eighty – two francs cheaper. You can also see a whole gorilla being roasted on a spit. Revolving above the embers, it looks strangely like a man. This eating of anthropoids, which to me carries a whiff of cannibalism, explains a great deal.

The forest-dwelling gorilla fears no enemy. Its only foe is man, and man hunts it far less often for the sake of zoos and circuses than, quite simply, for food. The local inhabitants are more often hungry than not. Gorillas mean meat, and hunger ignores campaigns and laws for the protection of animals threatened with extinction. Therefore they are killed. It is distressing that such a pacific animal should be slaughtered in its natural environment. Eye-witnesses have told me that a hunted gorilla which senses the imminence of death will turn imploringly to face its pursuers, groaning and weeping. It ends up as food all the same.

Gorillas of both sexes are killed, of course. There is little difference from the culinary point of view. The hands and brains are reserved for chiefs, the hands because they enhance a hunter's skill and the brains, naturally enough, because they impart intelligence. That leaves the babies. If they are very

147

young they will die unless saved by an exceptional combination of circumstances, as in the case of Annick Richard's baby gorilla. If they are old enough to survive, the hunters take them back to their village. There they serve as children's playthings and, quite often, as scapegoats. But they are gorillas nonetheless, and the villagers fear them despite their youth and small dimensions.

So, to render them harmless, they blind them. As for the parents, who have provided a few good dishes of meat, their skulls are often preserved and sold at market.

Where, you may ask, do the dealers come into all this? Are they the main instigators of gorilla hunting? They do not have to kill she-gorillas for the sake of their young. They need only tour the villages. Not all baby gorillas have their eyes put out. Some are consigned to little bamboo shacks and kept 'in stock'.

Do dealers contribute to the extermination of the species by sending a certain number of specimens to circuses and zoos? Yes, when they engage in illegal traffic. It is surprising that the gorilla, the first species to be officially 'protected', should be captured and exported in this way. At the same time, black market dealers may unwittingly and paradoxically be assisting in a rescue operation. Although Annick Richard's gorilla will probably die without issue, gorillas have bred successfully at Basle and various other zoos. The future of the species may no longer lie in the remains of its forest habitat, which man is invading and disrupting, so much as in some artificial and protected environment. We shall revert to this subject later.

In daily circus life, such questions are seldom pondered. The care of animals is an exacting business. Although it sometimes attains the status of devotion, as we have seen, it more often tends to be routine and unsentimental. But even at this less exalted level, it almost always breeds a good relationship between man and beast.

I once had to tend the aches and pains of a truly monstrous gorilla named Jackie, who belonged to the Cirque Bouglione in Paris. He stood six-foot-six tall and was broad in proportion. A mountainous beast looking more like King Kong than the original, he lived in an immense cage protected by bars as thick as a man's wrist. Suspended from the roof were his toys, a pair of tractor tyres on which he did gymnastics.

Jackie was quite composed as a rule, but there were times when he grew restive and rattled his bars – on one occasion much to Michèle's alarm. There was such a commotion inside the cage that one could not help wondering if the two-and-a-half-inch bars would bend or the roof give way. The idea of such a monster breaking out and venting its spleen on everything in sight was pretty perturbing.

I never ventured into Jackie's cage; he could have strangled me with two fingers. One day when Firmin Bouglione was standing just outside, Jackie caught hold of him by the jacket and tried to haul him through the bars. Firmin would have been crushed to death if we hadn't intervened in time. We managed to slit the back of his coat with a knife. He abandoned his sleeves to Jackie and escaped, breathless but unscathed.

This, as I later realized, was a game. Gorillas are far less aggressive than people suppose and wholly unaggressive in their natural surroundings. They are not jealous either. If a strange male comes to pay court to a female, he asks the chief's permission and receives a nuptial benediction in the form of an approving glance.

The essential intermediary between Jackie and me, as between Jackie and anyone else, was his beloved keeper. He alone was entitled to enter the cage. All his nights and days were spent with the 'monster' whose sole delight and distraction he was. He slept near Jackie in the spacious cab of the truck. The gorilla's cage was separated from this by a barred window through which the keeper kept an eye on him, talked to him or fed him bananas. The man himself adored Jackie and was always singing his praises. When he entered the cage Jackie would make a great fuss of him and fold him in his mighty arms. Sometimes he picked him up with one arm only, like a doll, and circled the cage with him before depositing him gently in the straw. Watching this trick from outside the bars, one could not help feeling a little apprehensive.

Jackie became seriously ill while I was away on a visit to the United States. Although the circus called in some distinguished veterinarians, he died. He had many friends during his life in captivity. I am sure that the closest of them, his keeper, mourned him deeply.

I have known trainers who, though decent enough folk in themselves, jeopardize their animals because of straightforward ignorance. One night I was summoned by an Italian circus trainer who shared his wagon with five chimpanzees. *'Pronto, pronto, signor – va malo!'* This was yet another New Year's Eve, as it had been on the night of the ocelot's blood transfusion. I had booked a table somewhere, Michèle was all dressed up, and we were just on the point of leaving. We would drop in at the circus, take a quick look at the chimpanzees, scribble a prescription and hit the road. We deserved a night out after twelve months' honest toil.

I tried to stifle my misgivings, but on reaching the wagon we were greeted by a chorus of hoots and screams which promptly put us in the picture. The chimpanzees saluted our arrival by yelling and rattling their bars in anticipation of a disturbed night at our hands.

They were, in fact, very ill. To judge by the way they coughed and spluttered and sneezed up blood-tinged mucus, they probably had pneumonia. Unless they received adequate treatment right away, they would not be long for this world.

The trainer was a rough type. No use trying to explain the course of treatment and leave it to him. Michèle and I would have to tackle the job ourselves.

We hadn't even brought any overalls in our eagerness to delude ourselves that it would just be a question of giving some good advice and zooming off to see the New Year in. I removed the jacket of my best suit and rolled up my snowy shirt sleeves. The Italian's wife did at least find Michèle an apron to wear. Goodbye champagne, pass me the thermometer . . .

Two of the chimpanzees were big strapping males, each confined to a cage of his own. The three smaller animals were caged together. Taking the temperature of these little youngsters presented no problem: I simply laid them across my knee face down.

As long as their trainer held them and told them a story, they made no attempt to squall or struggle. The big boys were quite another matter. Still undebilitated by illness and made irritable by high fever, they were snappish and suspicious of the strangers in their midst. What was more, they didn't 'speak' French any more than their trainer did. Not only my person but my words and vocal inflections were unfamiliar and consequently distasteful to them. I tried a little Italian.

Softly, softly, catchee monkey – apt advice, in the present context. I approached the first cage. Its occupant bellowed and rattled the bars. I kept talking until he deigned to listen. Was that the voice of an enemy? Perhaps not. I put my hand through the bars. This was risky – quite as risky, under the circumstances, as putting it into a lion's or tiger's cage – but I had to start the current flowing and simultaneously remain physically and mentally alert to any sign of danger. The big chimpanzee took my hand. Careful, now! One untimely move on my part and he might bite. Although I might elude him if I reacted quickly enough, contact would have been broken and the battle lost.

The chimpanzee neither bit my hand nor tugged at it. Still suspicious, he gently drew it towards his nostrils and sniffed. If he decided that the smell was hostile he would be perfectly placed to sink his teeth in it, but why should he fear a hand that lay completely relaxed in his own and betrayed no aggressive tension? No, there was nothing evil about my hand. Having sniffed it all over, he gave it a couple of exploratory but friendly licks. Finally, with two tentative fingers, he gave a renewed and decisive demonstration of friendship by plucking some hairs from my wrist as though delousing me. That was it. I had passed the test.

We could now get him out of the cage and stick a thermometer in his backside. He was too big to drape across my knees, so his trainer made him bend over. Reluctantly, he let me do my worst. His resistance did not signify any intention of attacking, as he would have done a few minutes earlier when my menacing and unfamiliar figure invaded his home territory. He had once more become a 'child' obedient to its 'father', the trainer whose authority and smacks he tolerated, and to someone he now recognized as a member of the family.

Meanwhile, Michèle had driven to the surgery to fetch some equipment. Now came an antibiotic injection. The secret here, after saying a few soothing and explanatory words, was to give the patient a smack – a short sharp smack on the thigh which was *not* destined for injection. Momentary alarm focused his entire attention on the point of impact. He turned to look and clapped his hand over the place. Simultaneously, I planted my needle in the other thigh. He hardly noticed and made no attempt to grab my hand, still less to rub or scratch the place. All his emotions and actions were concentrated elsewhere.

I had forgotten about our New Year's Eve party. It was all happening here, in the wagon. Michèle had gone off again, this time in search of a chemist that was open. I needed some mustard powder to make a poultice for each of the chimpanzees. Poulticing the chest of the largest specimen was a job requiring considerable patience. We also had to stop him tearing the plaster off when the heat began to penetrate. Kind words were not enough. He had to be rapped on the knuckles with a stick, good and hard. He tolerated these blows just as he had tolerated having his ears pulled. Chastisement was part of his scheme of things, but the blows he received from his trainer were far gentler than those inflicted by a dominant male on his inferior in the wild.

I had finished with the first chimpanzee. That left the other four, each of whom had to be treated in turn. The second adult needed handling as gingerly as the first. Then came the three youngsters. Although they were easier to deal with, I had to remain on my guard: a bite doesn't take long to deliver. Hours went by, and New Year's Eve was a memory by the time we finished.

But why had the apes caught pneumonia in the first place? The answer was obvious: the wagon and its cages were not only cold but streaming with moisture. The trainer explained as best he could that he had tried to give his charges an inhalation. This had only made the atmosphere more humid, so I recommended the installation of a ventilator and an electric heater. Meanwhile I told the man to open one of the trailer's two small windows.

The Italian's chimpanzees call to mind another of their species for whom I was again compelled to play the dentist. This chimpanzee had had its canines shortened in Frankfurt and the trainer suspected that one of them had developed an abscess. After going through the usual procedure of a tranquillizing injection in the thigh followed by an intravenous anaesthetic, I examined the chimpanzee's canines. Three of them were badly infected and the damage disclosed by x-rays left me no choice but to extract them.

They were huge teeth, over three quarters of an inch in diameter and more than two inches long – shorter than a tiger's but as broad. Removing them entailed the sort of drudgery I have already described: chipping away with hammer and chisel, sawing the teeth lengthwise while still in the socket, and carefully extracting every last fragment. It was a long job and a severe strain on the patient's constitution.

A young gorilla, happy and content in the author's arms
(*F. Gragnon, Paris-Match*)

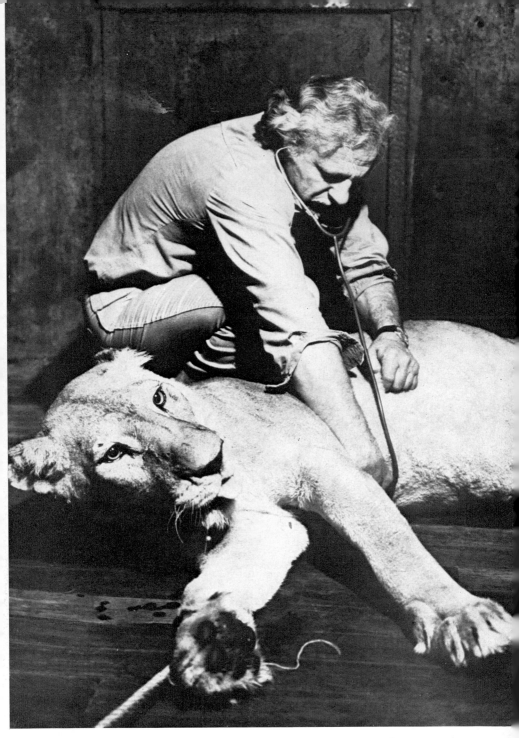

Dr Klein examines a lioness before she recovers consciousness
(*J.J. Morer*)

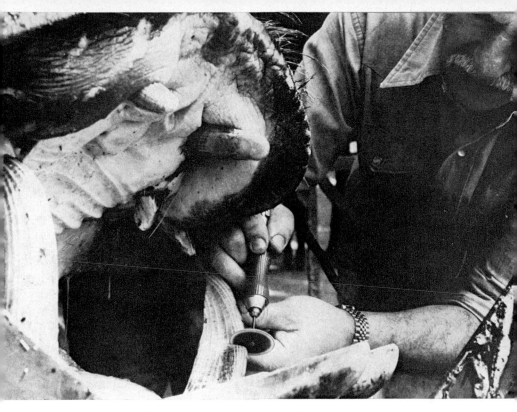

Dentist to a hippopotamus *(Gamma)*

Chiropodist to a giraffe *(J.J. Morer)*

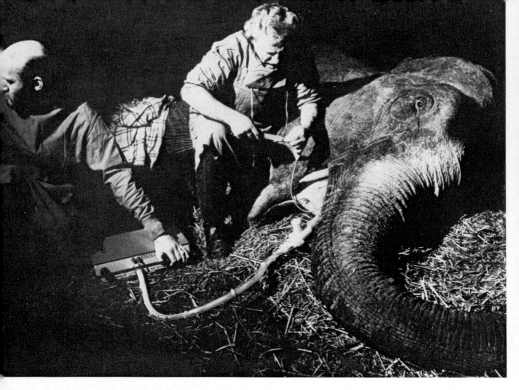

1974 – the first time an elephant was given a general anaesthetic in France *(J.J. Morer)*

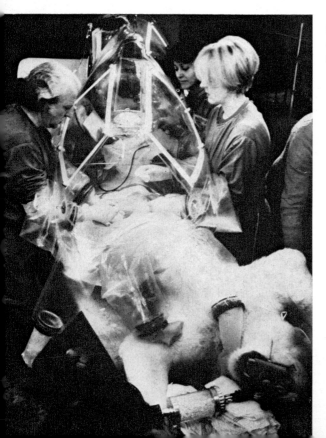

1975 – the first time an isolator was used in an operation on a wild animal *(Studio OROP)*

I had to keep him on a drip for several hours afterwards, and it was not until evening that he was able to leave with his master.

While still on the subject of teeth, a word about those of the elephant. Tiger's teeth are a picnic by comparison. One of my elephant patients belonged to a circus that had opened near Paris around Christmas one year. She wasn't eating, but why? She had something wrong with her, but where? Confronted by that mountain of flesh and blood I found these questions as perplexing as I would have done if confronted, at the other end of the scale, by a flea. I had already felt the same way about an elephant's ear. This time the sensation was even more disturbing because there was no immediate clue to the seat of the trouble. However, careful observation and reflection led me to conclude that there was something wrong with the animal's mouth.

But an elephant's mouth does not open wide like that of a hippopotamus. Relatively speaking, it is very small and narrow. It also contains a nonextensible tongue which takes up a lot of room and insists on delving in the very place you want to examine. Finally, whereas the hippo yawns readily, the elephant tends to shut its mouth just when you want it to say 'Ah!'

With patience and the mahout's help, I finally persuaded my patient to half-open her mouth. There in the lower jaw, of which even less could be seen than the upper, I spotted a molar in bad condition. It did not contribute properly to the process of mastication. Part of the tooth had formed a large excrescence which interfered with the masticatory movements and was lacerating the cheek. The solution was to extract it.

While working on this huge tooth in such a comparatively small mouth, I could expect no help or good will from my proboscidean patient, who was, as usual, a female. At the first tickle, one blow from her trunk might send me hurtling across the shed. She would have to be totally immobilized by general anaesthesia, but four tons of elephant cannot be put to sleep with a cotton wool pad soaked in ether or chloroform.

Fortunately, I had managed to get hold of a remarkable product unobtainable in France. This could only be imported if the requisite permits had been issued by the International Health Organisation, based in Geneva – quite a performance. There was a good reason for all these precautions. The product was not only easy to use but incredibly potent. One milligram would immobilize a creature weighing half a ton and keep it immobilized until death supervened unless the antidote was administered. Once this was introduced into its system, the animal got up and carried on as if nothing had happened.

Nobody in France had ever before anaesthetized an elephant in such a way or for such a purpose. Spectators, newspapermen and television cameras turned up to witness and record this French première. I had taken the precaution of bringing along some resuscitation equipment which would assist respiration by inflating the lungs with oxygen under pressure, alone or mixed with air in the required proportions and volume. My apparatus – a small box measuring $24 \times 12 \times 8$ inches – had been specially designed and constructed on this scale for the ventilation of an elephant's thorax.

The dose to be injected was 8 milligrams, or a little over 3 cubic centimetres. I administered it without difficulty. The drug took two minutes to act. During this time we tried to manoeuvre the patient so that she would lie down on her right side. Her bad tooth being on the left of the lower jaw, this would make things easier for me. She took a few steps, every movement anticipated by two men carrying a large mattress with which they hoped to break her fall. The drug would drop her in a heap, not cause her to subside gently. She began to sway from side to side, still standing, while we endeavoured to push her to the right. Her head and trunk swayed too, and her eyes widened, as if she were suffering from vertigo and trying to focus on a fixed point. Finally, still stiff-legged, she collapsed on her side – the wrong one, naturally. The men just had time to slide the mattress under her, but her four tons caused a minor earth-tremor all the same.

As usual, I had to make the best of a bad job and work in the least comfortable position. There I was, half kneeling, half crouching in front of the elephant's mouth, with a hammer and a long cold chisel. One assistant raised the trunk while another tried to keep the jaws open. I started banging away.

I had often used a cold chisel to dress bricks and mortar when doing odd jobs around the house. Compared with an elephant's molar, these materials are child's play to work on. They split and flake off in chunks. Ivory is so hard and dense that it neither splits nor flakes. You have to make a series of opposed cuts, like a man wielding an axe, and no chip will ever become detached until the two cuts meet.

It was back-breaking work. My chisel was too short and the elephant's mouth too narrow. In order to guide the chisel accurately I had to hold it near the cutting edge, whereas the best place to hold it for effective use under normal circumstances is near the head. Periodically, too, it slipped from my grasp and fell. Last but not least, there was that confounded tongue. Although the elephant was wholly unconscious, the reflex movements of her tongue were constantly masking the tooth to be disposed of.

Chipping away without a break, I took over an hour to remove the offending object. It was not, I might add, a little milk tooth, but a massive molar six inches long, two-and-a-half inches wide, three inches thick and over a pound in weight. Having filed and rounded the corresponding tooth in the upper jaw, I got up feeling stiff as a board.

Before bringing the elephant around I inserted the endotracheal tube of my resuscitation machine to test its efficiency. No problem: it functioned like clockwork. I withdrew the tube, removed my equipment and injected the antidote into a vein behind the ear.

The effect was as remarkable as I had expected. Twenty seconds later, the tip of the elephant's trunk quivered and emitted some snoring sounds, then stirred a little. Before long, the eyelids half opened. The eyes, which were still very sunken, resumed their normal appearance. Life and intelligence came flooding back. The ears flapped, and – quite suddenly – the elephant made an effort to rise. Four or five men tried to prop her up, but she subsided again. Two more attempts and she was back on her feet, asking for a piece of bread and gently nudging her mahout with her trunk as if nothing at all had happened.

9

Snakes and Pains

What can one say about sea creatures kept in captivity? Being inhabitants of spaces still wider and more open than the savanna roamed by lions and elephants, don't they suffer even more terribly than their terrestrial fellow prisoners when confined to a wretched little pool in some circus or music hall? Again, if a man can't feel friendship for a chimpanzee, which is closely related to his own species, what can he possibly feel for a sea-lion or even a dolphin? Is he prompted by self-interest alone?

I have had several encounters with performing dolphins. One of them, a young female named Kiki, used to undress a girl in a striptease act at the Moulin Rouge in Paris. Even without the sea at her disposal, she had a lot of fun. Although Kiki could not properly be said to have been on affectionate terms with her human partner, she was not indifferent to their relationship. There were shades of discrimination in her social behaviour. For instance, she reserved her squeaks and aquatic somersaults for the man who looked after her, fed her and tended her pool. Was she unhappy? Was her presence in the pool an indignity? The factors that determine the answers to these questions are the same in the case of an ocean-dwelling dolphin as in that of a forest-dwelling chimpanzee.

How much would we know about dolphins if we were not occasionally shown one? Would we ever have become interested in what happens to them at sea when lured towards the Japanese or Russian factory-ships that haunt the world's oceans? Using electronic equipment, these vessels track shoals of fish and induce them to congregate beneath their hulls. Fish destined for human consumption emerge ready canned. The others, including dolphins, are jettisoned – dead, of course. The same thing happens when they are caught in tunny fishermen's nets. Dolphins accompany shoals of tuna because they like to feed off them. International regulations prescribe that nets should have openings large enough to allow dolphins to escape, but regulations are sometimes ignored. In come the nets, tuna, dolphins and all. As many as two hundred dolphins may flop around on deck for hours before being thrown back into the sea, dying or dead.

In view of this wholesale slaughter, is it really such a crime to keep Kiki in a pool at the Moulin Rouge and train her to gambol around with a pretty dancer? Not that she knows it, she too has been entrusted with a mission of importance: she is an ambassador between species. She not only familiarizes us with the gaiety, grace and good-nature of her breed but she enlists human aid and protection against the true exploiters: those who destroy marine life with an equal disregard for dolphins and the future of mankind.

This, of course, is a human approach to the question. It is human beings who turn dolphins into hapless victims or devoted ambassadors, whichever you prefer. If we try to form a judgement from Kiki's point of view, I think our first duty must be to inquire whether she is biologically adapting to the artificial environment in which she has been resettled. The answer is anything but negative. Kiki has been living in her pool for eight years. She is thriving there and shows every sign of contentment.

I have had to treat her from time to time, on one occasion for erysipelas. I was familiar with the work of veterinarians in the US widely experienced in the field of marine mammals. Kiki was vomiting and had developed large blotches on her skin. I doubt if anyone in France had had occasion to treat a dolphin before. Taking a blood sample, for instance, posed considerable problems. A lively dolphin weighing 400 pounds can flatten you with one swipe of the tail, and the tail is just where your sample must come from. You have to find the particular vein beneath the creature's smooth skin and subcutaneous fat. You cannot feel it with your finger so much as guess at its whereabouts with a delicate touch and an accurate knowledge of its theoretical course. It follows the line of the tail, traversing a depression which also has to be located more by guesswork than by eye. Here you have to insert the needle vertically, aiming with the utmost precision.

Kiki showed no inclination to keep still while I was preparing

157

to do this. My assistant and I stripped off and joined her keeper in the pool, which had been partly emptied for the occasion. We managed to pin her against the side after a brief but vigorous wrestling match, but she struggled hard. Nobody likes the needle, and Kiki, who knew from past experience what I wanted, was no exception. We finally draped her in a net which enabled us to hoist her clear of the water on three hooks. I now had to take my sample from the right place, hoping that she wouldn't squirm at the crucial moment.

Not only an animal but an artiste in her own right, Kiki the dolphin received VIP treatment. A man was employed to wait on her night and day because the water in her pool required constant attention. He had to regulate its salinity and alkalinity, maintain a constant temperature, and ensure that the pump and filtering mechanisms functioned properly. Living in this artificial environment, Kiki would swiftly have succumbed to the least negligence or oversight.

Dolphins need very careful handling, particularly when being transported from one pool to another. They must first be loaded on to a special stretcher padded with foam rubber. Armed with one of these, you lower the water level and jump in. The whole secret is to manoeuvre the dolphin so that one of its fins lodges in a hole in the canvas. Once this happens the creature is immobilized and can be carried to the waiting truck. Even during a short trip, however, it cannot be allowed to dry off and must be constantly moistened with warm salt water. These days, automatic sprinkler systems have taken the place of the watering can. The stretcher itself is equipped with a sprinkler, pump and trough, and the whole arrangement functions on a closed circuit basis.

Despite their importance, these precautions are sometimes neglected. I was once consulted about a dolphin which was to be featured in an entertainment at a nightclub on the occasion of a big launching party. Could it be temporarily accommodated in the nightclub's pool, which was neither saline nor filtered and heated? I strongly advised against any such course of action, but my advice went unheeded. The nightclub owner had been offered a substantial fee.

My phone rang at 2 a.m. The owner informed me that his dolphin seemed to be in a bad way. He had tried to get it out of the water but failed. Could I help him? Privately consigning him to hell, I turned out for the dolphin's sake. There was no way of emptying the nightclub's pool quickly. Although I didn't feel in peak form at that hour of the morning, I had to don my trunks and brave 40°F in front of a bunch of party-goers whose innards were aglow with Scotch. The dolphin's indisposition had not affected its mobility, so capturing it in such a volume of water took quite some time. My antics must have set the cap on the night's entertainment.

Among other amenities, the nightclub boasted a sauna in which I sought refuge as soon as I emerged from the water. I was offered a drink afterwards – good man, you've earned it, etc. . . . . Suddenly sickened by all these people who had casually risked a dolphin's life for the sake of their lousy party, I refused it. I also told them – savagely – what I thought of them.

Blunders of this kind are necessarily rare because the usual penalty is death. Performing dolphins are too expensive an investment to warrant such negligence, so most of them receive the best of care and attention.

As for Kiki, she was even permitted to savour the delights of conjugal bliss. A male was introduced into her pool at the Moulin Rouge, and she gave him a warm welcome. The male dolphin has a nice big penis, like all mammals. Copulating with decorum, the two creatures circled their little pool long and amorously. I remain to be convinced that they really missed the wide open spaces of their native ocean . . .

Thanks to the care bestowed on them, the amours of dolphins in captivity have borne fruit – a triumph for man as well as beast. Not long ago, a great deal of fuss was made about the birth of a baby dolphin in the Soviet Union. The Russians, who hailed this as a world première, could not have been aware that Kiki's owner, M. Mauser, had already procured a birth at the Rapperswil dolphinarium in Switzerland, and that others had previously occurred at Harderwijk in Holland as well as in Britain and the United States. The mother gives birth near the surface, whereupon the baby dolphin rises quickly to breathe and then returns to suck. Because it cannot feed for long at a time, the mother is equipped with a muscular mechanism which injects concentrated milk into the baby's mouth under pressure, like an aerial tanker refuelling a plane in flight.

It is thanks to the exhibition of aquatic mammals such as

dolphins, sea-lions and grampuses, and to their prominence in marine zoos, that members of the public have – in some countries – come to realize that cetacea of every kind are being subjected to ruthless, selfish and inordinate destruction on an industrial scale, all international agreements notwithstanding.

The International Whaling Commission fixes annual quotas, but they are not observed. Although campaigns for the protection of marine mammals are developing in the United States, France, Britain and numerous other countries, the almost superfluous whaling industry persists in its depredations.

Even in the case of snakes or saurians whose psyche is so primitive that the average person would feel little sense of duty towards them, circus folk seem to me to have a humane attitude. For some time I had a woman client who made a speciality of such creatures. She transported them around in a light van, and I can still see myself sitting on a heap of alligators in the back, rummaging around in search of the one with a bad tooth. (I should add that they were not over-aggressive!) The patient had an abscess. Anaesthetic was useless in this case, so I wedged the jaws open with a piece of wood and extracted the tooth with an ordinary pair of pliers.

Living with reptiles had given my client an intimate knowledge of their aches and pains, and I more than once benefited from her experience. At the circus, her modest act consisted mainly in dancing with snakes wound around her body and posturing near the toothy jaws of somnolent alligators. Although I cannot pretend that her relations with them were as personal as those of a dog or cat fancier, she took good care of them and was mindful of their welfare – not only from self-interest but because of her simple and instinctive respect for animal life.

One day she phoned about her boa constrictor. 'I can't think what's the matter with him,' she told me. 'He won't unwind properly – he's all angles.' The patient was brought to my surgery for an x-ray. We put him on the table and unwound him as best we could. Sure enough, his coils were not very regular. The trouble? Arthritis: my patient was a rheumatic boa constrictor! We gave him some cortisone injections. He responded very well and was soon able to coil tightly around the warm and – to a boa constrictor – agreeable body of his mistress.

My client eventually sold all her reptiles. Like her snake, she had developed arthritis of the hip. That spelled the end of her dancing career. She ought to have gone for treatment long before, but how? Being alone in the world except for her snakes and alligators she could not go to hospital while they were dependent on her. Her case was a renewed illustration of the bonds that exist between human beings and animals.

I think it true to say that, whether or not their affection for them is profound, and whether or not it is outweighed by material considerations, circus folk do the best they can for their animals. But their best often amounts to a great deal and is more than pure self-interest would demand: it is a sense of professional responsibility carried to extreme lengths.

I doubt, for instance, if anyone could have done more than Jean Richard once did for a dozen tigers at Ermenonville. Nobody had procured them for him by depopulating the jungles of Asia. These tigers had all been born in captivity and purchased from a zoo. They were healthy, handsome animals, though a trifle short in the leg.

Then one of them fell ill and died. An autopsy seemed to indicate that the cause of death was gastroenteritis due to poisoning, but before long a second tiger sickened and died under similar circumstances. This time I performed the autopsy. I found a small abscess on the lung and had some tests made. The answer was tuberculosis.

This was extremely serious. The entire circus and zoo – and the remaining tigers first and foremost – were threatened with infection. It was absolutely essential to trace the source of the trouble and eliminate the agent that had carried the bacillus. Was it one of the tigers? I doubted it. They were sound when Jean Richard bought them. They were also young – only three years old – and had been with him for six months. Signs of illness would have declared themselves sooner if infection had occurred on the vendor's premises.

Against this, the rest of the zoo's inmates were all closely supervised and in good health. No blame could be attached to them, so the tigers had very probably been infected by a human being – but who? The whole of the staff, or thirty-odd people, were examined at my request. A mobile medical unit checked each of them on the spot, but the results were negative.

While waiting to discover the cause of the trouble, we tried to tackle its disastrous results. I was under no illusions: all the tigers would become infected. Should we slaughter them to prevent any spread of infection or try treating them despite our slender chances of success?

The implications of this question were very grave, if not dramatic. Could we – should we – attempt the impossible with these animals as we would have done with human beings? Should we turn a deaf ear to all but the chill dictates of reason, which prescribed extermination, on economic and hygienic grounds? Jean Richard was fond of these tigers, whose training had already begun. Repelled by the idea of ruthlessly destroying so many of the lives in his charge without a final attempt to save them, he reacted like the artiste and sensitive person he was. Accordingly, we plunged into the fray.

How do you treat a tuberculous tiger? Curing a human patient is difficult enough and takes at least eighteen months. Treatment must be strictly administered to avoid developing strains resistant to antibiotics – a regrettable phenomenon which is becoming more and more frequent because many patients treat themselves at home, often without due care. Antibiotics are bacteriostatic, not bactericidal. They inhibit the growth of micro-organisms but do not kill them, so treatment resembles a boxing match. To knock the bacillus out, you have to hit it long enough and hard enough. If you stop hitting or fail to hit with sufficient force, it will recover its strength. It will also learn to parry your blows, becoming resistant and jeopardizing the antibiotic's chances of success.

In the case of animals, these difficulties increase. Requests have been made during conferences between doctors and veterinarians that we should not treat tame or domesticated animals infected with tuberculosis. However, most dog or cat owners insist on having their pets treated. If we satisfy them by prescribing medication, they tend to discontinue it as soon as signs of improvement appear. The disease hits back with a bacillus that has become not only resistant but, when transmitted to other animals or human beings, more dangerous than ever.

When the laboratories perfected a new antibiotic called Rifampycin, we were again requested not to use it on cats and dogs. Although we complied, this did not prevent the development of resistant strains in human beings. Bacillus tuberculosis is particularly hard to eradicate. It will persist after a house or cowshed has been disinfected. It will even persist when the walls are repainted after disinfection. It can even revive after a layer of plaster has been applied. In a cowshed, the only way to eliminate it is to treat the walls with blowtorches.

Is the risk of infection increased by the growing numbers of cats and dogs in our towns and cities? No. Apart from the fact that vaccination against tuberculosis is compulsory in my own country, the presence of an animal may actually help to track the disease down. I was once asked by a neighbour's wife to examine her sick guinea pig, but the animal died before I could do so. An autopsy revealed that it was tuberculous. I asked the whole family – the wife, her doctor husband and their two children, all of them apparently bursting with health – to have a checkup. If the guinea pig was tuberculous, it must have been infected by someone on the premises. The chances of infection by a visitor were very remote because transmission of the bacillus requires uninterrupted contact with the carrier for at least a month. An x-ray examination disclosed that my neighbour's wife had a large cavity in the lung. It should be noted in this context that restaurant and café dogs run a greater risk than other animals because of their contact with regular customers, some of whom may be infected.

Thus tackling the tuberculous tigers at Ermenonville presented grave difficulties. The death of the first two was followed by signs of illness in a third, as I had foreseen, but how were we to administer daily antibiotic drips to a tiger? A human being would patiently submit to it, even for eighteen long months, but the tiger could not understand what was required of him. He had to be penned up in the restraint cage for two hours a day in order to receive the massive dose he needed. We gave him tranquillizers, which enabled us to reduce the pressure, but it was no good: he couldn't stand being imprisoned for so long. Physical restraint was an ordeal which accentuated the stress of the treatment itself. Before long he resigned himself to being more or less pinned between the walls of the cage. He abandoned his convulsive struggles and stopped trying to tear out the needle and syringe, but he also became sad and dejected. His frail feline psyche had been crushed. He refused to eat, even when the antibiotic used was Rimifon, which is reputed to stimulate the appetite.

This meant giving the tiger two drips, one for nutritional purposes and one for the perfusion of antibiotics, which only increased his exposure to the restraint that so distressed him.

His condition improved nonetheless. He stopped losing weight and his coat became more lustrous, but his spirits did not revive. We redoubled our efforts. We fed him by hand, gave him chicken and minced beef, petted him, talked to him and kept him company. Nothing made any difference. He hung on for a few months. Then, one morning, he was found dead on the floor of his cage. The autopsy revealed no bacilli. The infected tissue had healed over, so his death was due as much to depression caused by treatment as to weakness induced by disease.

So a third tiger had died after months of effort, but others had become infected in the meantime and were also undergoing the same drastic and desperate treatment. As soon as one emerged from the restraint cage, another was pushed inside. Jo Clavel, the man in charge, was as exhausted as the keepers who helped him treat the animals. Jean Richard was sick with worry. I paid periodic visits to the theatre where he was currently appearing. My news was rarely good, but neither of us felt like giving up. Although I had warned Jean that the odds against our saving any of the tigers were very long, he readily took the gamble. The animals were now isolated in a small building erected specially for the purpose. Jean sometimes came and watched us at our work, scanning each tiger for signs of improvement. There seldom were any, but his determination never flagged even when self-interest might have counselled surrender. Treating the sick tigers entailed hours of hard work and massive quantities of drugs. Another two died notwithstanding, and that was not the end of the story. From the financial aspect alone, the expenses incurred in trying to save the tigers had far exceeded their capital value.

In company with Jean Richard, Jo Clavel and their entire team, I waged this battle for two whole years. It took up a lot of my time, but I could not bring myself to abandon the struggle. As I saw it, I not only had an obligation towards animals in general but owed a duty to the sick, humanly as well as professionally.

Nine of the twelve tigers died. Of these, three or four were cured in the sense that my autopsies disclosed no lesions or bacilli – cured, but they had given up and died. Two of the zoo's panthers also became infected, despite our attempts at isolation, and one of these died too. All in all, we had suffered a defeat. The other side of the coin was our well-meaning but realistic expenditure of effort and perseverance. Although we failed to save the tigers, we had learned a great deal, and, above all, left no stone unturned from the medical and moral point of view.

I did not discover the cause of the outbreak until two years later. The zoo at Ermenonville employed a keeper named Charlie to look after the elephants, whose enclosure abutted on the tiger house. One day Charlie fell ill and was admitted to hospital. He died some time later of tuberculosis of the urinary tract. Only he could have carried the bacilli that had infected the tigers. What accounted for the failure to discover his illness, from which he must already have been suffering when checks were run on all the Ermenonville staff? I could only conclude that no bacteriological examination of urine specimens had been carried out. Although Charlie was not in direct contact with the tigers, he sometimes lent a hand with them. More importantly, he must have urinated in their vicinity. This would have been quite enough to infect animals particularly susceptible to Koch's bacillus.

The death of the nine tigers at Ermenonville caused something of a stir, but few people bothered to ask if human beings always did as much for their own kind as some had this time done for 'mere' animals.

I once received another urgent summons. Though just as distressing, this emergency had a happier ending.

My telephone rang at 2 a.m. It was the Cirque d'Hiver in Paris. Would I please come quickly; something was wrong with the horses. They were coughing and looked extremely ill. I stopped off at my surgery to pick up some equipment and reached the circus to find that two horses had already died. Panic reigned. The stables held forty horses, some of them belonging to Bouglione, others to Hagenbeck and others to a Hungarian who was due to leave for South Africa in the next few days. There were also five or six zebras, not to mention miniature ponies.

All the trainers were keeping vigil over their animals. The keepers, who slept near their charges, had quickly publicized the double fatality, and the local hotels and restaurants were buzzing with it. Nobody thought of sleep. Everyone had turned out, looking very, very worried indeed.

I saw at a glance that it was strangles. Horses suffering from this bacterial infection develop a high fever and a bad cough. If left untreated, it usually proves fatal. It is also extremely contagious, so the whole stable was in danger.

There was nothing for it but to tackle the animals at once. I had to give several series of intravenous injections – antibiotics and arsenicals – to forty horses. Unable to get the whole lot into them in one injection, I had to take each of the forty in turn and then start all over again. Although the trainers and keepers were a great help, it was a herculean task. Dawn was breaking by the time I finished.

I had raided my dispensary before hurrying to the stables, but I was already running short of drugs. I drove home for a shave and a bath. As soon as the laboratories opened I raced there to replenish my stock, then back to the circus, where I gave the forty threatened horses another series of injections. After that I had to go and see what was happening to my clients at the surgery.

I worked there till evening, as usual. Then I returned to the circus and continued my labours until 4 a.m. I did manage to snatch a little sleep before being woken at eight. Then back to the surgery again. I followed the same routine the next night, and the next, and so on for two whole weeks: nights at the circus, days at the surgery. Fortunately my efforts paid off. Every animal in the stable survived and none of the trainers had to miss an engagement.

Where emergency calls are concerned, I have known nearly every imaginable situation. I once had to work under the very trunk of an elephant which had something wrong with its right forefoot. One of the toes, which was badly swollen, had broken open and was bleeding copiously. I did not at that stage have any means of administering a general anaesthetic. The most I could manage was a local, but would it be sufficient?

I had four assistants to keep the patient still and persuade her to entrust her foot to my care. One of them was armed with some sugar and the other with a goad. It was quite obvious, however, that no sugar or goad would restrain her if her mood deteriorated. She hesitated for a long time, tossing her head and brushing my ear with her trunk. She put her foot out and withdrew it several times. Finally, she consented to rest her foot on a pedestal and submitted to a prolonged bout of soaping, brushing and rinsing. The site of my injections had to be absolutely clean or an abscess might result.

The elephant could not have found my preliminary work too disagreeable, because she did not protest when I administered the first injection of xylocaine. But one was far from enough. I gave her quite a number all around the foot – almost a pint of the product altogether. Technically, the foot should now have been desensitized, but surprises could never be ruled out. The trunk continued to hover near my shoulder and above my head, but not – or so it seemed to me – in an irritable manner.

I cut into the foot and exposed a large tumour. The anaesthetic worked – there was not much reaction – but the elephant became more agitated at the sight and scent of blood. Her trunk curled towards the foot to sniff it, nudged my shoulder and even tried to seize my instruments. My helpers tried to keep it away from the site of operations, but it disengaged itself – fortunately without violence – and resumed its gentle and inquisitive probing. I periodically had to brush it aside as I worked.

I had come equipped with a coagulator, or electric scalpel, but it was too small to cope with such an expanse of flesh. Quickly sending for a red-hot poker, I used this rather unorthodox instrument to achieve the same end.

I had to remove the entire toe, which left a substantial cavity. After disinfecting this, I packed it with a large quantity of cotton wool to inhibit bleeding. Then came the dressing. The quantity of bandages required to swathe the foot of a forty-year-old, four-ton elephant may give some idea of its dimensions: I had to use twenty or more six-foot rolls plus yards of adhesive tape to hold them in place.

The elephant had gradually grown used to me. Her investigation of the wound's environs and of my hands, which were definitely not inflicting any pain, became a little less intensive. She now took a rather more immediate interest in my person, sniffing my head and tugging gently at my hair with her trunk.

There were two more elephants quite close to us, heads turned in my direction. Their inquisitive trunks, which were also within range, followed the proceedings in their own way by applying themselves in a friendly but somewhat obstructive fashion to various portions of my anatomy.

Without dwelling on the fact, I knew that one blow from those probosces was capable of breaking the back of a fellow elephant sixty times my weight. But I also knew that there was little risk of aggression on the part of my patient or her neighbours unless I was grossly clumsy or committed some behavioural blunder. Mutual trust had been established. For all that, the elephant's gentle and inoffensive air can sometimes prove deceptive. However great the trust between man and beast, it is wise to be wary at all times. Plenty of handlers and mahouts have been flattened like pancakes before now.

This same trust may well underlie the relationship between man and beast in circuses. It is a trust which, on man's part, derives from his knowledge and experience of animals and, on the animal's part, from an instinctive knowledge that human beings in a circus environment mean them no harm.

Some will accuse me of painting an over-rosy picture of the relations between these captive animals and their jailers. Others may add privately, 'Oh, sure – lions and tigers are his bread and butter.'

It would be nearer the truth to call them my ruination. If I had been willing and able to charge a normal rate for all the hours, nights and weeks I have spent with animals, many of whose owners were as broke as their personalities were remarkable, I should long ago have become the gentleman farmer of my youthful dreams. I should not still be toiling like a galley slave under the spell of an enthusiasm which will always ensure that I am anything but a millionaire. I should not still be in two places at once, every day of the week including Sunday: one half of me at the service of the dogs, cats, parrots and ravens that visit my surgery, the other dancing attendance on the hippos, rhinos, gorillas and countless other creatures to whose side I am forever rushing with barely time to relax at home with my wife, children and friends.

10

Inside the Bear Pit

'Why don't you worry about your cats and dogs and stop meddling with our lions and elephants?' I was once asked by a celebrated big-game hunter and safari enthusiast. 'Animal protection is our business, not yours.'

That was his response to a comment of mine published in 1967 in *Le Figaro*. I had stated that there were only four or five thousand tigers left in Asia and that it was high time to take an interest in their fate. No press campaign on behalf of wild animals had yet been launched. I do not know if a slayer of such creatures – even a reformed one – is better qualified to undertake their defence than someone who ministers to their needs. Not being an extremist, I gladly concede that even a killer can come to know, love, and ultimately protect his erstwhile victims. But if the devil can become a hermit and the sportsman an ecologist, why shouldn't the animal doctor have a right to his own ideas on what should be done to preserve a few tigers, jaguars and other threatened species for posterity?

Big-game hunters developed their urge to protect wild animals by killing them. Mine came from tending them, but I was no more of a conservationist at the outset than they were. Just as they used to roam the bush and savanna in the hope of a successful kill, I roamed zoos, menageries and circuses for interest's sake and the pleasure bestowed by a successful cure.

Syringe in hand, I have stalked more animals than other men have killed or even seen in a lifetime of safaris. I have patched up countless bears, gnus, ostriches, elands, zebras, rhinos and other creatures. I have delivered and helped to rear a wide range of young animals in captivity. In doing all these things, however, I was gradually coerced into a process of self-interrogation. Whether confined to a simple cage or granted the relative freedom of a fenced enclosure, were all these animals in their rightful place? By helping them to live behind their bars – by contributing to a system that made them our prisoners – wasn't I doing even worse than the big-game hunter? Weren't wild animals hunted before being imprisoned? Didn't we kill the adults in order to capture their young? How many creatures had to die so that one might dwell in captivity? The public conscience is now tormented by such questions, which have dogged me throughout my professional career. They all boil down to the same thing. Are zoos good institutions or bad? Should they exist or not?

I now know the answer, more or less. For the time being, suffice it to say that my attitude inclines towards moderation and a middle line. Fanaticism in this field, as in any other, strikes me as reprehensible. I shall revert to the subject later, but ten years ago, when someone rang my surgery about a bear in difficulty, my attitude towards zoos was still rather nebulous. What counted, as usual, was the need of the moment. I was an animal doctor summoned to the side of a patient, nothing more. I never suspected that this call would mark the start of a new and enthralling adventure which was destined to unfold in the setting of a large wildlife park, teach me a host of things and give me much food for thought.

The man's voice at the other end of the line was different from the usual run – not jovial or familiar but reserved and extremely polite. 'I'm rather worried about a brown bear of mine,' it said. 'I wonder if you'd take a look at him some time, when you happen to be passing.' My prospective client did not sound too anxious. I could have taken his words at their face value, but my old instinct told me that something was wrong and warned me not to be misled by his dispassionate tone. I asked him a few questions. His answers conjured up a vivid picture of the bear. No doubt about it: the animal was in very bad shape. I said I would be there in an hour and a half.

This was my first contact with Paul de la Panouse, head of an enterprise which developed into the great wildlife park at Thoiry, twenty-five miles from Paris. At this stage, in 1967, all that existed was a sort of zoo near the château. The park and its numerous inmates were not added until later. I inquired the château's whereabouts and then set off, having entrusted the cats and dogs in my waiting room to the expert care of

Michèle and my woman assistant.

The keeper, Monsieur Nicolas, took me to the bear pit as soon as I arrived. It was a substantial structure incorporating tons of concrete. I went downstairs to the cages, which were brand-new and built of galvanized iron. Everything looked spotless. Monsieur Nicolas briefed me on the way. There were six bears in all: two white, two brown and two black. 'Three different species in the same enclosure?' I said. 'Doesn't that cause trouble sometimes?' The keeper agreed. The animals occasionally exchanged blows and bites. I made a mental note. My patient might be the victim of a scuffle of some kind.

We stopped outside his cage. The big bear was slumped at the far end with his back against the bars, mouth open and forelegs splayed. He emitted spasmodic growls but showed little other sign of life. Quite clearly, his condition was even worse than I had suspected. The same old problem: how to tackle a wild animal at long range? I could not apply a stethoscope to the bear's chest or check his temperature without taking special precautions. Although he looked completely done for, the risk of a bite or a swipe of the paw persists until an animal expires.

'Give me the key,' I said.

The uniformed keeper stared at me, aghast. 'What for?'

'I want to go inside, of course. You don't think he'll come over here, do you?'

I had to talk Monsieur Nicolas round and absolve him of all responsibility before he agreed to hand the big key over. The bear didn't stir when it turned in the lock. Leaving the door ajar so that I could make a dash for it if he turned aggressive, I edged towards him while the keeper waited outside.

No reaction from the bear. I prodded his paw with a stick. Still nothing. Just as I thought: he was at the end of his tether. I could save precious time by treating him without over-elaborate precautions.

As a form of insurance, I secured the bear's forelegs to the bars with the help of the keeper, who now felt authorized to break the rules and enter the cage. Then I hurriedly set up a drip in an attempt to revive him. It took me quite a while to find the vein, which was not only hidden under fur, tough skin and a thick layer of fat but attenuated by low arterial blood-pressure.

171

The bear remained inert throughout his drip. I took the opportunity to examine him and eventually found traces of scarring on the back which might have been caused by a bite. I did not discover its exact nature until three days later.

Despite my treatment, the bear died. An autopsy revealed haemorrhagic lesions in the right kidney which were more than sufficient to cause death. The wound was scarcely visible from the outside. The jaws had crushed the kidney, which gives some idea of their formidable strength.

I had failed to save the bear's life, but nobody blamed me for that. I had done more than was expected of me. I also contributed to the subsequent debate on how to prevent a recurrence of such accidents. How could the bears be dissuaded from killing each other? In nature, the weaker can resort to flight. What escape was there here, in a pit enclosed on all sides? How could we help? Bears of different breeds could often be seen tolerating each other and working together in circuses, but there they were supervised by a man who knew how to keep the peace. The bear pit presented a different situation. The occupants were not only in mutual contact but cut off from any means of escape. How could they be separated? There was no question of going down into the pit and leading them off to their respective cages. Several methods of curbing their aggressive behaviour were considered. One was a jet of water from a high-pressure hose, but the battling bears promptly ignored it after a moment's surprise. They reacted similarly to another form of intervention, even though it must have been more disagreeable: a pole long enough to reach them safely and armed with an electrified tip. They merely shook their heads and retreated for a moment, then returned to the attack.

We were up against a typical zoo problem. If we could persuade the animals to live in peace, their captivity might still arouse grave misgivings but would not be utterly inimical to life. If they were prompted to kill each other by captivity itself, the answer was plain: in this respect, zoos were an unmitigated evil. Issues are seldom as clear-cut, however, and a solution soon imposed itself.

To members of the public, what was interesting was to see different bears living together. To the bears, what was vital was to avoid confrontations between different breeds and the attendant risk of serious aggression. Although fights do occur

172

inside the same group and breed, the chances of harmony are greater. The solution, therefore, was to let animals of each breed out of their cages in turn, so that they could take the air and bathe in the pool without meeting a potential aggressor.

One of the functions of a zoo may be to interest man in the existence of wild animals and render him sensitive to it by displaying them under the best possible conditions. Clearly, any spectacle that proves lethal to them fails in this object. In this case, the animals' interests had been sacrificed to those of the public. What their separation really safeguarded was the dignity of man. If it is in the nature of our kind to exploit animals, use them, feed on them, make companions of them, take pleasure in them and love them, it is unworthy of us to be their executioners. A bear had died in a cage. Properly regarded, this incident and our reactions to it raise important questions affecting human nature and the evolution of man and beast in today's world.

The situation improved and was stabilized by the measures we took, but not in an altogether expected way. The black bears, being weaker than the others, were soon withdrawn from circulation, but the polar and brown bears finally learned to coexist. One day a brown she-bear gave birth to a cub which, when it first appeared in public after hibernation, turned out to be of a curious colour: neither brown nor white, but a dark shade of grey. Nobody had been present at her mating, but the keeper was in no doubt that the sire was Narvick, a big white ten-foot male. The birth of this crossbred cub went some way towards offsetting the death of the bear I had been summoned to treat. The battle was not completely lost after all.

As soon as I started to work for zoos, I first instinctively and then deliberately made the most of any opportunity for research into the best living conditions available to the animals in my care. I could not confine myself to being a vet in the narrowest sense. I felt bound to ascertain how and why an injury had been inflicted or a disease contracted and discover what steps should be taken to prevent a recurrence. I could not be a vet without becoming something of an ecologist as well.

Even before I alarmed the bear's keeper by venturing into its cage, I had been consulted by some of the handful of French zoos that existed in the early 1960s. Their numbers remained static until 1965. Then they increased, often under circumstances open to the gravest criticism, in response to a new public craze for the study of wildlife and nature in the raw. Before that, certainly in France though not in Germany, the United States and some other countries, ecological considerations were of very secondary importance to all but a few pioneering zoos of specialist status.

I myself had few worries of this kind, in theory if not in practice. Why was I summoned to the Jardin d'Acclimatation, that ancient zoo so familiar to the children of Paris? Not to study the lion enclosure and advise on its modernization, for example, but to treat Cora, a twenty-one-year-old lioness reared in the image of the nineteenth-century establishment where she spent her days. She was spiteful and dangerous. It was impossible to examine her through the bars, as some other animals had allowed me to do. I asked what the matter was. She hadn't eaten for about ten days, the zoo authorities told me. This had caused no immediate concern because lionesses often fast while in season. Finally, when she still declined to eat, they had called me in – but only to confirm that there was nothing to be done and sign the equivalent of a death warrant. The keeper, Fritz, saw nothing to fret about. The old girl was on her last legs anyway; the only solution was to put her down.

To salve my conscience I insisted on carrying out a brief preliminary examination. I used my dart gun to give Cora an intramuscular shot of tranquillizer, which put her to sleep without trouble. Then I entered the cage and examined her. She had a badly swollen abdomen. I came to the conclusion that she was suffering from endometritis, a fatal condition if left untreated. The uterus fills with pus as a result of hormonal imbalance, the wall stretches and finally ruptures. The pus spreads, causing pelvic peritonitis, and the animal dies.

I would have to operate at once if we wanted to save her, but the operation was one that could only be performed at my clinic. Cora had to be got there right away. Normally, she would have been housed in a travelling cage small enough to be loaded into a van. The only trouble was, no travelling cage.

Our problems were solved by an emergency call to the police. A few words on the phone, and the superintendent went out of his way to be helpful. For the king of animals nothing is too good. A few minutes later, with a blare of sirens, a police van and motorcyclist turned up to clear the road and guard against all eventualities. I put another shot of tranquillizer into Cora, who had no idea of the honour that was being done her. Then we loaded her into the van and set off at top speed for the Boulevard des Batignolles.

Our arrival caused a sensation. A crowd gathered quickly, and I and a couple of policemen bore Cora into the clinic down a line of interested spectators. Once inside, we laid her on the table and secured her legs so that I could anaesthetize her for surgery. Lying there with her belly distended and her legs splayed, she looked curiously human and feminine – almost like a fat old lady.

I relieved Cora of the pus that had burdened and threatened to kill her. There proved to be a prodigious quantity of it – a whole bucketful.

Stitched, cleaned-up and still asleep after her ovario-hysterectomy, Cora was transported home in the same regal fashion by her police escort. She made a good recovery, healthily surviving for several more years.

The old lioness had taxed my ingenuity and tested my talent for improvisation, but in a sphere which could not be called veterinary in the strict sense. The day when the same keeper from the same zoo passed a comment on one of his she-bears, casually and by the way, I embarked on quite a different train of thought.

The fact was that Fritz suspected that his bears had mated but couldn't be certain. He hadn't actually seen them – bears are very discreet in these matters – but felt sure they had. So what about the cub? If a female bear mates she usually conceives and gives birth. Precisely – that was just Fritz's problem. He thought she had mated in the past and given birth, but he had never actually seen her at it. What was more, he had never found any trace of a cub. Strange, wasn't it?

These far from uninteresting remarks gave me food for thought. What became of the young, if any? I pondered the question. My veterinary studies had been silent on the subject of ursine reproduction. I knew that she-bears usually mated in spring and threw their young in October or November, at the start of the hibernation period. A new mother had to be perfectly concealed and shielded from noise, light and any kind of contact with the outside world. There she remained, fasting while she suckled her cub, until spring. Then, accompanied by her now sturdy offspring, she emerged into the light of day. Any disturbance during hibernation would immediately cause her to kill and devour her young.

That was why Fritz had never seen any cubs. The bears' living quarters afforded the female no means of keeping her offspring. During the day they lived on a bare rock surrounded by water. At night they returned to their equally bare cages. If the mother had ever given birth, she must have disposed of her young at once – and even more discreetly than she mated, because a bear cub is relatively tiny. The mother may weigh one-third of a ton and measure seven feet from muzzle to rump, but the cub is a little sausage twelve inches long and two in diameter.

This setback to the vital process dissatisfied me. I itched to get a bear cub born and reared on that desolate rock, but how? The only way was to create the prerequisites for hibernation artificially. The female had two communicating cages at her disposal. Two-thirds of the first cage I walled off and lined with bales of straw. Using more bales to line the other three walls, I reinforced them with planks, a tarpaulin and more bales still. I left a hole through which the she-bear could pass if she wished, but not so that she emerged straight into the bare expanse of the rest of the cage. Still using bales of straw, I built a staggered entrance which provided the inner sanctum with additional protection and allowed air to circulate without affecting the darkness inside. This exit granted the female some degree of freedom. According to preference, she could either hibernate or refrain from doing so and divide her days between the rock and the pool.

These arrangements were very simple and easy to make. They also cost next to nothing, yet it took me two years to persuade the zoo authorities to try them out. Why? Sheer lack of interest. Besides, they found it inconceivable to leave a she-bear unfed and her cage unswept for four whole months.

I eventually got my way, with results that were soon apparent. One day Fritz told me that a cub had been born and could be heard grunting and snuffling inside the 'cave'. By March the mother was out on her rock with the cub in tow. This time, life had triumphed.

Zoos and their problems were destined to play an increasing part in my life. Although circumstances had a lot to do with this, I realize in retrospect that, even before settling on a career, I had an abiding interest in the life of 'wild' animals. So does everyone, no doubt, but mine was a trifle different.

As a child, apart from the shaggy dogs that became bears in my imagination, I occasionally saw a real bear owned by a forester uncle of mine – a real live bear around which my mind wove half-remembered tales, like the one about the woman who came face to face with a bear in the forest, offered it her basket of raspberries and so escaped unharmed. I suspect that, between them, my uncle's bear and the above anecdote go some way towards explaining why I feel at ease with bears, even though I realize – and am forever reminding myself – that I should be even more on my guard with them than with lions or tigers. They also explain why I have always been fond of strolling around zoos, and why after the war, when I thought I had abandoned a veterinary career, I once found my-self paying a professional call on the Bronx Zoo in New York.

While I was travelling around the world I met many doctors and vets. I went to the Bronx Veterans' Hospital, where I became acquainted with the American medical technology of intricate monitoring equipment designed to keep patients under constant observation, which did not yet exist in France. As for the vets of my acquaintance, most of them were with zoos. Although unaware that lions and tigers were my 'line', I was already steeping myself in a whole new world without suspecting that I would enter it a few years later. I felt peculiarly at home in the working atmosphere inhabited by American veterinarians. I noted that they had a serious, patient and objective approach to animals and their problems which entirely accorded with my own idea of the profession. Above all, I was struck by the consideration they showed for both patients and clients – not, in the latter instance, because they paid the fees, but because they could, if you encouraged them, communicate small but vital pieces of information capable of influencing diagnosis and treatment. I myself had an instinctive tendency to treat animals in this way. Although I cannot claim a similar attitude towards every owner, I believe I have been appreciably influenced by my encounters with those whose affection for animals is not only intelligent but devoid of excessive or abnormal sentimentality.

In Germany too, circumstances were later to guide my steps towards zoos at Hanover, Gelsenkirchen, Hamburg, Duisburg, Frankfurt and elsewhere. There I met animal dealers whose families had been in the same business for more than a century. One of them, who had a big moustache and sported a cane, looked like Emperor Franz Joseph of Austria. These people had long ago realized that their material prosperity depended primarily on a respect for capital – in this case, animals – and that amateurism, chaos, bad handling and straightforward negligence could be ruinous. They had more than their own interests at heart. They not only respected the animals they bought, transported, housed and resold; quite often, they developed an affection for them as well.

At the time of my visits, many German zoos were run by these animal dealers. Now they are administered by local authorities. To give only one illustration of how carefully such establishments were run, food destined for animals was kept in air-conditioned stores equipped with temperature and humidity controls. I am bound to say that even today nothing comparable exists in France despite the progress made by a handful of zoos.

Respect for animals on the part of these professionals is also induced by the psychological and social climate in which they operate. They carry on their business under the vigilant gaze of public opinion, not simply under municipal supervision and control. In Germany, the bear or lion is not just another comparatively weird and wonderful creature but a local figure – even a sort of honorary citizen. Its background is known and publicized. If it is ill, people show interest and concern. For example, between seventy and eighty per cent of the population of the German town of Gelsenkirchen visited its zoo at least once a year. The whole zoo reflected this popular interest in zoophilia, from the junior keeper to the director himself, who was neither a businessman nor an enthusiastic amateur but a qualified zoologist.

These lions, bears and monkeys lived in captivity, but they also lived in comfort: well fed, well tended, well treated and able to breed. What is more, they enjoyed the good will of thousands of men, women and children, some of whom cherished an almost fraternal affection for them. Even if man bore some measure of guilt in this respect, he was at least doing his utmost to reduce that guilt to a minimum.

Unhappily, quite another situation prevailed in many of the French zoos that began to spring up as soon as animal protection and environmental conservation came into vogue during the 1960s.

I was once asked to call on such an establishment, which shall be nameless. Its serious defects filled me with misgivings, but I had been summoned in a professional capacity. If animals were sick, it was my duty to treat them. I could no more refuse to do so than a physician can decline to treat a human patient on the grounds that he lives in a hovel.

There were cages all over the place: bears here, lions there. Animals were arriving with little sign that any preparations had been made to house them properly. I could see that the staff had no idea how to handle them. They were merchandise intended for resale, nothing more. But panthers and parrots cannot be stacked in a corner like so many shoe boxes waiting for a customer. I soon discovered that the person in charge was a businessman who knew nothing about animals. He could claim credit only for having sensed what was going on in the minds of his contemporaries. 'Wild animals are all the fashion,' he told himself. 'Fine. We'll buy some, sell some, and make money.'

But animals do not readily lend themselves to this kind of speculation. They are too animate and delicate a form of merchandise – one that requires too much in the way of humane treatment to withstand the effects of guesswork and improvisation.

I was not, however, dealing with an evil-hearted bunch of people. Their inexperience was a mitigating factor. They also did their best to put things right. As for me, my job was to tend the sick. I should have violated the principles of my profession had I refused to accept any patients but those whose owners happened to suit me.

The situation made me uneasy all the same. I began to doubt if there were any way of remedying the incompetence of these dealers. Convinced that they could not maintain their present policy for much longer, I backed off.

They duly went out of business, as I had foreseen. Justice had prevailed, but at the cost of how many precious animal lives? The profit motive had still further contributed to the impoverishment of nature and destroyed some more wild animals. That was a grave matter. If there were more establishments like this, not only in France but throughout the world,

179

where would the slaughter end? Was it right to let such businesses proliferate? Was it right to authorize anyone to traffic in 'wildlife' just as our ancestors used to traffic in human slaves?

In my long experience of bears, I never once relaxed my vigilance, as I had so often done with felines of all sizes. On one occasion I had to treat a Polar she-bear in her cage. She was slumped in a corner when I arrived. I had been told that she was vomiting, slavering and suffering from diarrhoea. I studied her for a moment. What was her trouble? Toxaemia, probably, or some kind of food poisoning with infectious complications. She already seemed to be in a semi-comatose condition. As soon as the keeper prodded her with his stick through the bars, she scrambled up and swung round to face him with her cub frisking close beside her.

The existence of this youngster made us even keener to get the patient back on her feet as soon as possible. The mother's prolonged illness or death would threaten the survival of her cub, who was a universal favourite and the pride of the wildlife park at Thoiry. His birth had been a further demonstration of the fact that, by suitably modifying the environment of a captive she-bear and providing her with man-made facilities for hibernation, one can enable her to give birth and rear her young in a normal manner.

The first thing was to lure the cub out of the cage. This was quickly achieved by distracting the mother's attention. Next came the old, old question: how to tackle the animal in order to give it suitable treatment? Mouth open, tongue out, let's have a look at your throat . . . No, that was out. Kindly swallow these tablets . . . So was that. I could try to persuade her to take them in food. Fine, except that she was refusing food altogether. Injections and medicines? We should have to get them into her sooner or later, but how? Although there was no time to lose, we could not subject her to excessive strain. She was weak enough already.

Would I have to fire the drugs into her by dart gun? I might be compelled to. It was a spectacular technique, but thoroughly inconvenient in the bear's case. To inject the requisite volume of drugs into a huge animal weighing nearly 900 pounds I should have to fire a substantial number of projectile syringes, each containing a limited amount by comparison with my patient's needs. Besides, the thickness of a bear's subcutaneous fat always casts doubt on the proper penetration and diffusion of the substance injected. Finally, projectile syringes carry a danger of abscesses. In her present weakened state, our she-bear could well dispense with that additional hazard.

The zoo owned a restraint cage, it was true. We could butt it up against the bear's cage, coax her inside, pin her between the two walls and, having immobilized her in this way, give her the requisite injections by hand. However, it so happened that this cage was a mechanical monstrosity. It weighed a ton and was excessively complicated. As far as I could see, its only purpose was to make money for the man who had built it. Even getting it into position would be quite a job. The bear would then have to be persuaded to enter. She would only do so after prolonged resistance, which was bound to tire her still more and delay the start of her treatment. Finally, all these operations – manoeuvring the cage and pushing the bear inside – would require the cooperation of at least ten men.

Wouldn't a little foolishness be far more practical and effective? By foolishness I mean an unexpected course of action employing methods so simple, yet so subtle, that they shock the practitioners of technology on a grand scale; a course of action which conforms to reason but carries risks that render it slightly reprehensible in a world where total safety is the general rule; a piece of foolishness such as the use of baskets by Chinese peasants who, in default of bulldozers, contrive by this and other primitive means to move vast quantities of earth for the construction of dams.

In the case of the she-bear, my Chinese dodge – the equivalent of the basket as opposed to the bulldozer and my own crude substitute for the dart gun and restraint cage – was half a common-or-garden broomstick.

Although this is one of my favourite defences when in contact with wild animals, it can only be used at very close quarters. Such was the problem confronting me: when all was said and done, my only way of administering any worthwhile treatment was to enter the cage and get within arm's reach.

I spent some time watching the bear and observing her various attitudes. In the end my instinct – my sixth sense –

gave me the go-ahead. After all, a trainer sometimes manoeuvres as many as six assorted bears around the big circular cage in a circus ring. I realized that this particular animal hardly knew me, that she was ill and possibly irritable in consequence, and that she-bears with young tend to be more than usually aggressive. Besides, I was going to have to subject her to some novel and unpleasant experiences, not make her repeat an exercise she had performed a hundred times. Finally, I was a vet, not a trainer. For all that, she did not seem in a particularly vicious or aggressive mood. I had managed to give or throw her some apples in the past. Although we were not on intimate terms, she might have a vague recollection of me. Anyway, she made a good general impression. I began by paying her all sorts of compliments from outside the bars. Although I wouldn't claim that my voice had a seductive effect on her, she didn't appear to find it distasteful. Was that an illusion born of my long-standing empathy with bears? Hard to tell, but I seemed to feel the current flowing between us. My confidence grew: she wouldn't pounce on me. I prepared to go in.

At once there was a chorus of dissent from the keepers and zoo people who had been studying the situation with me. I was crazy, she'd have me for breakfast, I'd look lovely without a head . . . They were all very nice about it. It would genuinely have distressed them if I had got myself knocked down or killed. Besides, they felt in duty bound to uphold the precious safety regulations. I decided to set them straight. 'Listen, the responsibility's mine. The boss won't go to jail if I get eaten, and neither will you. You're absolutely right: safety regulations are taboo, but it's the vet who'll be breaking them in this case. It's my job to take risks and I never run any without a very good reason. Anyway, let's not exaggerate. I'm not saying it's an odds-on certainty, but I've taken worse gambles before now. All right, let's have some quiet. I don't want anyone talking to the animal but me. Don't make a move unless I ask you.'

There was one elementary precaution we could take, and that was to fasten one of the patient's legs to the bars of her cage. Working from outside with the aid of a pole, a keeper slipped a noose under her paw, tightened it gently and secured the loose end to an upright. No trouble. The bear turned to resist this assault on her person. She tugged at the noose, but only halfheartedly, then lay down on her side. The fact that her captive paw was in the air exposed her belly and would make my job easier.

I was now at liberty to enter the cage. I knew that she could not reach me as long as I kept my distance, but there was no point in entering the cage at all unless I came within effective range. I was carrying my length of broomstick – not as a weapon, of course, but as a means of occupying her jaws and keeping her head away, if it came too close, for just long enough to cover my retreat. I continued to ply her with sweet nothings: she was a nice old thing who wouldn't hurt a fly, and she was going to behave for her own good and that of her cub, who needed his dear old mother, and so on. She seemed to accept these kind words in the right spirit. No sign of protest, no jaws angrily straining to repel the intruder's steady advance. She merely turned her head towards me when I came within reach of her belly. I watched her warily, poised for sudden flight, but did not even have to raise the stick. The bear made no demur. Still keeping guard with my right hand, I felt her belly with my left.

It was hard, distended and unquestionably painful, but she suffered my attentions as if realizing that I meant her no harm. I palpated her even more deeply, and still she made no effort to resist. I decided to take prompt advantage of her amiable mood, which might not last, and get a good dose of drugs into her. I had got my things ready before entering the cage. Gingerly my assistants passed them to me through the bars. I gently inserted my needle into the thigh of the captive limb. There were no unwelcome reactions, so I was able to inject her intramuscularly with five good syringefuls, or about 100 cc of an antibiotic and adjuvant 'cocktail'.

That was one good job done. Since the bear seemed so cooperative, why shouldn't I go one stage further? Come on, old girl, give me that great big paw so I can take a blood sample – don't worry, you won't feel a thing . . . This was a tricky operation because I needed one of her forepaws. Taking blood from a hindleg might have upset her and provoked a fierce response. She would probably find me less objectionable if I worked right under her nose.

I slipped a rope round her right forepaw, inserted the end through a loop and pulled gently. From behind, someone had released the tension on the bear's hindleg so that she could stand up, raise her forepaw and surrender it to me. I went over and gave the end of the rope to an assistant outside the bars. I pulled a little with one hand. The paw yielded readily and the rope was kept under the requisite tension.

The next stage was even trickier. I had to put a tourniquet around the elbow and tighten it, feel for a vein hidden beneath thick fur and a layer of fat, insert my needle in the bend of the elbow, attach the barrel of the syringe and draw off some blood. The bear's jaws were very close indeed to my head and hands. Psychologically, however, they were a good deal further than it seemed. To both of us, my length of broomstick offered a chance of escape. Thanks to its presence, the bear felt that she could get away, was not immediately threatened and need not show aggression. It was, of course, a wholly illusory obstacle. She could have brushed it aside in a flash, but psychologically it formed a very solid barrier between us.

I put it down nonetheless – I needed my right hand – but kept it within reach on the floor of the cage. I took the blood sample, still without opposition, and carried on. The needle was still in the vein. This afforded an opportunity to attach my patient to a drip. Something convinced me that she sensed she was being treated for her own good. She glanced at me occasionally, but I could detect no hint of impatience in the movements of her head or the expression in her rather lack-lustre eyes. I did not retire while the drip was up because I had to prevent her from removing the needle. From time to time, she put her muzzle to her paw. I made a slight movement with the stick, and that was as far as it went. The treatment proceeded without incident. When it was all over I offered her a fish by hand. She sniffed it gently but declined it. Was she going to lick me like some of the tigers and lions I had treated? It wouldn't have been in character – and besides, I doubt if I'd have let her. Bears have long pointed tongues, but her teeth were too close. Though generally predictable, a bear's behaviour is more capricious than that of the lion or tiger. You must never put out your hand for a bear to lick. On a few very rare occasions, when my desire for physical contact becomes irresistible, I risk it with a black bear named Peluche, of whom more will be said later. His is a special case, but I freely admit my imprudence. As a journalist friend sometimes tells me: 'He'll get you one of these days . . .'

Up to date, however, my instinct has served me well. Polar bears have always been regarded as exceptionally dangerous. I am bound to say that they have never given me that impression. In general, they strike me as reasonable, good-natured and unaggressive. I once treated another white bear at Orléans under similar circumstances. This one, a male, belonged to the Pinder-Jean Richard Circus, which was installed in the middle of the town. He was slavering, vomiting and grunting pathetically in his cage behind the scenes. The circus had no restraint equipment, so I climbed straight into the cage. I was able to take his paw and administer an intravenous injection, followed by a drip, with no resistance from the jaws that hovered so close to my hands. I worked like that for two hours, watched by a growing crowd of spectators who assembled regardless of the wintry morass of mud round the cages. The bear never caused me a moment's real anxiety, but still . . . I may simply have been fortunate enough to come up against two relatively placid subjects. The wisest and most prudent policy is to adopt the general view that polar bears are exceptionally dangerous. I am probably biased in their favour by one of my childhood prejudices.

I am also bound to concede that I have never had dealings with any but bears that are half tame and accustomed to man. In fact, zoo bears quite often hail from circuses where they have worked with a trainer. Last but not least, I benefit from a natural disposition in which I take no pride and for which – at the risk of repeating myself – I claim no credit whatsoever: I never feel afraid. Although I don't pride myself on my lack of fear, it can be a useful asset when not allied with recklessness. Animals are highly sensitive to fear in others, which excites aggression.

The white she-bear and her male fellow patient in Orléans made a complete recovery. A course of action which might have seemed foolish in theory had proved sensible, swift, effective and economical in practice, but I would naturally hesitate to advise anyone to base a general rule of conduct on these two isolated examples. Everything depends on the animals, their species, their environment and mood of the moment, as well as on the temperament, experience and technique of the person approaching them. What succeeds in one case may very well fail in another. I nonetheless feel that one rule of procedure can, for all that, be derived from my face-to-face encounters with bears. Commonsense and experience must at all times dominate the instinct or sixth sense that prompts you to be bold, improvise and take short cuts. Otherwise, boldness degenerates into carelessness, improvisation becomes confusion and short cuts end in failure or disaster.

11

Rhino with a Complex

Commonsense allied with bold experimentation – is this the principle that has governed the development of zoos in my country for the past decade? I would hesitate to make such an assertion. I have seen and sometimes contributed to a few laudable endeavours. I have registered some partial successes. Exceptions apart, however, the results obtained in France have yet to match the standard of those I have observed in Germany, the United States, Britain and elsewhere.

What brings a wildlife park into being? As always, a combination of motives and circumstances ruled by human interests rather than those of the animal world. Just occasionally, however, the latter's interests come to assume greater if not paramount importance. This more or less applies to Thoiry, the establishment that has claimed so much of my time in recent years. My veterinary status entitled me to treat the sick and take preventive measures, but I could hardly interfere in the running of the park. It nonetheless became the scene of some enthralling experiences. I have not only learned a great deal there but feel satisfied that I have often been of service to my animal patients.

Thoiry dates from the period when owners of French châteaux were debating their future. The income from such properties was not as a rule sufficient to cover expenses. English landowners had already pointed the way by throwing open their country houses to visitors in return for an admission fee. One of them, Lord Bath, had been inspired by the former circus proprietor Jimmy Chipperfield to establish a model safari park on his estate at Longleat in Somerset. Could his admirable example be followed in France?

The la Panouse family had begun by creating a zoo at the Château de Thoiry, not far from Paris. One rainy October day, when I had already paid several professional calls there, I visited Thoiry to treat Fanny, a she-elephant with serious growth problems, arthritic joints and enlarged ganglions. I was giving her trace elements intravenously. This was a rather awkward proceeding because Fanny was a nervous creature and fidgeted the whole time. Instead of immobilizing her by force, I kept the drip bottle moving in time with her head to prevent the needle from slipping out of the vein. Meanwhile, a keeper fed her continuously with sugar and other delicacies.

Pathé had sent a camera team to film this operation, which later figured in a newsreel, and a reporter from *France-Soir* had also turned up.

During the lunch that followed my performance on that bleak and dismal day, Paul de la Panouse outlined his problem. How was he to save his ancestral home? Receipts from admission charges to the zoo and château were not enough to solve his difficulties. It became clear, in the course of discussion, that he would have to mobilize the full resources of his estate if he wanted to save it. Why didn't he use all that land to establish a wildlife park where animals could live in semi-freedom? Visitors wishing to see them would have to drive through without leaving their cars. For once, I emphasized, the habitual relationship between man and beast would be reversed: the animals would be at liberty, the visitors in a sort of cage. Similar experiments had been tried in South Africa, the United States and Britain, but in France we felt like pioneers, which was something of a thrill. I cannot pretend that I regarded this scheme as an opportunity to pursue objectives of an ecological rather than a veterinary nature. Those preoccupations were still only a vague blur on the horizon of my professional activity. What weighed most with me was the dream image of a large assortment of animals whose health and comfort would be my personal concern. I could foresee masses of work and hosts of problems – a magnificent field of activity providing ample scope for research and initiative.

We had almost everything to learn in this field. Although there was a sudden surge of public concern for wildlife, the interest of the French public in animals still lacked the quality I had observed in Britain and America. Simplifying, one might say that people considered animals more as a show than as living creatures to whom they owed a duty. Although this interest was far from negative, it tended to steer zoos in an undesirable direction and turn them into amusement centres rather than places of conservation. Even the best zoos will always have difficulty in striking a tolerable balance between the need to provide a spectacle and the requirements of animal protection.

The organizers turned to Germany for advice on laying out the park and stocking it. As the vet appointed to look after the health of the park's many hundred inmates, I made it my job to examine our acquisitions before they were transferred, observe environmental conditions in their places of origin and study the problems posed by acclimatization after their removal to new surroundings. It was an enthralling trip. The vendors showed me round and briefed me on everything in a remarkably competent and conscientious manner.

At last the animals arrived – truckloads of them, and almost simultaneously. It wasn't a question of two or three lions, a few gazelles and half a dozen monkeys. The whole of Africa descended on us at one fell swoop: forty-odd lions, as many zebras, ostriches, elands, gnus, kudus, giraffes, white and black rhinos, and scores of others. The sight of them was enough to make a strong man quail.

It was 1 May, and the park was barely finished. Bulldozers had been bludgeoning their way through impenetrable clumps of oak trees for the past three months. The loamy soil was still sodden, muddy and unstable. The fences were in place and had been checked in theory, but the animals would be quick to detect any human error and take advantage of it to escape. It was impossible to be sure of every last thing. The finishing touches could only be added once we had tested the fences in practice – though not, of course, after the public had been admitted.

It took several days to install the animals in their various enclosures. Growling with fear and fury, some of them flatly refused to leave their cages. The thirty ostriches had travelled in crates covered with tarpaulins. When the latter were removed, thirty diminutive heads on thirty long necks turned this way and that, trying to discover what had happened. It was hard to coax them into the open. One of them, having finally made up its mind, took off so impetuously that it fractured a leg on the spot. My first patient!

One of the zebras, equally panic-stricken, fell into a drainage ditch and lay there unable to move, flailing the air with its legs. Its movements became even more frenzied when we tried to approach, so we eventually retrieved the animal by lifting it out on planks sufficiently long to keep its formidable hooves out of range. Fortunately for it and for us it escaped without injury.

But the animal that scared us most was one of the white rhinos. These had been installed on an island enclosed by a moat. One of them managed to cross the moat and galloped towards the double gates along a brand-new road which had been laid on a causeway several feet high. After a brief run, the rhino decided to scramble down the slope, probably noticing that the field below was covered with green grass which, though not exactly the colour of his native savanna, might well be good to eat. No sooner had he left the asphalt road than he sank in up to his middle. The sides of the embankment were like a quagmire: the more he struggled, the faster he stuck. Before long he was buried up to his muzzle.

The rhino's panic was matched by that of his human pursuers. An ostrich with a broken limb or a zebra flailing its legs in the air are unapproachable enough. Our half-buried rhino presented problems of a different order. He was lunging in all directions with his head, which was still free, and making fitful but titanic attempts to extricate himself. If he succeeded, we would be better out of range. There was no possibility of lifting his three-ton frame on planks as we had with the zebra, so what? A crane? Whatever the answer, we should have to hurry if we didn't want him to drown in the mud or break something in his efforts to escape. We had to save him, not merely because he was worth a great deal of money but because his life itself was precious and did not deserve to be cut short in this way. He was already a member of the Thoiry family, and we had all become attached to him. Despite his predicament, the animal did not seem unduly aggressive. I put an apple on the ground near his mouth. He took it and ate it. Then I gave him another by hand, and another. He sniffed me before accepting these offerings, like a dog. I appeared to find favour. We simply had to extricate him somehow.

The solution was simple enough – once it occurred to us. We realized on reflection that it would be impossible to get the rhino back on to the road he had left. A better plan would be to take advantage of the slope and help him to slide down it on to firmer ground. At the foot of the bank, however, stood the stout perimeter fence. This would put us back where we started. The only answer was to breach the fence, allow him to escape, and solve the ensuing problems as they arose.

Wire cutters, picks and shovels were brought. We set to work as planned, digging the mud away from in front of the rhino's forelegs and evading any lunges from his great horned head. Our efforts encouraged the animal to redouble his own, with consequent risks to those who were nearest. Before long, the left forefoot was almost clear. We beat a hasty retreat as the rhino struggled with all his might. Now he tore his right foot free and floundered furiously, dog-paddling in the mud. Was the idea working? Yes, he made a couple of feet at least, only to get stuck again lower down. We repeated the process all over again. The method had proved its worth. With a lot of care and hard work on our part, he would get out of there in the end.

Once the forelegs were free again, we dug away some of the mud clinging to his flanks and shoved him from behind. Caked with yellow mud, he barged through the hole in the fence, as intended, and trotted off across the green meadow. It was the Ile-de-France, not Africa, but even its limited extent spelled freedom to a rhino on the loose. However, the park's Land-Rovers were there to shepherd the fugitive back to his island. Freedom is always relative. Our rhino needed no second bidding. Wearied by his ordeal, he didn't bother to turn and charge. Instead, he fled the unpleasant noises behind and on either flank – roaring engines, blaring horns and raucous yells – and soon returned, after a few minor detours, to the companionship of his own kind.

This escapade was never repeated. The rhinos behaved so peacefully that they were permitted to leave their island and roam freely in the far larger antelope paddock, where they caused no harm to anyone.

We also had a black rhino of particularly gentle and sociable disposition. His behaviour was so good from the outset that he earned the special distinction, during a presidential election campaign, of bearing the name of one of the candidates whitewashed on his back.

He was, it is true, still young at the time. Although born in captivity and used to human beings, he later became less docile. One day he developed severe dyspepsia and had to be given a course of injections – a new problem from my point of view. My patient was accommodated in a concrete pen with a wall five feet high and fifteen inches thick. The gate, which consisted of welded steel pipes four or five inches in diameter, had to be strong enough to withstand blows from the snout of a creature weighing over a ton. From over the wall, which came up to my shoulder, I tried to plant a large needle in the rhino's epidermis. It bent at once. I tried the base of the ear – theoretically a softer area – but failed to penetrate it by so much as a millimetre. The rhino started to fidget a little, as though tormented by a fly. He was not normally aggressive. I had entered the pen before now without his showing any inclination to flatten me against the wall. On this occasion I naturally took shelter behind it, but I still had to be on my guard. He began to toss his head. His horn protruded well above my concrete shield. One blow from his snout alone would have acquainted me even more intimately with the toughness of his hide.

After these initial setbacks I went and got a hammer. Surreptitiously, I took a new needle and tried to drive it home with a few judicious taps. I might as well have tried to pierce concrete. The rhino saw me off with an irritable toss of the head.

That left the dart gun. I selected a needle designed for rhinos: a colossal thing three inches long and nearly a quarter of an inch thick. Loading the gun with a maximum-charge cartridge, I stationed myself behind the wall. I was too close to fire over the top without protection. If one of my projectiles rebounded it might catch me in the face. The next thing was to hit the right spot. I needed a neck shot, as close to the skull as possible. Needless to say, the rhino took a malicious delight in presenting every portion of his anatomy but the one I wanted. All right, I muttered grimly, turn . . . At last he did. I aimed, ducked my head and fired. This time the needle went home. The rhino gave a start. He must have felt something but checked in mid-charge. Where was the enemy? Nowhere to be seen. A moment later he was his usual placid self.

I later had to treat a white rhinoceros whose hindfoot had developed a nasty whitlow. Attempts had been made to treat the infected toe by dousing it with warm water and disinfectant, but the condition failed to improve and the infection spread to the whole foot. The affected area really needed bathing for long periods – either that or an operation for the removal of all purulent tissue. On the other hand, how much would be left of the foot if I decorticated the toes? Undoubtedly, it was too late to embark on such a course.

I nonetheless had to do something or the rhino would die. Antibiotic injections? These were normally given in the neck, but only a massive dose would have been sufficient to act on such a huge beast weighing over a ton and a half. The drugs available were relatively dilute and my projectile syringes held only 16 ml. I should have had to administer numerous injections daily for several days on end – not a very practical or effective course of action.

It occurred to me to try to concentrate my antibiotics on the affected limb and administer a massive dose which might do the trick at one go. I could not, however, inject straight into the foot. A big needle designed for implantation in the shoulder might do damage and break a bone, even in a rhino's foot. I decided that my best available course was to aim for the thigh.

A game of hide-and-seek began. I had to fire at a given range and be sure to take cover each time in case I was hit by a ricochet. As if stalking the creature on safari, I squinted around posts, over the parapet or through the bars of the gate. To ensure that the drug acted properly, I had to place the projectile syringes all around the limb. This meant changing my position after each shot. The rhino countered by taking evasive action. His leg undoubtedly hurt him, so he tried to mask it and largely succeeded. I had the greatest difficulty in bringing my gun to bear.

One by one the syringes went home, but the rhino's agitation increased with each successful shot. He now charged every time he was hit – quite an alarming performance. Although he could not take much of a run, his massive body shook the entire pen as it thudded against the walls and his horn struck sparks from the metal gate. I felt more and more tempted to leave him in peace, but I knew that I must persevere to the bitter end if I was to have any chance of saving him.

I should add that the wardens in charge of the rhino and antelope enclosure didn't exactly stand around twiddling their thumbs. They doused the affected foot with a warm antiseptic solution several times a day. Although our patient sometimes enjoyed his foot bath, he often demonstrated that looking after undomesticated animals can be a hazardous occupation.

We eventually won the battle. I fired half a dozen syringes into the rhino every other day without getting a single one in the face. The pen stood up, the steel bars held, and the walls did not come tumbling down. Most important of all, the rhino recovered.

To revert to an earlier case, the love life of one of our white rhinos seemed to have been affected by emotions experienced at the outset of his captivity, coupled with immaturity and other more or less obvious factors. The wardens reported that he tried to do his duty by his mate but was not very successful. For the benefit of those who may be interested in the male rhino's anatomy, I should explain that his sexual organs display certain peculiarities, notably a pair of small fins on the penis. The function of these is not, as might be supposed, to maintain it at a suitable height but to retain it inside the vagina during ejaculation. It must also penetrate fully – something which seemed to elude the rhino in question. Although I tried to help him by injecting hormones, they did not, as far as I could tell, impart the requisite tonicity. Thoiry's rhino island has yet to celebrate its first birth. I still believe, however, that the male will succeed when he grows older and that we too shall have the satisfaction of producing a little white rhino whose birth will go some way towards justifying the presence of its father and mother in our midst.

Where bears were concerned, releasing them into the park *en masse* was a particularly enjoyable experience. Thoiry already owned a certain number of bears, but these, as I have already said, lived in a confined space under traditional zoo conditions, dividing their time between their cages, their ditch and their pool. This time, forty-odd North American black bears were to live in semi-freedom in a wooded enclosure covering several acres.

Black bears are handsome and reputedly peaceable creatures. The preparation of their spacious abode had presented a variety of entertaining problems. Rhinos or elephants can be isolated by digging a ditch or moat of suitable dimensions. Keeping a bear inside a fence is appreciably more complicated. He not only climbs and digs better than any other large animal but

194

likes to go roaming where roaming is forbidden. No fence constructed of ordinary wire mesh would have been adequate. The enclosure had therefore been fenced with concrete slabs superimposed to form a wall. But a bear would have been capable of scaling this wall by clinging to the cracks between them, so the cracks had been carefully pointed all around the perimeter. The bear's aptitude for digging had additionally entailed burying the concrete fence to a considerable depth. But there were also field drains and culverts which would have made ideal escape routes unless blocked at suitable points with stout gratings. Finally, the enclosure was fringed with trees via which a determined bear could have gained the outside world. These had prudently been cut down.

Despite all these precautions, a few cunning individuals spotted gaps in the defences and hightailed it for the surrounding countryside through a drain which had been left unbarred. They were recaptured with some difficulty. In general, however, the inmates seemed tolerably satisfied with their new home, and the measures taken to keep them there proved sufficiently effective to rule out any further escapes once the teething troubles were over. Three large ponds were created for the bears' benefit and stocked with fish, which multiplied with surprising rapidity. The bears sometimes amused themselves by fishing. Bordering the ponds were large trees and bushes where they could hide. Some of the animals dug enormous earths beneath these oaks the winter after their arrival, hibernated there and produced young.

The black bears arrived in May, precisely twelve months after the bulk of their fellow inmates. The trucks delivered the cages one evening, and it was decided to release the animals at dawn next day, a peaceful hour when they could be introduced to their new domain without fuss. Also present on this occasion was a young American vet named Bob Olds, who later became a senior surgeon at the Animal Medical Center on the East River in Manhattan, the largest American clinic for small animals. We were both in high spirits. Although it was chilly, the day promised to be fine and springlike. The woods were sweet-smelling and moist with dew – a bear's paradise.

Together with Paul de la Panouse, his brother Raoul, their father Antoine and the wardens, Bob and I had climbed on top of the travelling cages to raise the traps, partly for our own protection and partly for the sake of better visibility. A few of the bears took quite a while to emerge, unhurriedly sniffing the air with their hindquarters still inside. Some lolloped into the undergrowth while others made straight for the trees and climbed them.

One big specimen calmly sat down in the middle of the asphalt road running through the enclosure and appeared to become engrossed in drowsy contemplation. Another bear, also of considerable size, ambled over to the small truck containing the food we had planned to distribute later on. He circled it, sniffed it, and glanced up at us on our perch. I liked the look of him. My old soft spot for bears proved too much for me. I promptly christened him Peluche and decided to make friends.

Peluche looked so genuinely amiable and peaceable that I joined him beside the truck. He neither retreated nor betrayed any sign of displeasure. I took out some apples and lumps of sugar. Peluche, who seemed to get the message at once, slowly drew nearer. Unless I was much mistaken, this bear was thoroughly accustomed to human contact and had been on good terms with man – either that, or he possessed an exceptionally quiet and trustful temperament. Once again, I did something rather rash. The bear could easily have chewed my hand as well as the apple or removed them both with one swipe of his paw, but something told me that I could trust him just as he apparently trusted me. At all events, he spent our first encounter guzzling sugar, apples, pears and dates. The larger fruit he held in one paw and demolished with his teeth, periodically glancing at me with a look that conveyed satisfaction at having struck it rich. I dug out some more food at the expense of one of his friends, and Peluche soon returned for a second helping. He was a good sort – certainly for as long as my supplies held out.

The bears spent the next week getting used to their territory and forming new habits. There were no incidents, except that one mischievous animal discovered a bulldozer parked near the entrance and calmly installed himself behind the wheel. I visited the bears several times, partly for amusement's sake and partly to check that all was going well. A week after their arrival, a press conference was held in one of the château's annexes to announce the opening of the new enclosure. There were journalists, a television team, a cold buffet and numerous invited guests. Why shouldn't Peluche attend the party too, if he was so well behaved? Confident that he would enjoy himself and help to enliven the proceedings, I asked Paul de la Panouse to come and help me fetch him. Paul looked faintly perturbed. A bear in the middle of all those people? Was that wise? I told him that the responsibility was mine – that Peluche was as meek as a lamb and would do anything I wanted in return for kindness and candies. On reflection, Paul decided it would give the reporters a good story and went along with the idea.

We climbed into the car and drove about a mile to the bear enclosure. We did not have to spend long hunting for our quarry in the undergrowth; he might have been waiting for us. The car had only just pulled up when Peluche appeared from behind a large oak tree, probably because the very sight of it made his mouth water. We hadn't brought a collar, chain or muzzle. I simply lured him over with a few lumps of sugar and some well-chosen compliments, opened the rear door of the hatchback and deposited another sugar lump on the floor. Peluche climbed in without more ado.

There he sat, propped on his hindquarters and grunting contentedly. The sound of him chewing and chomping away behind us might have deterred the more impressionable. I detected a trace of uneasiness in Paul's face, but he trusted my judgement and we arrived without incident at the former stables where the press conference was being held.

Peluche climbed out of the car as he had entered it, cool as a cucumber and preoccupied with one sole objective: more tidbits. He followed me into the room without the least nervousness. I invited the guests to gather round, but at a safe distance, and gave them a brief summary of the bear's career to date. Flash guns went off in all directions and television cameras whirred. Peluche, who was under no kind of restraint, gazed calmly around him as if he had been a star since birth. He left with us shortly afterwards, gladly obeying the voices that, to him, signified food and companionship.

At the time, I felt that my action had been a signal success. I had established good relations with an animal. I had enjoyed myself and entertained others. I may have even provided a little interest and instruction by showing them my bear at close quarters and introducing them to a 'wild' animal – an encounter publicized in thousands of homes by press and television. I had, or so it seemed to me, done a good 'propaganda job' on behalf of the animal world.

Later on, I delivered a harsher verdict on myself: I had not only run a personal risk – which was my business – but put others in jeopardy as well. However well a person knows his business, he is never exempt from error or miscalculation. This was soon brought home to me.

One of the lions in the park had developed a limp and seemed to be in pain. I discovered that he was a cryptorchid, or animal with one retained testicle. For the purposes of a film on animal care, it was proposed to operate outside in the lions' enclosure, rather as if we were in Africa. The weather was fine and summery, and we would find it no harder working in the open air than inside the lion house.

To whet public interest, it was arranged that the patient should be captured in a spectacular 'African' manner instead of being simply neutralized with a good dose of tranquillizer from a dart gun. For safety's sake and to avoid overexciting him, however, we decided to give him a small shot of tranquillizer before the camera started rolling – just enough to quieten him but not enough to put him to sleep and spoil our little act.

On the appointed day, three striped Land-Rovers entered the reserve. One of them isolated our patient while the others stood by to repel the rest of the lions if curiosity got the better of them. I stationed myself at the window of the first vehicle, dart gun in hand, accompanied by three wardens armed with poles cut from branches to make them look cruder and more authentic. Attached to the end of these poles were nooses.

The patient trotted along in front of our Land-Rover, limping but unafraid. We shepherded him gradually towards the fence. At last, when he was only a few yards off, I fired and hit him in the thigh, as planned. We pulled up and waited for the drug to act.

The lion did not seem to have noticed the impact at all. He halted too, and sat down without trying to put any more distance between us. Like all his kind, he had a leonine dislike of needless exertion. We waited another ten minutes. The lion continued to sit there, yawning and showing no interest in us. He was just the way I wanted him.

We all got out and walked over. The men levelled their poles, which did not appear to upset the lion unduly. He raised one paw as if to defend himself, but lazily and without conviction. He might almost have been holding it out and saying: 'If that's what you want, carry on.' A noose was slipped around the paw and pulled just tight enough to prevent it from escaping. We had no intention of hobbling the animal in view of his total compliance. The tranquillizer had done its work.

We repeated the process with the second paw. The lion offered just as little resistance. This time, the paw was held a few inches clear of the ground to enable me to administer an anaesthetic. Now it was my turn: 'All right, old boy, give me your paw.' I squeezed a little but there was no reaction. The lion half closed his eyes as if already lapsing into sleep. I could detect no muscular resistance. Leaning forwards, only eighteen inches from his jaws, I fastened an elastic tourniquet round the paw to make the vein protrude as an aid to injection. Though on my guard as usual, I had little to fear. Thanks to the tranquillizer, the big fellow seemed more in the mood to lick my hands than sink his teeth in them. It was a real pleasure working under these conditions.

A few seconds later the lion submitted to his intravenous injection without the slightest fuss. Another few seconds and he slumped on his side, this time fast asleep. Our contest between man and beast had been a walkover. Whatever the film might have lost in the way of excitement, the lion had benefited because his 'capture' had not subjected him to any pre-operative stress.

When it was all over I gathered up my equipment and retrieved the dart from the animal's thigh. Examining the projectile syringe before cleaning and replacing it in my case, I felt my heart stand still. This time I *was* afraid – after the event! I discovered that the mechanism designed to inject the tranquillizer fluid into the animal's body had failed. The barrel of the syringe still contained the entire dose. All the time I was working under the lion's nose, not a drop of tranquillizer had penetrated his system.

Why hadn't he got rid of me by crushing my skull between his jaws or flattening me with his paw? Why, a few minutes earlier, hadn't he sprung at the men who dared to corner him against the fence and torment him with their poles? We had already been importunate enough to pursue him in our Land-Rover and fire a dart into his flank. Just when he might have hoped to resume the slumbers that had been so rudely interrupted, his troubles had started again. He would have been

199

quite entitled to turn and rend the intruders who presumed to mill around so close to him within his legitimate and guaranteed domain, yet he suffered our attentions as if genuinely tranquillized. All of us – and I in particular – had been outrageously lucky.

I looked for explanations. He was not accustomed to us as a lion is to the trainer who makes him repeat and accept the same procedures over and over again, but he must have been a former circus animal inured and resigned to the peculiarities of man. His skin must have been so tough that neither the dart in his thigh nor the needle in his vein was sufficient to cause him real annoyance – after all, what was an injection compared to the teeth of another lion? He might also have been weakened by his undescended testicle and unaggressive in consequence. He may even have sensed that we meant him well, like several other animals whose instinctive benevolence I had experienced in the past. Or was he just exceptionally placid and lazy by nature? Had he been in such an uncommonly good mood, despite his troubles, that he could not be bothered to resist my manipulations? Whatever the truth, I must have chosen a time when he wasn't hungry and had no problems with a female or rival male; otherwise I shouldn't have survived to tell the tale.

The possibilities were legion. I even speculated whether he might have wanted to indulge us by playing his part in our little wildlife drama. I am not alone in having noticed that lions sometimes develop a theatrical sense of occasion and agree to play man's game. For whatever reason, he had spared my life; that was the main thing. For the rest, perhaps it was better to admit my ignorance and accept the mystery as it stood.

It took another incident to give me a full grasp of the lion's potentialities and prove conclusively that it was wiser to keep one's distance.

The wardens in charge of the lion enclosure at Thoiry had been concerned to note that visitors were behaving rashly and seemed unaware of the dangers that threatened them if they failed to observe the safety regulations. These rules prescribed that they should only tour the park in cars and that all windows must be fully raised. The wardens had noticed that many people drove through with their windows down. Some of them even went so far as to get out with children in

Removing a small wart on the tiger's eyelid *(J.J. Morer)*

Female leopard and her three cubs about to travel to a zoo in a glass cage *(Nice-Matin)*

Inspecting the teeth of an alligator *(author's photo)*

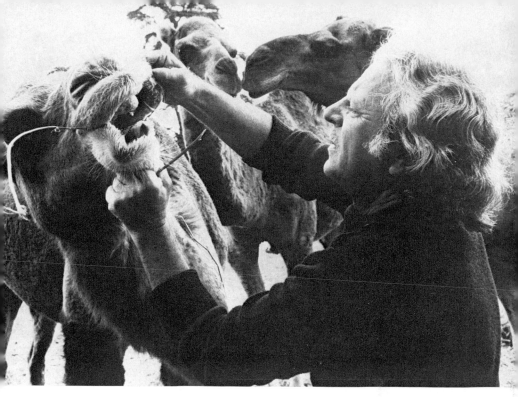

Judging the age of a dromedary *(Gamma)*

A medical examination of Kiki in the pool of the Moulin Rouge *(W. Piquemal, Paris-Match)*

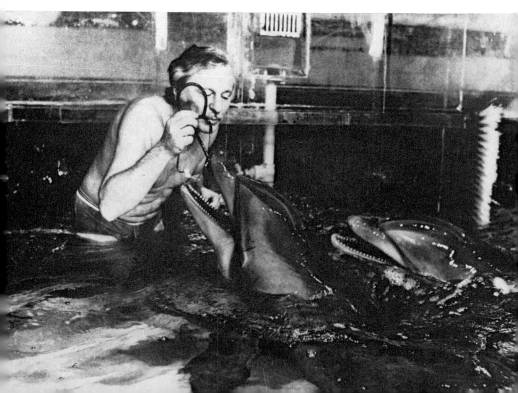

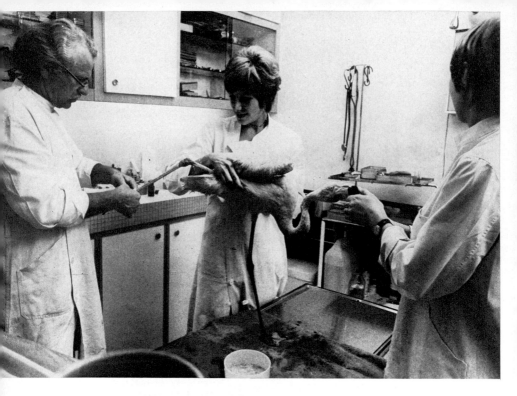

Treating a flamingo – or a dog, all in a day's work *(J.J Morer)*

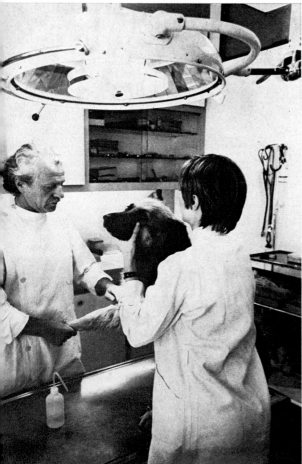

their arms and pose for photographs with their backs to the animals. The lions made a wholly innocuous impression. Most of the time they slept, quite indifferent to what was happening round them. Visitors sometimes complained about this and asked if we kept them doped. Needless to say, we didn't. The lion is a lazy creature. As long as he has eaten well and is not within range of a rival or a female in season, he sleeps.

But he sleeps with one eye open, and that is what we planned to impress on the unwary by filming a small experiment. Somebody would take the wheel of an ordinary car with a dummy beside him on the passenger's seat. A piece of meat would be attached to the dummy and the window on the passenger's side would be wound down. The whole idea was to film the lion's reaction – if any.

The chief warden was radically opposed to such a scheme. He wanted us to expose the dummy and the piece of meat outside the car on the end of a pole, with the window closed to its fullest possible extent. I felt that it would be far less impressive to stage the experiment under those conditions and decided to execute the original plan on my own. My main fear was that nothing would happen at all.

I duly drove into the lion enclosure at the wheel of a normal saloon car. The back seat was occupied by a television cameraman and his assistant. The dummy lounged beside me with the window down. Lions were dozing here and there in the usual way. Quite suddenly, the car was struck by a thunderbolt. I had no time to see it coming, no time to duck or cower away. A sort of maned projectile materialized in the window space beside the dummy. With incredible speed and precision, a huge paw lunged into the car's interior. I just glimpsed a flash of claws at my elbow, and it was all over. The dummy and its bait were gone. The lion dragged it through the dust, biting and rending it in a strangely agitated way. He even seemed more interested in the dummy than the piece of meat. Roused by the commotion, other lions ambled lazily over to watch.

We now had documentary evidence of the power, speed and precision displayed by a charging lion. That placid old creature which we had been accused of doping – which scarcely seemed to have the strength to drag itself a few yards between naps – was really an awesome mass of muscle capable of discharging strength in a way that defied the imagination. My own reactions are fairly quick, but even if I had seen the lion take off I should never have had time, before it reached the car, to lean over, grab the handle and wind the window up. The animal would still have had ample time to drag the passenger from his seat.

But this experiment did more than illustrate the danger that threatened a driver and his passengers if they neglected to wind up their windows. It also brought home my own imprudence because, on this occasion too, I wondered if the lion had not to some extent played along, as his fellow lion may have done during our little piece of African make-believe. The lions in the reserve were well aware that the duty Land-Rovers represented instruments of man's power. They knew that those who drove them were not just animated lumps of meat, not prey animals, but human purveyors of food. Something tells me that the one who snatched the dummy knew he was dealing with a toy, not a man. Did he sense that we were offering him a simulacrum instead of an authentic prey? Did this lion, too, mean to gratify us and himself by play-acting? I wouldn't swear to it, of course, but the combination of these two behaviour patterns, observed under different but comparable circumstances, persuaded me that my theory might not be so far from the truth. In any case, game or not, the incident taught me a lesson: no more liberties with adult lions save on the exceptional occasions when certain forms of treatment required me to break the rules. In general, I resolved on an even stricter compliance with regulations.

In particular, I promised myself that I would never again do what I had done the day before the dummy incident. Some reporters had come to interview me inside the lion enclosure. For the sake of a good picture, the cameraman asked me to answer a few questions standing beside the Land-Rover with some lions twenty or thirty yards away in the background. I agreed without a second thought. The absence of any reaction on the lions' part did not make this any less of a mistake on mine.

The same incident called to mind a remark once made to me by the wife of a friend. She and her husband had asked to accompany me on one of my routine visits, so I took them and their seven-year-old daughter on a guided tour of the enclosure in a Land-Rover. The mother and child were left alone for a few minutes while I went to deal with a problem inside the lions house, escorted by the father. Becoming bored, the young woman and her daughter had got out of the car. Because they were close to the double gates, and the nearest lions, though visible, were a hundred yards away, there seemed to be no danger.

For all that, my friend's wife later confided that she had been scared stiff. One lioness, apparently dozing on a bare mound of earth, suddenly rose to her feet. She stared, fixedly and intently, in the direction of the human figures. 'I'm sure she was looking at us,' the woman said. 'She seemed to be wondering: shall I or shan't I? It was like a nightmare. I couldn't move. Half of me refused to believe there was any danger – we were with you, after all – but the other half felt there was something wrong. I looked around for the gate, wondering if we ought to make a dash for it and completely forgetting about the car, which was the obvious place. The lioness took two or three steps in our direction. Just at that moment you reappeared and shouted to us to get back in the car.'

Instead of paying much attention to this story at the time, I put the woman's alarm down to imagination. What I mainly recalled was that she had got out of the Land-Rover. I considered this a bad example to others but not particularly dangerous. Still later, she confessed that she was often haunted by the memory of the lioness staring intently at the child and herself. I now suspect that she may have appreciated the true situation better than I did.

Today, having witnessed that lightning assault on the dummy, I am inclined to believe that the lioness surveying the woman and child from the top of her mound was about to charge. If so, neither of them would have had time to get back in the car and slam the door. The animal would have covered three quarters of the distance before they even realized what was happening. Like the dummy's attacker, the lioness had obviously asked herself some questions. Outside the Land-Rover, which to her represented a formidable but familiar human sanctuary, two strange figures had appeared within charging range.

What were they? A choice offering of fresh meat? The child

would have aroused her special interest. To a lioness, young children must resemble little monkeys, an easy and succulent prey for which lions in the wild have a particular liking. Under these circumstances, there can be no doubt of her desire to investigate the nature of what confronted her. It was a test which could only have been performed with tooth and claw . . .

12

My New Year's Eland

Little by little, these and many other experiences made me more conversant with the animals I had to tend, more familiar with their physical needs and quirks of behaviour. The wildlife park at Thoiry proved to be the field of operations I had always dreamed of.

Although I was still enthralled by my professional dealings with domesticated creatures such as dogs, cats and birds, I had begun to feel constricted in my clinic. Circumstances had steered me towards veterinary medicine and Paris, but I still missed the country and its animals. These were what I rediscovered by becoming Thoiry's veterinary consultant. From the geographical aspect, my life fell almost by accident into a pattern that enabled me to meet my commitments in full. By setting up house at Garches, on the outskirts of Paris, I installed myself at a point equidistant from my surgery in the capital, the wildlife park at Thoiry, where I called regularly, and Jean Richard's zoo at Ermenonville, which had long employed my services. I thus seemed to have struck a successful balance between town and country, wild animals and domesticated. In short, life was good and I had received my share of its blessings.

I would have paid to work at Thoiry. It was a joy to me to wade around in mud and handle animals as large as cattle and horses or even larger. I also continued, in this rural setting, to explore a world which, though already familiar to me from the circus, assumed new dimensions amid those many acres of woodland and pasture: the world of wild animals. I bore responsibility for the health of a vast population of wild animals ranging from the kudu to the elephant. My duty towards them was, above all else, a pleasure of the first order. Tending such a multitude of animals presented me with a steady stream of problems to solve.

The immense pleasure I derived from working with the animals in this wildlife park environment brought a growing awareness of my duty not only towards the individual patients I had to treat but also towards the species of which those individuals were members.

What did protecting a species entail? First and foremost, helping it to breed and survive – an exciting task which posed innumerable problems whose solutions had to be found gradually and empirically, not by consulting books.

A large proportion of the park's inmates lived together. The lions and tigers did not share the same enclosure, of course, because they would have killed each other, just as neither group of felines had access to the territory of the gnus and oryx because they would have preyed on them. But the gnus, oryx, dromedaries, kudus and elands all roamed the same vast enclosure, where they were sometimes joined by the rhinos. The cohabitation of all these different species sometimes caused trouble. That was how we eventually discovered that the zebras were harassing the gnus.

Large ruminants with something of the bull about their heads and horns, equine tails and manes and antelope-like bodies, the gnus had soon settled down in their man-made setting and established a rigidly hierarchical society of the sort found in their native environment. Gnus maintain a permanent alert and keep their females and young ringed with male sentries. Though far from frail – an adult male can weigh more than 600 pounds – they are nervous creatures whose main defence against their natural enemies consists in vigilance and flight.

Our gnus were about twenty in number. We found that they adapted to their new life extremely well, though they declined the shelters provided for them. They remained outside even in winter and did not appear to suffer from the snow and cold weather. Something was wrong nevertheless: the females gave birth but their offspring were found dead – apparently trampled to death.

By observing the course of events with binoculars, we at last identified the cause of this systematic slaughter. For some mysterious reason, our forty-odd zebras seemed to resent any new addition to their neighbours' herd. Even when a female gnu gave birth in a secluded spot near some bushes or trees, well screened by the rest of her kind, the zebras were immediately aware of the event. They approached by slow degrees, grazing with no sign of evil intent. When they came close enough, the gnus retreated. Although they made something of a commotion, they failed to stand their ground against their powerful and aggressive tormentors. The baby gnu, which would still be recumbent in the grass or just trying to stand, soon perished beneath the zebras' hooves.

What was the reason for this strange behaviour? Early on, when the gnus were already breeding fast, the zebras had yet to reproduce. I wondered if their aggression might be a form of jealousy, particularly as mares seemed to be in the forefront of these genocidal forays. What seemed to support my hypothesis was that when the zebras' female ringleader later had a foal she seemed to lose interest in newborn gnus. However, this may simply have been because we took vigorous steps to save the gnus' offspring as soon as we realized what was happening.

Our only solution was to capture the newborn calves and preserve them from the zebras' murderous hooves, but we also had to capture the mothers because their offspring would be rejected by the herd even if we managed to ensure their survival by intensive care. Simple as it seemed in theory, this operation proved awkward in practice.

It was midwinter and snowing. The birth was expected at any time, so we could not afford to miss it. The zebras would be there within half an hour. We stationed ourselves at a fair distance so as not to upset the gnu herd and the expectant mother. I was joined in my vigil by some wardens equipped with two-way radios to help coordinate our movements. I tried to observe the female's behaviour through binoculars. It wasn't easy. Judging by the way she always contrived to put a tree or bush between us, she might almost have been averse to the presence of witnesses. I worked my way round. I had to see how she was looking and breathing. After a few minutes she lay down, a sign that birth was imminent. Still through binoculars, I studied her contractions. Everything seemed to be going well. The calf's muzzle appeared. Then, from one moment to the next, the little creature was literally ejected into the snow. The female rose almost at once, ate the placenta and started to lick her young. We couldn't intervene yet. The mother must be given time to establish contact with her offspring. The process of cleaning and licking would trigger a number of vital functions and build up the emotional bond which any calf needs in order to survive and thrive. To break that bond before it had a chance to form would impel the mother to abandon her young. The calf was now making efforts to rise. The mother helped it with her muzzle. It subsided again, but not for long. There it was, up on its feet at last and looking for the teat. A few moments later it was trotting along beside its mother.

The zebras were already on their way. They drew closer, nosing out tufts of edible grass in the snow. At the risk of indulging in anthropomorphism, I would describe their manner as slyly hypocritical. It was time for us to step in – the most delicate part of the whole operation.

The female, who had already played hide-and-seek while I observed her through glasses at a distance, dodged me even more stubbornly when I tried to approach her with a dart gun. To score an effective hit without injuring her, I had to get within twenty yards. I made some artful manoeuvres, but every time I had her in my sights she made a movement which masked my target.

I communicated by walkie-talkie with the wardens who were helping me. Very quietly, without alarming the female, they guided her into a space sufficiently unobstructed for me to fire my shot of tranquillizer under good conditions, in other words, at a moment when the animal presented her flank to me. It was important to future relations between the calf and its mother that she should only receive a dose large enough to facilitate her capture. We could not go to the lengths of anaesthetizing her altogether, because that would have separated her, physically and psychically, from her offspring. The shot she received did not put her to sleep or enable us to lead her off quietly. Although the drug prevented her from fleeing at a full gallop, calmed her nerves and weakened her resistance, it took several of us to capture and immobilize her. That left the calf. It had already developed a fair turn of speed but did not stray far from its captive mother.

Meanwhile, we had steered the zebras away. All that remained was to put the mother and her calf in a special enclosure not far away, where they would be safe from the zebras but not completely divorced from the rest of the herd. Contact would be maintained through the wire mesh by sight, scent and even touch. This isolation would not be maintained for longer than the few days needed to banish the zebras' recollection of the incident.

Following these procedures, we saved an appreciable number of calves. Most of the males had to be sold because their excessive numbers led to fighting and serious injury. We kept only one dominant male plus a few young bulls in reserve. This dominant male was the victim of a typical accident, I might add. He had lost one horn, a fact which transformed him into a holy terror because his single horn proved more effective than any pair. We decided to cut it off. Both horns would grow again in due course and all would return to normal.

But his capture was a dramatic operation. Despite all our efforts to stalk him carefully, he displayed an extraordinary talent for flight and evasion. Nine projectile syringes of tranquillizer had no perceptible effect on him. In the end, mustering all his prodigious strength and vitality, he cleared a Land-Rover and the fence in one mighty bound and galloped off into the countryside. We took up the chase outside the enclosure. Thanks to our Land-Rovers and the action of the drug, which had started to work, we finally caught him and sawed off the lethal horn. But we had only just finished with our patient when he abruptly gave up the ghost. After a struggle which taxed his physical resources to the limit, his heart had failed. Even the strongest creatures can die of fright. This accident well illustrates the frailty of organisms capable of bracing themselves for an extreme physical or nervous effort. It also illustrates the extent to which the use of the dart gun and projectile syringe may seem simple – you fire and the animal goes to sleep – but is, in reality, complex.

What is a dart gun, anyway? A means of projecting a syringe tipped with a needle that buries itself in an animal's skin and muscle at long range, propelled by an explosive cartridge. The antecedents of the modern gun were a kind of crossbow, a pistol and an air rifle.

Once the syringe and needle have reached their destination, how does the fluid in the barrel of the syringe penetrate the animal's skin? The impact of the projectile detonates another cartridge at the base of the piston. A small quantity of gas expands, causing the rubber piston to expel the fluid through the needle.

All these mechanisms are highly refined and extremely

delicate. The needle, for example, is considerably larger than that of an ordinary syringe and its outlet is not always situated at the point. It must also remain embedded for a while in the patient's body, so it sometimes incorporates a little collar or barb which holds it there.

Given these and other characteristics, the vet has to take certain additional factors into consideration. The choice of cartridge will depend on range, which may vary from about 20 to 80 yards, and on thickness of skin. Syringes must not be fired from a vantage point too close to the patient or they may ricochet and hit the marksman in the face. They must also be fired at a perpendicular surface, otherwise they will fail to penetrate the skin, which is invariably tough, glance off and go astray. Finally, they cannot be fired at random. A projectile that pierces the chest may cause pulmonary complications and even death. If the marksman hits a bone he may break it; if he perforates the abdomen, peritonitis will result. Therefore, his aim must be good. But there are ballistic problems as well, because the trajectory of the projectile differs from that of a rifle bullet. Personally, I had to put in a lot of target practice in my garden before going to work in earnest. Apart from anything else, projectile syringes are extremely expensive and have to be retrieved after use. This poses no problem if the animal is unconscious. If not, you have to manage somehow by quietly removing it while the patient is semi-immobilized. Sometimes the syringe slips out of its own accord. If you spot where it falls, all to the good. If not, you search for a while and then give up.

Next comes the question of what drug to use – the most complex problem of all. There is a whole range of products available: immobilizers, tranquillizers, anaesthetics, analgesics. The choice of a drug and its dosage depends on a variety of factors including the animal's age, state of health and environment – whether it is confined in an enclosure or allowed to roam freely. Its species must also be taken into account. Products that act well on rhinos and elephants are much less effective with giraffes, and those that suit giraffes are unsuitable for elephants. In the case of red and fallow deer, nothing is very much use.

A thorough mastery of these techniques was essential to the work that lay ahead of me. Our failure with the one-horned gnu had given me some idea of the difficulties they posed.

On another occasion, by firing at the wrong range with the wrong cartridge, I managed not only to plant my needle in a gnu's neck but to embed the whole syringe as well. Fortunately, that accident had no dire consequences.

Not the least of my difficulties has been to procure drugs of good quality, most of which are unobtainable in France. My connections on the other side of the Atlantic have often proved a help in this respect. It was thanks to some overseas colleagues, for example, that I was able to operate on elephants with the aid of the remarkable anaesthetic mentioned earlier, one milligram of which is sufficient to immobilize half a ton of living flesh.

Immobilization with the dart gun could not be my habitual means of approaching, restraining and treating animals that lived in semi-freedom. It was too expensive and time-consuming. In order to tend an animal population numbering several hundred head, I had to employ other methods. I could not use my dart gun every time I wanted to help an animal in labour. There was no question of stalking an expectant mother, putting her to sleep and taking her home for treatment. Anaesthesia could not be used except in the last resort. It always presented certain risks, quite apart from keeping the patient isolated from the herd for a certain time and exposing her to the risk of rejection phenomena. Finally, there was the safety factor. Gnu, antelope and oryx are not as dangerous as lions and tigers, but their strength is herculean compared to that of the feeble human frame. A single butt from any of them can break a limb or stave your chest in, as I learned by bitter experience when dealing with a mild tempered eland. Once again, luck rather than judgement should be credited with the fact that I was not crippled for life.

Belle was an amiable creature, but hardly an innocuous sheep, with her 1500 pounds of muscle and fine pair of horns. She had arrived at Thoiry with an old fracture of the pelvis which must have healed spontaneously. Although it caused her no pain, she had a depression between the haunches. She adapted well to her new environment and was soon in calf.

One afternoon I received a telephone call. Not for the first time in my career, it was New Year's Day. Would I please come at once? Belle was pushing but the calf seemed to be getting nowhere. We had a houseful of guests and the mood was festive, but I can't say I groaned at this urgent summons. On the contrary, I felt a familiar thrill of pleasure at the prospect of dashing off to Thoiry for a paddle in mud and dung. I was happy, once again, to put the animals first. The more they claimed my presence, the happier I felt. Having so many of them under my wing was a joy to me. One of our visitors had just presented me with a magnificent red cashmere sweater. It looked so handsome that I had put it on at once. Without stopping to change, I went off to celebrate the New Year by helping to deliver an animal wearing something appropriate to that festive and friendly day.

The situation at Thoiry did not seem too bad. The calf's forelegs were already visible. This indicated a normal presentation, so I prepared to deliver it in the ordinary way, as with a cow. The eland is almost a domesticated animal in any case. There are farms in South Africa where herds are bred and reared like cattle. They are docile and approachable and can even be fed by hand. No need for me to race back home for my dart gun and stage a safari in order to capture the patient. Belle was standing in her stall, as good as gold. Although her old pelvic fracture might possibly affect the birth, my mellow mood inclined me to think that all would be well.

I didn't even bother to remove my nice red sweater. Simply rolling up the right sleeve, I pulled on a shoulder-length delivery glove and prepared to conduct an exploration. The fracture was a nuisance all the same. If the pelvis was too constricted I might have to perform a Caesarean.

Before starting work I took the precaution of having Belle tethered by the head. A stout halter was wound crosswise around the base of her horns and secured to a post. This kept her head still and facing the wall. I was at Belle's hind end, far from her redoubtable 30-inch sabres. She could still kick, of course, but I was on my guard as usual. Every animal lashes out in its own way: the horse straight backwards, the zebra straight and crisply, the cow and the camel sideways. The eland kicks like a cow, but this danger can be averted by standing in a certain position. Besides, any intention of kicking is prefaced by signs which, if heeded, give you time to get out of the way.

I had just begun my examination when, quite suddenly, all hell broke loose. Hardly had I slipped my hand into the vagina past the calf's legs when its gentle mother snapped the halter with a single jerk of her head. Almost simultaneously, she rounded on me. One of her long pointed horns caught me on the right side of the chest and sent me flying ten or twelve feet through the air. I hit the top of the pen, which was well above head-height, and flopped back into the straw.

Dazed, I felt myself all over. No bones broken, no sign of blood. I took a closer look, trying to grasp what had happened. At last I discovered that my nice new cashmere sweater had acquired a large rent, but there wasn't even a scratch on the skin beneath. The horn, that sensitive instrument, had not been intended to deal a lethal blow. Its purpose was to eliminate the source of Belle's discomfort. As soon as it felt the sweater, it pierced it. If there had been no sweater it would have travelled a millimetre or two further. If I had stripped to the waist, as I often did when delivering a calf, the horn would have perforated my skin instead. Failing to encounter the tough resistence offered by a brand-new cashmere sweater, it would then have pierced my ribs.

So I had got off with a fright – no, not even that. The experience left me unmoved, probably because I had more to do at the time than contemplate my navel. The calf had to be delivered, sweater or no sweater. Having achieved her object, which was to get rid of me because I was hurting her, Belle made no move to follow up her attack. I decided to tether her more securely and go back to work.

This time my assistants used a heavier rope and took two turns around the post and horns. They also hobbled the eland's hindlegs. I resumed my examination. A moment later there was another loud crack. With consummate ease, Belle had snapped the second halter despite its greater strength and firmer attachment. Once again she spun round and lunged at me with her horns. This time I was more on my guard. I dodged, but she was too quick for me. She caught me behind the knees and flung me against the wall, not in a rising curve but parallel to the ground for a change.

I didn't beat a retreat even then. The baby eland's forelegs were still protruding. Although its mother was being difficult, she needed my services. Not for me to lodge a complaint with my union or claim compensation from an industrial injuries tribunal. I returned to the front – or rather, Belle's backside – telling myself to be even more careful. She wasn't going to get me a third time.

Strong as Belle was, we loaded her down with enough ropes

to ensure that she could not break loose again without demolishing the entire stall, which exceeded her powers and intentions. I also gave her a tranquillizing injection, and this time she let me work in peace. I was limping a little and had lost my sweater, but I felt as good as new. More than that, my hand had retained its touch and was discovering numerous points of interest.

The passage was narrow, and I could feel that the calf was suffering. Probing further, I realized that there was a second calf. Poor Belle's narrow pelvis had placed her in a very awkward predicament. I got the first calf out as fast as I could, but it had been subjected to too much stress and died at once, so I went in search of the second. Belle cooperated as best she could, and out it came. It was alive, but for how long? We held it up by the hindlegs to help it expel the mucus from its respiratory passages and clear the lungs. We chafed it and put some salt on its tongue. It stirred and began to wag its tail. We presented it to Belle, who turned her head and started licking it. It was going to live.

Even so, my New Year's goring gave me food for thought. In the interests of the patient's welfare and my own safety, the ideal thing would be to transfer every animal requiring my services to a place where it could be conveniently kept in conditions that enabled me to work without any danger of being bitten, trampled or gored. It should also be separated as little as possible from the herd during my ministrations to lessen the risk of its being rejected on release.

The answer was a pen and crush, an old stockbreeders' contrivance which had to be modified for our purposes because an antelope could not be manhandled like a ewe. My talent for tinkering and improvisation was exercised once more.

The pen was a sort of large funnel which opened on to the park where the animals lived. Two barriers could be used to cut off the narrowest section, which provided room for only one animal, and the other end of the narrow passage also gave on to the park. If the patient were to be persuaded to enter it at all, the crush had to have an exit as well as an entrance.

The crush itself was like a lock which could be shut at both ends when the animal was safely within. It had only one fixed side. The other three were mobile and allowed the patient to be placed under sufficient restraint to immobilize it. Each of these partitions consisted of heavy planks which could be inserted or removed separately by sliding them into channel irons and secured with eyebolts. We could thus make apertures anywhere we chose – in front, behind and at the side – and gain access to any part of the animal's body at the required height while remaining comparatively well shielded from its teeth and hooves. Total protection was an impossibility because we had to deal with very powerful creatures capable of superhuman spurts of energy, so it paid to be vigilant.

Thanks to this contraption, the animal retained some degree of contact with the other members of the herd. The latter, who were chary of the whole arrangement, would approach the crush and call to its occupant; indeed, one bull evinced signs of agitation which suggested that he had half a mind to free his captive mate. It was a form of isolation, granted, but it was the best we could do.

In the wild, animals live and die in accordance with the constraints of natural selection. Although we did not leave our charges to fend for themselves and provided them with an artificial environment, we still had to conform as far as possible to natural conditions. Our own version of the crush did its best to meet this requirement. It was more satisfactory in this respect than a constant recourse to immobilization by anaesthesia. Experience showed that it was quite well received by the animals and did not give rise to any rejection phenomena.

It was in this crush that Belle subsequently gave birth to another calf despite her infirmity and without putting my life in danger. I administered an epidural anaesthetic and then, through an aperture in the side of the crush, performed a Caesarean. Raoul de la Panouse stood beside me holding a cloth-covered plank. I extracted the calf through the aperture and laid it on the plank. Highly delighted by this birth, we watched it kicking for a moment. All of a sudden the umbilical cord ruptured flush with the navel. Bleeding started, but some prompt work with a clip and a needle soon restored the situation. Another young eland was going to survive.

We used the pen area as often as possible to assist delivery and birth among grazing animals. Many animals were introduced to it only after lengthy preliminaries. They had first to be habituated to these premises and convinced that they could feed and shelter there in winter. Here again, easy access had to be provided between the park, the yard surrounding their quarters, and the interior. Habituation was effected by distributing food closer and closer to the building until it was finally deposited inside. We also installed a system of zigzag passages built of straw bales, both in the yard and inside the building itself, to enable the animals to withdraw and isolate themselves in accordance with their needs and relationships. Only the gnus with their wild and mistrustful nature, stubbornly rejected our blandishments, preferring the harshest, snowiest climatic conditions to the home comforts at their disposal.

13

A Bison for Whitsun

At Thoiry there was thus no end to the host of problems requiring solution or the myriad details that merited careful observation. The relations between the species which living conditions inside the park had artificially brought together were an occasional source of surprise. This applied particularly to the bull oryx and the female dromedary. Although the former cohabited with his mate and relations between them were entirely normal, he also cherished a passion for the she-dromedary. He not only ran after her but often tried, by craning his neck, to sniff a place that might have been thought uniquely of interest to male dromedaries. It was comical to watch the pale-grey oryx haunting the female dromedary's backside – possibly because its scent stirred memories of his native continent. Although the object of his attentions did not seem to mind these goings-on, which we observed with amused interest, they aroused fierce resentment in her mate, who occasionally charged his strange rival. The oryx, who hardly came up to his belly, was wise enough to turn tail.

One day, however, we found the male dromedary with a perforated abdomen. Investigation proved that the wound had been inflicted by the oryx. Nobody witnessed the incident, but it seemed likely that the dromedary had once more taken the field against his mate's eccentric little admirer. Steadfast preoccupation with areas to which he had no real access except by sense of smell may finally have convinced the bull oryx that he enjoyed legitimate rights over the female dromedary and that it was his duty to defend her against a male intruder. He had used his horns, which, being just the right height, had not unnaturally pierced the underside of the dromedary's flank.

Although this drama would not have happened in the wild,

instances of drama are never lacking even under the most ideal conditions. Another accident – this time one that might easily have occurred in the natural state – proved to me how helpless we sometimes were in the face of circumstances which no amount of experience and good intentions could control.

A zebra had fractured a leg. In Africa, his end would have been quick: a lion or some other predator would have finished him off within minutes. Here in the park he was under the protection of human beings who felt bound to go one better than nature.

To be precise, the animal had sustained a fracture in the cannon bone between the hock and fetlock. As soon as the wardens spotted this, they tried to coax him into the zebra house for treatment. This was easier said than done. With very few exceptions, zebras are totally intractable and extremely aggressive. They have something of the donkey's obstinacy. They bite on sight and kick at the drop of a hat – very hard and very much harder than a horse. There is no question of opening their mouths to examine their teeth, as with horses, or of lifting their feet to shoe them. They refuse to tolerate the lightest harness and are extremely difficult to mount.

Paradoxically, they are also sociable and inquisitive creatures. They will approach your car in a wildlife park, crane inside for food if you leave the window open and readily take sugar, carrots or bread from your hand. A few very rare individuals can even be models of gentleness. Our own herd included a young female named Zozo who was so accommodating that she would allow my son, Jean-François, to sit on her back when he was six or seven, and some of the others were bold and inquisitive enough to make an occasional tour of the public lavatories.

There is much mutual biting among zebras, particularly on the neck. It is a strange fact that these wounds, which are notoriously slow to heal in horses, form scar tissue with great ease. To treat such cases, the animal is cornered against a fence and doused with water and disinfectant. No direct contact is attempted.

These diverse characteristics and apparent conflicts of behaviour make the zebra a rather unpredictable and untrustworthy creature. It is, after all, a wild animal. Given these facts, I could well understand why the wardens had been hard put to it to coax the injured male into the building where it was hoped to treat him. He tried to elude them, mostly on three legs, but had aggravated his condition by sometimes putting weight on the fourth. He ended by limping on the bone itself, which had pierced the flesh and skin.

This was the pitiful condition in which I found him when I reached Thoiry in response to an emergency call. Would it have been possible to avoid getting him into such a state by on-the-spot treatment? Darkness was falling, which made his capture even more difficult. Besides, treatment of the sort I had to administer would scarcely have been practicable in the open.

What, in fact, could I do? Reducing the animal's fracture and immobilizing him effectively were major operations requiring equipment which I only kept at my clinic. I could not perform an immediate operation in the zebra's stall. I could either destroy him – as I was half inclined to do – or put a temporary plaster on his leg while waiting for a chance to operate.

With some reluctance, I decided on a plaster. The zebra was anaesthetized, the wound disinfected and dressed. I fashioned a really heavy plaster, bulky and tough enough to withstand teeth and hard knocks. Then I waited for the patient to come round.

The result was horrific. Once back on his feet, he behaved like a mad thing. Frantic with fear and regardless of the terrible pain it must have caused him, he proceeded to lash out and batter his plaster against the side of his stall. It was a maddening din, a devil's tattoo. The unfortunate creature's life force seemed to have transmuted itself into a mania for self-destruction. He had no wish to be treated, no wish to recover, no wish to live. The impression he created was genuinely suicidal, though his frenzied struggles may only have been an attempt to escape intolerable pain.

Whatever the truth, he soon achieved his object. Thick as the plaster was, he soon kicked it to shreds. I was horrified to see the remains of his foot fly off with a fragment of plaster attached. We had failed. There was nothing we could do but put a bullet in his head, regretting the agony our well-meant efforts had caused him, and ponder on the implications of the tragedy.

Why had it been necessary to destroy him when his injury was not apparently fatal, just as one still destroys a horse with a broken leg? Why did a lion take quite readily to having a fractured limb in plaster when this zebra had refused to tolerate it? Perhaps because a feline's constitution and the suppleness of its muscles and joints enable it to dispense with the use of one leg if the worst comes to the worst. In the wild, a lion with a broken leg is just as surely doomed as a zebra. It is finished off by its own kind and devoured by scavengers. Very few free-ranging lions survive the loss of a limb.

Equine quadrupeds, however, have an even greater need for all four legs. They spend far more of their time standing than felines. They stand up to eat, an activity to which they devote themselves for at least twelve hours out of every twenty-four. They sleep standing up, at least for part of the time. Their bodies are very heavy in relation to their limbs, so the loss of one leg has a profound effect on their balance. Finally, their entire physical mechanism is centred on their four limbs. This may help to explain why any impairment of one of these is considered fatal, and more so than in the case of a lion or tiger. It is also probable that the innervation of their limbs is such that any injury to these parts of the body is particularly painful – once again, more so than in a feline.

It nonetheless appears that certain animals whose legs are as important to them as a zebra's sometimes try to heal a broken limb. Red deer in this condition have been seen to embed themselves in mud and spend days without moving. By drying in contact with their bodies, the mud immobilizes the limb like a conventional plaster.

I was luckier with another zebra which had something seriously wrong with one foot. It was not fractured, but there was an abscess on the coronet at the top of the hoof, above the heel. The hoof was partly detached and the foot had begun to suppurate.

We transferred our patient to the horse clinic at Grosbois, near Paris, where I was to operate. First came the usual difficult routine: immobilization and anaesthesia. At last I could set to work on the foot. I began by trimming the hoof. Cut as I would, I failed to reach healthy tissue. By the time I finished I had removed four-fifths of the sole. This exposed the quick. All that remained of the hoof was part of the inner wall connected to the heel by a sort of bridge – a suspension bridge, in a sense, because it was detached.

How was my zebra going to stand on this leg without laying

the pedal bone bare? I had to make him a shoe at once, but how and with what? Then an idea occurred to me. I asked the nurse to go and buy me a tin of peas. I emptied out the contents and started tinkering with the can. I cut a sole, fashioned an upper with folds and flaps, flattened the sides and stuck the flaps together with adhesive. The shoe took shape.

Meanwhile, I had sent my assistant to the nearest chemist to fetch a powder compounded of tannin, charcoal and picric acid, a traditional remedy for grease in horses. Having packed the bottom of my tin shoe with this mixture. I fitted it over the foot of my still unconscious zebra. A few adjustments, some more adhesive, and he was shod at last.

I was slightly apprehensive of what he would do when he came round. Would he make every attempt to get rid of the contraption as the other zebra had done with his plaster? No, he accepted it quite gracefully and proceeded to walk around on his tin of peas with barely a limp. I boarded him out at the Grosbois clinic. Three months later he had grown a brand new hoof. The foot healed and required no further treatment.

In the case of our first zebra, nature had demonstrated the limits of human ingenuity. Fortunately for our self-esteem, we are not invariably doomed to failure.

Some other zebras which turned up at the park one day did not have broken limbs but were little better off. Their owners, a wealthy couple who lived in Brittany, had fancied the idea of keeping the animals on their estate. They probably thought it a picturesque way of embellishing the landscape and impressing their friends and neighbours. However, zebras are not statues capable of resisting the elements for centuries. They are living creatures which can only survive in a controlled environment, as their owners discovered with some dismay after a few days of bitter winter weather. There had originally been a dozen zebras. Six of them had died within the space of two hours.

A despairing plea by phone: the others seemed to be in a bad way; what did we suggest? We tried to explain how to treat and nurse them, but the people at the other end either couldn't or wouldn't understand. 'All right,' I said, 'crate them up, put the crates in a truck and send them here right away.' The job was tackled by some professionals. We were warned to expect the zebras by nightfall.

Into action. It was January, and exceptionally cold for the time of year – several degrees below zero. The patients would probably be in poor shape, so our first task was to find them suitable accommodation. All the buildings were occupied and we could not risk exposing the other animals to possible infection. Not far from the park, however, we discovered a disused barn which might lend itself to our purpose. Although the building was secure enough, there were chinks all over the place and the interior felt just as cold as the outside world. Our only course was to improvise something less draughty inside this outer shell. We sent for a truckload of straw bales. Using these and an assortment of planks, we built a shelter large and weatherproof enough to house the new arrivals. This was to be our field hospital.

We waited for the truck at the main entrance to save time, stamping our feet in a vain attempt to keep warm. It finally turned up at 10 p.m. We led the way to the barn, where the crates were unloaded and deposited side by side in the shelter of the straw bales. One of the occupants was already dead and I would not have bet much on the chances of the remainder. A cursory examination by flashlight – the barn had no electricity – revealed that they were in a highly feverish condition. They were also coughing. Everything suggested that they had infectious pneumonia and were going downhill fast. We offered them water but they refused it, nor would they accept food.

There was no time to lose if we wanted to try to save them. I had to give them a drip with the 'cocktail' of corticosteroids, arsenicals and antibiotics I had prepared in advance. This was easier said than done. The crated zebras were not only ill but doubly aggressive in consequence. How was I going to give them an intravenous injection in the jugular? I already knew what a reluctant patient of their species was capable of.

It was no use searching the veterinary manual for a chapter entitled 'How to treat dying zebras in arctic conditions by flashlight'; there wasn't one, so I had to cudgel my brains and make the best of it.

The first thing was to get at the animals' necks. I had holes sawn in the sides of the crates. Even this minor exercise proved awkward. Ill though they were, the zebras kicked and fidgeted to such an extent that the saw came within an inch of doing them an injury.

I tackled the quietest zebra first. The problem was to locate the jugular by hand, exert pressure to make it protrude, plant the needle and attach the syringe – simple movements, but the zebra refused to tolerate them. As soon as I put my left hand through the hole in the crate, he turned and bared his teeth. Who would be the first to give in: I, in my attempt to treat him, or he, in his stubborn resistance?

I tried to inject him unawares with a drug which could be administered intramuscularly. The zebra jibbed violently, bucking and kicking inside his crate. The planks were not as strong as they might have been; what would we do if he kicked them apart? Besides, he might easily break a leg, and that would be the end.

Surprise hadn't worked, so I decided to try persuasion. We sealed off the crates by separating them with more bales of straw. Leaving the first zebra to calm down, I tried my luck with the next. I called for absolute silence and forbade movement of any kind. The beams from the flashlights steadied, concentrating on the shoulder-height aperture in the side of the crate. Then I turned myself into an animal charmer. I spoke to the zebra like an old friend, melodiously coaxing and cajoling him. He still turned his head towards me and bared his teeth whenever my hand approached his neck, but I could tell that he was only halfhearted. His threat to bite was largely show.

I went a stage further. My fingertips brushed the zebra's neck. His head returned. I withdrew my hand. Gingerly, I replaced it. Before long I was able to rest my palm on his neck. Like horses, zebras have lateral vision. To allay my patient's nervousness, I took a small board in my left hand and screened my right, which was still resting on his neck. He made fewer and fewer attempts to turn his head. I started to stroke him, still murmuring kind words. I was soon able to remove the board and continue my stroking without the head turning to investigate.

Had the moment come? Still stroking, I took the prepared syringe in my free hand and moved it slowly towards the neck. But the zebra, having consented to the touch of one hand, balked at the approach of another. He got upset again and tried to bite me. I surrendered. Removing my left hand, I detached the needle from the syringe and secreted it in my right before resuming my caresses. The zebra tolerated them.

223

Very gently, I moved along the neck by stages towards the jugular furrow where the big vein lay. At last I thought I felt it. Gripping the needle between my index and middle fingers, I felt around with my thumb. Still no reaction from the patient. I compressed the vein with my thumb and inserted the needle.

There it was. Blood seeped out all over my fingers: I had hit the right spot. The animal did not seem to have noticed anything. I rinsed my hand and then, still as gingerly, fitted the syringe on the needle. Masking it as best I could, I injected the antibiotic.

I moved on to the next zebra to allow the last one to recover his composure before returning to him and his predecessor. Having learnt from experience, I tried to improve my technique. The third patient was as aggressive as the first, with bloodshot eyes and a tendency to squander his dwindling reserves of energy on convulsive efforts to escape. To keep his head away and enable me to tackle him with greater ease and speed, I tried giving him something to bite on. My preliminary attempt to placate him with a lump of sugar was a failure. Better results were obtained with a stick on which he could vent his wrath. While I stroked him, an assistant inserted this through the cracks in the side of the crate every time he turned his head towards me. He attacked the stick and gnawed at it, but his aggression soon waned and the use of the stick became less and less necessary.

Thanks to our new technique I was able to go to work with both hands almost at once, thus gaining time and accuracy. For this patient's benefit I rigged up a little arrangement with a plastic tube attached to a 50 ml syringe held ready outside the crate. This was an improvement on the 10 ml which were all I had managed to inject in the first instance.

The next zebra benefited from further technical refinements. I had so far encountered some difficulty in locating the jugular, which is finer in the zebra than in the horse and lies at a greater depth. In addition, my patient was a sensitive creature. Even when he had quietened and was accepting the touch of my hand, he lowered his head as soon as it neared the jugular furrow and tried to prevent me from touching it. All my cautious attempts to push his head away provoked fresh irritation and a renewed baring of teeth.

I asked a stablehand to climb on top of the crate with a

noose and dangle it under the zebra's nose. The animal promptly opened his mouth to bite it. This enabled the noose to be tightened around the upper jaw and meant that the head could be raised while I was looking for the jugular. It did not solve all my difficulties because the zebra, furious at being trapped, struggled violently and made the crate shudder like a house in an earthquake.

It wasn't until the fourth zebra that our improvised technique received its finishing touches. This time I coupled my plastic tube not only to a syringe but to a drip bottle suspended outside the crate which enabled me to treat the patient with all the drugs prepared in advance.

I had to repeat the process with all five zebras three times in succession. The five men who assisted me were just as unsparing in their efforts. Our work became better and better coordinated. We no longer bumped into each other when changing places. The beams of the flashlights were always levelled at precisely the right spot. Two a.m. came and went, then 3 a.m. It didn't matter much. We had forgotten about the cold. Between the second and third laps we stopped for a little snack of bread, sausage and wine, perched on bales of straw. We might have been more comfortable tucked up in our beds, but it was a joy to work and be alive even at that unearthly hour.

After the second round of injections, three of the zebras seemed to be improving but the other two still looked very ill indeed. I stepped up their intake on the third lap. Another two hours went by and the zebras started to accept food. By the time we had finished – for the moment – a January day was belatedly dawning. The five survivors had all come through the night. It was a journey back from the brink of death.

I resumed the zebras' treatment after a few hours' sleep. All the patients survived. While not erasing my memory of the death of the zebra with the broken leg, this success rendered it less painful.

Another unfortunate experience offset by an almost simultaneous success caused me to make a renewed assessment of all the problems posed by acclimatizing and rearing wild animals in an artificial environment. The park at Thoiry owned a pair of bison. The bull, an exceptionally large, powerful and magnificent beast, was our pride and joy. One day he began to suffer from what at first seemed to be a minor complaint: inflammation of the penis. Scrutinizing him more closely through the heavy tubular steel fence, I suspected that the trouble might be more serious. Observation was no easy matter. The European bison is an awkward customer and charges very readily, but I thought I detected a large tumescent abscess. It could not be left untreated.

Firing from behind the fence, I tranquillized the bison sufficiently to enable me to approach him. I opened the abscess, then bathed and disinfected it with a small hand-pump. The affected area was thereafter bathed daily with a jet of warm antiseptic solution. The bison allowed himself to be coaxed over to the palisade and treated in this manner. He apparently got used to these shower-baths, which doubtless imparted a sense of well-being.

But his condition failed to improve. One morning I made another attempt to examine him through the fence, dousing him with lukewarm water as usual. What happened next remains a mystery. Whether something had hurt him, whether he had had enough of our concentration upon an intimate part of his anatomy, he suddenly took off. Dumbfounded, we watched him back away and lower his head. Then, with an agility almost incredible in an animal built like a tank and weighing nearly three quarters of a ton, he soared over the two fences that enclosed his paddock. One of them, the tubular metal fence, was four feet six inches high; the other, a protective wire mesh barrier designed to keep visitors at a distance, was six feet high and five feet from the inner fence. It was a spectacular jump from the aspect of both height and length. Landing safely, the bison galloped off into the blue with us in hot pursuit on foot and by car.

We spent the whole day chasing him up hill and down dale. Getting close enough for a shot with the dart gun was fiendishly difficult. The bison outmanoeuvred us time and time again. He had the advantage of us because he could, for example, cut through woods while we were forced to skirt them by car. He could also outdistance any human pursuer on foot. I did manage to get in a shot from time to time, but not under ideal conditions and to little outward effect. The drugs available to me at this time were not very satisfactory, and a certain number of projectile syringes must have ricocheted or fallen out before absorption was complete. These difficulties illustrate that a dart gun is not the answer to every problem. The bison was still holding out when darkness fell. We kept after him, searching by the light of our headlamps.

Although he eventually started to show signs of fatigue, he did not collapse. Finally we sighted him lounging on the outskirts of a wood like a bull at rest in a field, not sprawled on his side like an exhausted animal. His various doses of tranquillizer had at last begun to act. Besides, he was naturally tired by the chase.

I walked over to him carrying my equipment. He looked passive and resigned. Still by the light of the headlamps, I started to examine the bison and prepared to revive him. Quite suddenly, his head dropped. He was dead. The cause, once again, must have been fear and excessive fatigue allied with the cumulative effect of the tranquillizers that had been injected into him by dart gun.

The only immobilizing drugs available to me at this time were nicotine-based. They caused many serious accidents, not only to animals but also to those who administered them, and have long been superseded.

It was heartbreaking to lose the animal, but we discovered during the autopsy next day that his illness had been a contributory factor. It was not a minor ailment after all. His tumour proved to be malignant and was already giving rise to secondary growths elsewhere. He would never have recovered, so his death in action – in the heat of battle, as it were – had only stolen a few weeks' march on the inevitable outcome of a fatal disease. Not for the first time, I speculated whether the bison's prodigious leap and desperate flight might have held some deeper significance – whether his last struggle had been less a revolt against the human beings who were imprisoning and tormenting him with their attentions than a final surge of life on the threshold of death.

As it turned out, the bison had already given new life before relinquishing it himself: his mate was in calf. Not unnaturally, this birth was eagerly awaited because it would go some way towards compensating for the loss of the sire. Everyone followed the expectant mother's progress with more than usual care and attention.

One Sunday, when she was almost at term, we were lunching at the restaurant installed in Thoiry's converted seventeenth-century stables. It was a fine Whit Sunday, and the park was already attracting plenty of visitors. I had just started on my crème caramel when the warden in charge came to tell me that calving had begun. The mother was having contractions but the calf did not seem to be moving.

We set off at once. A crowd had already gathered round the enclosure. The visitors must have sensed the importance, solemnity and beauty of the occasion. Their children craned to look, half curious, half comprehending. This time, life had to triumph over death.

The mother needed help urgently, but she was not a mare or a cow. As soon as we approached the outer fence she lowered her head and charged. The bull near by was more aggressive still, and circled her with all the proud irascibility of a legitimate sire. After the death of the big bison, he had assumed the protective and proprietory rights that had been denied him during his rival's lifetime.

The enclosure could be divided into two sections. A shot with the dart gun, this time fired under favourable conditions, enabled me to tranquillize the bull sufficiently to isolate him in his own half. I had meanwhile concocted a mixture of drugs more suitable for use on bisons than the 'cocktail' which had helped to kill his predecessor.

Another shot containing a weaker dose enabled me to tackle the mother without more ado. I stripped to the waist and pulled on shoulder-length gloves lubricated with antiseptic jelly. Exploring the mother's genital passages, I soon discovered that the baby bison was rather big for her – especially as this was her first pregnancy. To make matters worse, the head was slightly to one side and not properly engaged as a result. Last but not least, one of the forelegs was flexed.

Although I did not take long to manipulate the head and legs into the correct position, the mother still failed to give birth. And so, while she continued to push, I and my reinforcements pulled.

The baby bison advanced by slow degrees for seven or eight suspenseful minutes, its progress followed intently by the crowd. I got ready to break its fall and prevent the umbilical cord from snapping. Cheers greeted the new arrival when it finally tumbled into my waiting arms.

It was a moving and satisfying moment, but the battle was not yet won. The calf, which had suffered considerable stress, lay limp in my arms. If we failed to revive it, it would not be for want of trying. We held it up by its hindlegs to help clear the mucus, massaged its heart and rubbed it down with straw. Then I washed its face, rinsed out its mouth and throat with salt water and administered a whiff of smelling salts. It began to stir. More murmurs and cheers from the crowd.

We laid the youngster against its mother's flank. It was a red-letter day in every sense. Not content with giving us an eland for New Year, the fates had sent us a bison for Whitsun. We had no cause for complaint.

14

Tiger in Hospital

Nearly all the wild animals that were being acclimatized at Thoiry received veterinary attention on the spot. In some cases, however, they had to be transferred to my clinic. All kinds of wild animals turned up at my surgery under the strangest circumstances.

A female panther was once brought to me by a team of Romany showmen. She had been living in a semi-zoo, semi-circus environment. Her owners occupied a suburban house with a small garden in front and an all-purpose outbuilding behind. The men and their animals shared these cramped quarters, all living cheek by jowl. Apart from the panther there was an elephant housed in the small shed used for hanging out laundry, two bears, a lion, two cheetahs and a pair of chimpanzees for whom a couple of rooms were reserved inside the house itself. Everyone lived in harmony, but under rather primitive conditions.

As often happens, I had been consulted at the last possible moment. The panther's life was hanging by a thread when she reached my surgery. She was almost inert, completely dehydrated and vomiting blood. The diagnosis was paraleucopoenia and the prognosis extremely gloomy, but we tackled her case with grim determination. Hours of intravenous drip-feeding, nights of nursing, days of treatment. Everyone at the clinic awaited the outcome in an agony of suspense. However conscientious a vet's treatment, however devoted his care and advanced his techniques, he is subject to harsh criticism nonetheless. If the animal survives, you're a man in a million and fully entitled to a halo; if not, you're politely branded an incompetent of the first order. The panther made a full recovery after three or four weeks' treatment on the premises, during which time we got to know her well. She proved to be extraordinarily docile and gentle.

I soon yielded to the temptation that overcame me in the case of Youyou, my adopted Beauceron. The panther was not caged, but roamed the surgery as she pleased. She used to jump on a stool in the canteen where I and my assistants ate our midday meal, which she often shared. She was quite as tame, housetrained and friendly as a contented and intelligent cat. Her owners pleaded poverty and swore they would bleed themselves white to pay for the treatment she had received. Meanwhile, they appealed to my kindness of heart, my generosity, my humanity and several other qualities customarily invoked on such occasions. Not being a complete monster, I let them soft-soap me. They did more than take their panther back. In token of their gratitude, friendship, confidence and other glowing sentiments, they brought me a bear to treat.

I could hardly slam the door on a poor old bear half paralysed with rheumatism. It wasn't his fault if his owners hadn't a sou – or swore they hadn't. I gave him the full treatment: shortwave, manipulation, physiotherapy, infiltrations, massage . . . Using those two classic and ultra-sophisticated aids, half a broomstick and a pocketful of tidbits, I got him to perform a wide range of movements. He was muzzled, of course, but he wore no gloves over his claws. Thanks to some effective help from his trainer, favourable results were obtained.

The patients I have just mentioned were only three of the many large animals that have passed through my surgery. Bears were particularly frequent visitors. One of these sometimes accompanied me when I visited the bar on the boulevard for a drink with its trainer. The animal would rise on its hindlegs, take a flower between its paws and amuse the customers by obeying an injunction to 'give it to *la patronne*!'

I was once landed with a very rare and far from docile creature. The arrival on my examination table of this valuable black jaguar raised a serious question, namely, the right of certain zoos to exist.

The call came one Saturday lunchtime. The manager of the zoo, a small and out-of-the-way establishment, explained the situation: an animal worth several thousand pounds had suddenly fallen ill. (I didn't believe a word of this hoary old tale: the trouble must have been brewing for quite a while, but nobody had noticed.) He had phoned X and Y, only to be told to bring the carcass along for an autopsy, so he was calling me for advice.

I was up to my eyes in work. The whole of that Saturday afternoon was earmarked for an autopsy on a dolphin. Still, black jaguars were rare and beautiful creatures, and I hated the thought of abandoning this one to its fate. There were only two in the whole of France. I had never seen one outside the United States, so I gave in. 'All right,' I told the man. 'If your animal's still alive when it gets here, we'll see what we can do.'

My client's representative arrived at the end of the day. I joined him at the clinic, feeling pretty exhausted by my afternoon's intricate post-mortem work on the dolphin. We laid the almost inert animal on the examination table. It was a limp rag, not a jaguar. Its nose oozed blood and its skin was dehydrated. The diagnosis was obvious: haemorrhagic pneumonia. The jaguar had probably been ill for some time. It had not been treated early or efficiently enough.

I began by rehydrating it. I administered massive antibiotic injections, intravenous drips of proteins, glucose and – despite the patient's haemoptysis – corticosteroids. Everything now depended on patience and supervision. Would the animal pull through? Three hours went by, then four, and still it clung to life. At about 11 p.m. the local café sent in some coffee and sandwiches. The keeper who had accompanied the jaguar was a likeable fellow and devoted to his charge.

The jaguar's near-inertia persisted. While the drip continued I cleaned its fur and cleared its nasal passages with an inhalation atomizer. Some time after midnight, it finally showed signs of life and began to stir. It would quickly become dangerous if it revived, so we had to secure its legs. Its temperature started to fluctuate. Hypothermic on arrival, the jaguar had now become feverish. Its temperature dropped again, only to soar alarmingly. By the time it nudged 41°C, we felt the battle was lost.

But we didn't give up. I injected a variety of cardiac stimulants, aromatics, respiratory analeptics, and so forth. I also persevered with drip-feeding. The patient's temperature remained extremely high, but he hung on. So did we.

Morning came. The jaguar was still alive and had regained some of his beauty. Although it was Sunday, my only day of rest, I could not leave the patient in his present condition, even for a few hours. The vigil continued. I had been working for twenty-four hours without a break, but if the jaguar could stand it so could I.

I kept him permanently drip-fed on the operating table until Sunday night. Cats and dogs would be turning up when the surgery opened on Monday morning, so our patient could not occupy the premises indefinitely. Meanwhile, a cage had been delivered. We bedded him comfortably down on some straw and carried him upstairs into the apartment which served as my office. The steel cage was deposited in the passage with a plastic sheet beneath it to protect the floor.

The jaguar was not yet out of danger. I had to continue his intravenous injections and drips. Luckily, the cage had a mobile partition which enabled me to restrain the animal and keep his paw immobilized. Though still in a weakened state, he was becoming more aggressive and needed careful handling.

I could no longer give him inhalations directly into the nose, so I saturated the entire passage – and ourselves too, more or less. To ensure that he inhaled the solution, I had to keep the atomizer working full blast and the doors and windows shut. The walls and floor benefited as much as the patient and were soon coated with a sticky film.

He seemed to be on the mend. The nasal bleeding had lessened and his coat was looking better, but I did not take his recovery for granted. He remained on a drip for half the day. I persevered with all sorts of treatment and intensified them in accordance with the results of daily laboratory tests. I also kept an eye on the electrolyte levels and all the biological parameters which it was possible to measure.

One lunchtime I saw the jaguar sniff the air. There were some fillet steaks on the grill. I had already tried feeding him with pieces of beef cut up small so that they would not require much chewing, but he had always refused them until now. Was he hungry at last? I took my steak between two fingers, walked over to the cage and raised the trap. He crawled towards me. Although he subsided on his belly almost at once, he condescended to sniff my princely offering. He showed no sign of displeasure even when I rubbed it against his nose. Eventually he licked it, took it delicately between his teeth and proceeded to chew.

Our four fillet steaks all went the same way, one after the

233

other, each one offered by hand. Another stage on the road to recovery had been reached. I felt a thrill of pleasure but superstitiously refrained from showing it. Next day I brought the patient some diced stewing steak. He didn't even deign to sniff it. Our own lunch that day was rabbit. I took a piece of the saddle and proffered it as I had the fillet steak. That did the trick. Piece by piece, he devoured the entire carcass. We gave up our lunch with good grace. Although the jaguar might not be eager to take the bread out of our mouths, his manner certainly conveyed an insistence on the same menu as ours. Next day I tried offering him some more stewing steak. I might have saved myself the trouble. He was still too frail to be denied his little whims, so I sent out for a few fillet steaks from the butcher and he devoured them eagerly. All attempts to vary his diet failed. Fillet steak alternated with rabbit for a full month. Our jaguar was a lordly creature with refined tastes. He was no fool, either.

For the first forty-eight hours the jaguar's keeper slept beside the cage on a mattress in the corridor. His job was to deal with any emergencies and keep the animal clean. Our patient was still so weak that we could enter the cage, keeping a weather eye open, and had no need to use any form of restraint. The keeper soon left because he was needed at the zoo, so my wife and I had to play the lion tamer and handle the cleaning ourselves.

The jaguar showed an initial reluctance to leave his cage; in the end, it was all we could do to get him back inside. On one of the early occasions I opened the door and prodded him gently through the bars with a broomstick, my intention being to coax him into the kitchen and shut him in while the cage was being cleaned. Prodding had no effect. I had to catch hold of one paw and extract him by force, then drag him towards the kitchen. But coercion was tiring and unpleasant for both of us, so I tried a gentler method. I left a dismembered rabbit in front of his door. That worked. He ventured halfway out. Next day I put a fillet steak farther down the passage. The day after that, more rabbit, this time in the kitchen itself. He ended by going there of his own accord.

As soon as he was safely shut up, Michèle dived into his low cage on all fours – it was less than two feet high – and extracted the litter, which was stuffed into plastic bags for disposal.

To begin with, the jaguar was docile. He purred as he strode towards his rabbit or fillet steak and needed no inducement to re-enter the cage. It was still his favourite refuge – his home and haven.

What with the fillet steak, vitamin injections and the rest, however, he became more independent and refractory. He developed a taste for promenading in the kitchen and the corridor. He posted himself on the roof of his cage and insisted on staying there. His behaviour in the kitchen became more and more audacious, especially when he grasped that the refrigerator served us as a larder. One day he opened the door and scooped out the entire contents, chewing anything that seemed of interest and playing with the rest. I was increasingly compelled to act the lion tamer with a length of broomstick in each hand. But the jaguar resisted, pawed at the sticks, drew his black lips back over his handsome white teeth and made playful lunges in my direction. He was turning into a tough customer. My job was done. I decided to send him home, hoping that he would receive better care in future.

I was understandably delighted to have saved the life of such a rare and splendid beast. The jaguar is an animal that needs cosseting in a really first-class zoo where it can live under optimal conditions, so my pleasure was somewhat blighted by the thought of returning him to an environment unworthy of him. I knew that his owners were not professionals and that the zoo he inhabited was typical of those make-shift establishments that had sprung up in response to growing public awareness of ecological problems. Some businessmen had spotted a chance to make money, so another self-styled zoo had come into being. It was wrong that such a valuable creature – valuable zoologically, not financially – should have become the chattel of inexpert people for whom the health, well-being and propagation of animals were subordinated to material interests. They undoubtedly made an effort on their jaguar's behalf, but only just in time. If they had not hit upon a fool who spent his nights administering drips and his days sacrificing fillet steaks, the animal would never have survived.

The story of the black jaguar exemplifies the modern tendency towards better and more elaborate veterinary treatment. This is being fostered by the development of new attitudes, new techniques and a greater respect for the animal world. I systematically did as much for each of my animal patients as I would have done for a fellow human being. I was particularly pleased when we were able to secure, this time for a tiger, the benefits of the very latest medical technology in a hospital designed for human patients.

Tambo lived in a small zoo whose inmates, though not all kept under ideal conditions, enjoyed the proprietor's personal attention. Tambo was a tame but well-built adolescent tiger weighing a little over 200 pounds. His owner brought him to see me at the surgery without any special precautions, holding him on a short leash and armed with nothing more intimidating than a small truncheon. The animal appeared to have a heart condition. Even a gentle walk around his enclosure made him pant and slump to the ground.

I listened to his chest and took an electrocardiogram. Tambo submitted quietly and did not have to be tranquillized. Although I could hear a murmur, I was not fully satisfied by an examination conducted with the resources at my disposal. I recommended a more exhaustive cardiac examination. This could be performed in a brand-new and superbly equipped clinic – and not a veterinary one either – where I had some friends who were specialists. There were even facilities for landing patients on the roof by helicopter.

My cardiologist friends expressed interest. It was possible that we would discover an interventricular opening. In that case, surgery would be necessary.

It was decided to examine Tambo as thoroughly as any human patient. This would entail catheterization, or the introduction of a probe into the heart. Opaque substances injected into the bloodstream by way of the probe enable the movements, the chamber outlines, the state of the valves and the opening – if any – to be scanned on a television screen. Pictures can also be taken where necessary (in fact, we made ninety x-rays). Catheterization further enables one to determine and record the pressure inside the various cardiac chambers. In this instance we would be rechecking the electrocardiogram tracings on the monitoring screen throughout the examination and keeping records.

On the day of the appointment, an estate car pulled up behind the hospital in the area reserved for delivery vehicles. Although Tambo could not be admitted via the main entrance for fear of alarming or offending the uninitiated, he received

VIP treatment. He dismounted from the car on his leash, watched by a large audience ranging from the medical superintendent and surgeons to the nurses and orderlies. Few film stars could have been accorded a better reception.

The tiger entered the hospital at basement level, so he did not have to change floors in order to reach the x-ray room where the examination was to take place. Tambo gazed around him with interest, making an occasional friendly flutter with his lips. He surrendered his paw without fuss, suffered the tourniquet gladly and was not upset by his intravenous injection. On the contrary, he gave me a companionable butt with his head, like a domestic cat. A few moments later he went to sleep. We picked him up and put him on the brand-new examination table.

We were personally pleased for Tambo's sake but a little disappointed professionally when catheterization disclosed nothing positive. We had drawn up an entire plan of battle with my friend Dr Bernard de Parade, the cardiovascular surgeon, and his team. The decision to operate would have called for heart-bypass equipment and a quantity of compatible blood – tiger's blood, of course – for the transfusion of our patient.

I felt entitled to conclude that Tambo's cardiac arrhythmia had an emotional origin. The tiger was growing fast. Although this rendered him more vulnerable to certain forms of stress associated with cardiovascular trouble, there was naturally no question of operating under such circumstances. Tambo came round two hours later. We had stretched him out on the floor in advance. He stood up and glanced at his master as though nothing had happened. Then the two of them left the way they had come.

I saw Tambo again the following year. I walked over to pet him and pass the time of day. All of a sudden he sprang at me. Fortunately, he was muzzled and tethered to a tree. I received a mighty thump in the chest which sent me reeling backwards, but my only injury was a twisted ankle.

I have always wondered what came over him. Had he simply become vicious with adulthood? Had his master given him one tap too many on the nose? Was he annoyed at being muzzled and tied up? Had catheterization left some ill-defined scar on his psyche, and had the sight of me triggered an unpleasant memory? Why, on this one occasion, should hostility have

237

flared up in an animal I had always been on good terms with? What gulf had suddenly opened between Tambo's animal nature and my own? The incident posed questions to which I could find no real answers. At all events, it was yet another reminder that I must never drop my guard. These artificial reserves for wild animals, these wildlife parks, these zoos large and small – were they a curse or a blessing? Did they do more good than harm or vice versa? I had witnessed many happy births and many harrowing deaths. From the animal and the human point of view, did they add up to total failure or partial success? Was I entitled to draw up a balance sheet at all? Was I, even now, in a position to pass judgement?

I say 'even now' because I still had one experiment to conduct.

15

Summary Execution

'Why shouldn't *I* have a try?' This is the question which ultimately and inevitably occurs to the doctor who yearns to apply his therapeutic methods in a clinic of his own, the technician who yearns for a factory in which to test some manufacturing process of his own devising, and many other people. So it was with me. Why not a wildlife park run by myself? Why not a park which possessed the attributes I dreamed of, which would enable me to fulfil objectives distilled from years of personal experience? I knew what was lethal to the bear, tiger and monkey, the oryx, kudu and numerous other creatures. I had an ever-expanding knowledge of what they needed in order to live and reproduce. I was now convinced that unless we established havens for wild animals, almost on Noah's Ark lines, many threatened species would soon vanish from the face of the earth. Why shouldn't I found such a sanctuary myself?

It would not be one of those mushrooming zoological 'collections' which pander to the public craze for entertainment by herding the maximum number of animals together under deplorable conditions.

By contrast, I planned to create a protected and specially designed environment where a limited number of species could thrive in groups, or at least in pairs. The park would be as spacious as possible and provide them with living conditions favourable to breeding. It might also become one of the first animal banks for wildlife threatened with extinction.

I gradually discovered that a wildlife park is hard to make pay. When animals are exploited by straightforward business-men whose sole preoccupation is a return on capital, they assert their natural rights and dignity by dying. This wipes the capital out. But a wildlife park is no more profitable when it happens to be a cultural venture which respects and protects the animal for its own sake as well as the welfare and dignity of mankind. Running it is an expensive operation requiring outside help – a local government grant, for example, or some other form of subsidy.

Undaunted, I joined forces with an associate and took the plunge. Thanks to population density, a municipal subsidy and the regional importance of tourism, our choice of a site on the French Riviera offered some chance of making the place a going concern and fulfilling at least a few of my pet objectives.

Visitors to the park would, of course, be charged an admission fee. As things stood, there was no other way of financing our capital outlay or covering the park's subsequent upkeep. Though established for the benefit of animals, the park would also be designed for the public. Our first objective – a haven for species threatened with extinction – had a natural corollary. We proposed to introduce the townsman to this world of wild animals, kindle his awareness of their beauty and demonstrate what was necessary to their survival. By so doing, we would help our contemporaries to regain an equilibrium subjected to increasing disturbance by their estrangement from nature, which they were destroying in the belief that they could dispense with it while clinging to their nostalgic memories.

We would thus be doing a service to man and beast alike.

It was an immense undertaking by my own modest standards. I was compelled to immerse myself in a sea of real estate, commercial and financial transactions where I felt like a fish out of water. The experience taught me a great deal, if not about animals, at least about economic and political life and the interests of man as opposed to beast. There were times when I felt like backing out, but it was too late. I had tackled the problem. Now I had to see it through.

Little by little, the project took shape. The outlines of the park became visible. I sometimes tore my hair, as for instance when I arrived from Paris to discover that my plans had not been implemented, that the layout of the lion enclosure conflicted with my intentions, or that the contractors had wasted and mutilated precious space by bulldozing the pool out of the hillside instead of siting it at the foot, where it would have better suited the lions' convenience and the visitors' angle of vision.

Sometimes, too, I experienced keen pleasure and moments of great enthusiasm. The elephant pool was a case in point. We dug and concreted it between Sunday lunchtime and Monday night. This time I was on the spot. The bulldozer carved away the soil under my direction, pausing only when the rocky site required a dose of dynamite. I occasionally took over the wheel and controls myself. As I watched, the pool gradually assumed its pre-ordained shape: oval, with undulations designed to help the elephants wade in and out. This time, everything accorded with my wishes. The retaining wall was vertical to prevent the animals from climbing out on the near side and persuade them to use the far slope, where the edges of the pool were well-rounded. The job was done in a way which would not only suit the animals but create a pleasant setting from the spectators' point of view. My design was followed in every detail. When I wanted the undulating approaches to the pool faced with rough cement to prevent the animals from slipping, my instructions were understood and obeyed. It obviously paid to be on the spot. If I wasn't, nothing matched my original intentions.

As for the animals that were to live beneath the cork oaks and pine trees in our park, my main aim was to acclimatize some cheetahs. The threat to the cheetah's survival was extreme. A magnificent but once unappreciated animal, it had suddenly become fashionable and was being ruthlessly slaughtered in consequence.

The preservation of these animals presented even greater difficulties than those besetting the survival of many other threatened species. Unlike lions and tigers, cheetahs not only faced extermination in the wild but were failing to breed in captivity. I had laid down a barrage of public statements imploring people not to buy cheetahs to embellish their country estates or entertain their visitors, but to no avail; fashion and one-upmanship proved all-powerful.

So why imprison cheetahs in my future park? I was not surrendering to fashion but responding to a need. The park would be an establishment devoted to the experimental breeding of cheetahs.

It only remained to find the cheetahs themselves. Deciding that it would be best to acquire them on the spot, I left for East Africa with all the equipment needed for their capture. But my well-meant safari did not turn out exactly as planned.

We drove nearly two thousand miles through the bush. We saw plenty of ostriches, Thomson's gazelles and gerenuks, or gazelles that browse on thornbushes by rising giraffelike on their hindlegs. We startled guineafowl, francolins and warthogs, saw bushbucks, dik-dik, waterbucks, Grevy's zebras, oryx, baboons, hornbills, bustards and so forth. On one occasion, as we were crossing an expanse of semi-desert, I rather annoyed the driver of our Land-Rover. There was a slight risk of guerrilla activity on the part of the Dankali, so we all had our rifles loaded and within reach. Suddenly my travelling companion braked to a halt, raised his rifle and took aim at a bull kudu with a fine pair of horns. I knocked the barrel up. We had plenty of meat and nobody wanted any trophies, so why kill the creature? I was disappointed enough with my quest for cheetahs as it was, despite the pleasanter aspects of roaming the Ethiopian bush. Futile slaughter would only have increased my dissatisfaction.

Personal inquiries yielded no positive results. We had too little time to spare and could not spend months on the prowl. Although we did see a handful of cheetahs, panthers and lions in Somalia and Ethiopia, we returned from the bush empty-handed. I soon found out what happens when an enthusiastic amateur decides to acquire such animals.

Like other foreigners before and since, I was visited at my hotel by young Somalis eager to sell me cheetah cubs secreted in baskets or enveloped in the garments they wore. They were baby cheetahs, captured before weaning and already in such poor condition that I could tell at a glance they would not survive. The Somalis probably killed the dams as soon as they gave birth and kept the cubs for some time without knowing how to feed or tend them. How many died before one survivor could be offered for sale? Trying to assess these losses at the time, I estimated that every baby cheetah acquired by a misguided animal lover represented a score of dead animals. In fact, the malady assumed such proportions that it soon bred its own cure: the animal lovers finally realized that the cheetahs on offer were not viable, so the sellers lost their market. The result has been that live cheetahs are only hunted to order. Although this must have reduced losses, cheetahs are still slaughtered for the sake of their skins. All these activities are illegal. The trade in cheetahs is strictly controlled in principle and their exportation theoretically prohibited. An official at Addis Ababa once showed me rooms in a warehouse stacked with confiscated cheetah and panther skins. Although this was better than nothing, it did not bring the animals back to life. Who can hope to control hunting in vast areas where tribal warfare rages and rebels dispute the authority of the central government?

I nonetheless bought two little cheetahs which had been offered for sale under these circumstances. My wife took charge of them as soon as I returned to France and reared them on the bottle like Sacha the lion cub and various other young animals. Both these cubs survived, though a baby cheetah is far more of a trial than a lion cub. Cheetahs are the most sensitive of all felines. A cub will not be separated for an instant from its real or substitute mother. If she leaves its side, it protests with earsplitting vehemence – so much so that one can readily grasp why deprivation spells death. Charlotte, our little female chimpanzee, also needed permanent contact, but at least she had her own means of clinging to a thigh, arm or skirt and thus enabled my wife to retain some freedom of movement. Not having prehensile paws, a baby cheetah must be cradled in your arms the whole time. At night, on pain of more earsplitting squeaks, it insists on sleeping on your bed or even under the covers.

Unlike a tiger cub, however, a young cheetah does not lend itself to housetraining. My wife had consequently to protect our bed from the baby invaders with voluminous plastic sheets. What still further aggravated the thralldom in which they held their adoptive mother was that our youthful lodgers declined to be fostered by Rinka, the Alsatian bitch. Although Rinka had reared lion and tiger cubs in our garden, no bond developed between her and the two little survivors. This put a severe strain on their human mother, who swore she would never repeat the experiment. She also began to ask herself a number of questions. Did she have the right to rear wild animals which became so deeply attached to her but could not be kept indefinitely? Was it fair to inflict the pain of separation on them (and, to a lesser extent, ourselves)? Weren't we condemning our protégés by making them unadaptable, incapable of associating with their own kind – incapable too, perhaps, of breeding?

The answer to these queries must depend on a number of observations which have still to be made. Be that as it

243

may, our two little cheetahs became inmates of the park a few months later. The other twenty I acquired from a dealer in South Africa – another German – who offered them for sale under firm guarantee. His animals hailed from South-West Africa, where cheetahs are still quite plentiful. They differ from those of East Africa and the Tibesti Mountains. Though darker in colour and a trifle less elegant-looking, they are more robust.

Would they become acclimatized? Would I persuade them to breed? What price all our efforts if I failed? How could I justify my participation in a seemingly contradictory system which set up wildlife parks to safeguard animal species but contributed to their destruction by so doing?

We kept our cheetahs under observation. When did they mate? It proved impossible to catch them in the act. Was captivity completely extinguishing their reproductive urge, or did the fault lie with our ignorance of their habits? We failed to observe any births, either, though the behaviour of certain females suggested that they were pregnant. Were we to conclude that they behaved like she-bears unable to hibernate, and devoured their offspring at birth?

My current theory was that cheetahs needed privacy when mating and giving birth, and that we ought to provide them with secluded nuptial chambers. Accordingly, we dug shallow caves out of the hillside where mating couples and pregnant females could enjoy peace and quiet.

The results are still inconclusive. Perhaps we should also have enlarged the cheetah enclosure, large as it already was in relative terms. I tried to provide the animals with extra space but failed. Three births have since taken place but only one cub survived, almost certainly because it was removed from its mother at once. Does this setback damn the whole enterprise? Some will claim so, but I disagree. Cheetahs have bred successfully in London, Frankfurt, Montpellier and other zoos. Environmental factors conducive to their reproduction are still under study and will almost certainly be identified in due course. Our venture was a step in the right direction, and the last word has yet to be spoken.

Other animals joined our Mediterranean Noah's Ark. They included giraffes, zebras, bubals, kudus, waterbucks and gazelles. The trials and tribulations of the lions and elephants were particularly significant.

The presence of the lions proved that a wildlife park can be stocked without any drain on natural reserves. They all came from the Paris area, their birthplace, and had previously been patients of mine.

Some time after their birth I received an emergency call from the zoo. Four lion cubs, all members of the same litter, appeared to be dying. I set off at once, well aware that every minute can count in such cases. They were still breathing when I got there. All were suffering from toxaemia, a fatal condition unless treated with speed and determination, and all required a continuous series of drips and injections lasting many hours.

At last, after a fortnight's fight for survival, the cubs began to mend. Titus grew up into a splendid male and the dominant member of the quartet. Nounours, the other male, was a robust animal but did not dispute his brother's authority. Louva proved to be a rather touchy lioness, more fearful than the males and therefore more aggressive. Chicha, another female, was the gentlest. My relations with all four were extremely affectionate.

While still young – only two-and-a-half – but almost fully grown, these survivors were transferred to our wildlife park in the South of France and released into the large enclosure which, though not laid out to my liking, suited them very well. Whenever they heard my voice, and especially when I had not seen them for some time, they galloped up to greet me – sometimes from the back of their enclosure. They rubbed against the wire, growled in a caressing manner, licked my hand and rolled over on their backs. I could still reach through the mesh and tickle them all over from the ears to the tail, running my hand over their bellies and testicles or even down the inside of their thighs.

I must make it clear, yet again, that physical contact of this kind is dangerous save in the most exceptional cases. It should never under any circumstances be attempted by an outsider. In a zoo, members of the public are separated from wild animals by a barrier which precludes any contact, but there are always a few incautious and unwitting spirits who succumb to the urge to touch them or picture themselves as lion tamers qualified to disregard the safety regulations. For them there awaits the terrible paw-stroke whose speed and power surpasses the layman's imagination. To grasp this you must, like me, have seen a lion launch itself at your person. You must have seen the injuries inflicted by lions on each other. You must bear in mind that an angry lion can, as I have recounted, bite off a fellow lion's tail at the root – a tail whose bone at this point is thicker and infinitely stronger than a human femur.

Our four lions were admirable and extremely well behaved animals, accustomed to man and ignorant of any world save that of the wildlife park, their native habitat. They had food in abundance. They had courtship and sunshine, long siestas, pleasant bathes and the friendship of their keepers. They even had room enough for an occasional little gallop. It might perhaps be claimed that they led the ideal existence of which lions in the natural state may cherish hazy dreams when drought prostrates them, prey eludes them and human beings hunt them: in short, they dwelt in semi-paradise.

What was more, these happy leonine existences were a high tribute to the human race. The animals had not been wrested from their natural environment. Far from impoverishing nature, we had enriched it. Nobody could think otherwise who witnessed the grand passion with which Titus, when in rut, made the hills ring with amorous roars which suggested that he was engaged in repopulating the entire globe. I have watched many animals mating in my time, but I am bound to say that the lion is something of a king in this respect.

I can still see and hear Titus at his lovemaking. I can picture him taking a brief nap in the sunbaked centre of the enclosure, one paw resting on the neck of his mate, Louva, whom he has covered a few minutes earlier. It is a proprietory paw, as the other lions are well aware. When Titus is feeling amorous, they keep their distance.

He wakes, yawns and rises. The time has come again. Louva looks less sanguine. She and Titus have been mating for the past four days. Well endowed as she is, the act has begun to lose its charms for her. Titus, who is far from spent, gently stirs her hindquarters with a massive paw. Louva finally gets to her feet – not very graciously, or so it seems. Titus asks no more. He does what needs to be done in a brief fifty seconds. Having emitted a deafening and enthusiastic roar at the crucial moment, he lazily resumes his siesta.

Nothing very surprising so far, but ten minutes later Titus is at it again. Not stopping to eat and resting only occasionally for one or two hours at a time, he maintains this rhythm – prodigious by human standards – throughout a period of four or five days!

Such were our four splendid lions, soon to perish in a terrible accident.

But by then I no longer wielded any control over their destiny. Financial considerations had compelled me to relinquish my interest in the wildlife park of which I was a founder. I had discovered that, while it is impossible to create a wildlife park worthy of the name without money, the intervention of money renders it almost as difficult. I had turned my back on the whole affair. Although I did not repudiate what I had done, a wide gulf still separated my intentions from their fulfilment. This relative setback, which occurred despite all my hopes and plans, was comparable with the problems I had observed in other zoos.

However, I still took an interest in the fate of the animals whose lives I had shared almost daily for four long years, spending more time flying between Paris and the Mediterranean than commuting by car between Garches and Paris.

That was why, one Sunday morning in January 1975, I received a telephone call from Josiane, my former veterinary nurse. Two people had been torn to pieces by the lions: the director in charge of animals, and an unfortunate youth, aged sixteen. As for Titus, Louva, Chicha and Nounours, the lions I had tended as cubs, they had been dispatched by a long double fusillade of pistol and rifle shots.

What had provoked this slaughter, which was promptly publicized by every newspaper and radio station in the country?

Our wildlife park had originally been subject to rigorous safety regulations of the sort observed by all good zoos. To take just one example, nobody could enter the lion enclosure without obtaining the only key to the gates. This was held, day and night, by the one person authorized to grant access: the chief warden.

It was also forbidden to enter the enclosure except in a specially protected vehicle modified in accordance with my own specifications. This was a narrow-bodied but powerful cross-country vehicle of Austrian manufacture. Having been adopted by the Swiss army for use in mountainous country, it was particularly well suited to our own rugged and wooded terrain. A cage enclosed the driver's cab as well as the loading platform, and the door and roof opened on the sliding principle. The bars were close enough together to prevent any lion from reaching inside, so the occupants were fully protected.

Only when travelling in this vehicle was the warden authorized to shepherd his lions from place to place, break up fights, isolate individuals and guide them to the restraint cage if they were sick, or conduct them back to their quarters at night. The lions were rather scared of the noisy great contraption and generally complied without protest. They did gnaw its tyres, but only when it was parked with no one at the wheel. Thanks to these two precautions – the single key and the field car – all possibility of accidents was eliminated. I should add that the vehicle had to pass through a 'lock' before entering the lion enclosure.

After I severed my links with the zoo at Fréjus, the staff changed and a new chief warden was appointed. He was a nice young fellow, an amateur who cherished a passion for wild animals and had reportedly wanted to become a trainer.

Given the setting in which he worked, this ambition should have been firmly restrained. Unfortunately, it was encouraged.

As a result of various business deals which sorely tried my patience and were partly responsible for my resignation, a small safari-style zoo had been established next door. All that separated it from our own park was an intermediate fence behind which, only fifty yards away, the public could watch a professional trainer leading twenty or twenty-five lions around like sheep. Under these circumstances, the ambitious new warden at Fréjus must have felt that the competition warranted his playing the lion tamer inside his own enclosure.

The new director actually joined in, leading his lions around on foot. All the ingredients of tragedy were now present. One little slip would be enough. Without the protection afforded by a vehicle, it promised to be fatal.

One of the chief warden's daily tasks was to conduct the lions from the lion house, where they spent the night, to their enclosure. The operation fell into two phases. First came the 'old' or adult lions, that is to say, Titus, Louva, Chicha and Nounours, and then the 'young', a group consisting of fifteen animals less than two years old.

The two groups were, in fact, kept apart. Each had been

An American black bear at Thoiry *(M. Descamps, Télé 7 Jours)*

At the Fréjus Zoo *(J.J. Morer)*

Titus likes being stroked (*J.J. Morer*)

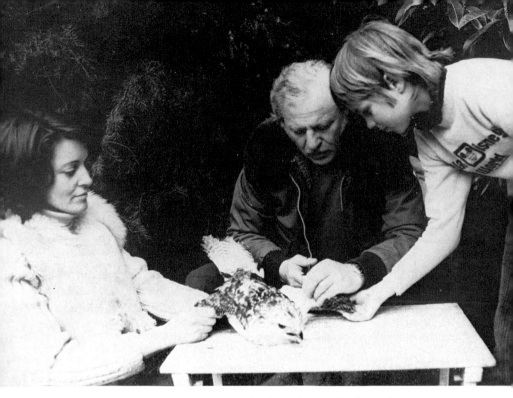

A Bonelli's eagle has his broken wing set by the author,
helped by his wife and son *(P. Vals)*

The twins, Isabelle and Florence, doing their homework
watched by Charlotte, a young chimpanzee *(author's photo)*

allotted its own enclosure to prevent friction. The young males would have tried to sniff females in season and been violently repulsed. Far from tolerating the presence of youthful strangers, the adults would have killed them. To reach their enclosure, the adults had to cross that of the youngsters. The warden consequently had to release them first, coax them into the wire mesh tunnel leading to the first enclosure, conduct them across it to the second and shut them in before going back to fetch the fifteen young lions and herding them into their own territory. Simple as it sounds, this manoeuvre called for careful handling. A number of gates had to be opened and closed. Above all, the warden had to shepherd the four adults across the first enclosure to the second.

On this particular day, the adult lions trotted towards their domain as usual, growling a little to preserve their dignity. They reached the pool, always a tempting sight, where they showed signs of loitering. The man in the rear called and waved to urge them on, and suddenly the game was up.

A boy of eleven, the victim's own son, witnessed the scene through the fence at the other end of the enclosure. Did one of the lions adopt a menacing stance? Did their escort flinch? Did he simply lose his footing and slip on the side of the pool? Whatever the truth, his fall spelled disaster.

Animals find man a threatening and intimidating figure when erect: once on the ground, he is reduced to the status of any other prey. Louva, who was nearest, could not have failed to be disturbed by this change in relative status, which aroused her predatory instinct. She pounced at once. Three hundred pounds of muscle armed with claws descended like a thunderbolt on the frail human body of her victim, who was immediately overpowered and knocked unconscious. But the well-fed lioness was not hungry. Having immobilized her prey, she abandoned it to the rest without devouring it. Her companions also retired after sniffing the recumbent form of their warden. It is probable that he was still alive. If the field car had entered the enclosure at this stage, the lions would have withdrawn and their victim's life might have been saved.

But who came to the rescue? Not the field car but a youth of sixteen, alerted by the combined screams of the warden and his eleven-year-old son. He was in the kitchen between the lion enclosure and the establishment next door. He came running. With a mixture of courage and ignorance, he entered the enclosure on his own.

More often than not, lions will quietly retreat at the approach of an erect and determined man. Faced with a child or adolescent, however, they react as they would to a monkey. To Louva and the other lions, the figure bearing down on them was not really that of a man: it was a prey they were entitled to seize, especially as the youth was unknown to them and had little direct contact with the inmates of the park. Just as she would have attacked a young and incautious baboon in the savanna, Louva leapt for a second time. The result was a second victim, not of animal ferocity but of human error.

But it was man who made the animals pay for his own mistakes. Some employees of the safari park next door had also heard the screams. Using walkie-talkies, they summoned their boss, who hurried to the scene with a pistol. He blazed away. The lions were hardly touched, by all accounts, but fear and agitation drove them back to their victims. It was only at this stage that they really started to maul them. The safari park director, who had run out of ammunition and saw that he would achieve nothing with a pistol, went to fetch a rifle from his home half a mile away. By the time he returned the lions had dismembered their prey. Although little of the latter remained to be salvaged, he opened fire regardless. This time, four lions bit the dust after a fusillade of thirty or more shots.

Would *I* have spared the lives of wild creatures that had just devoured two human beings? Certainly, though some may disagree. It all depends whether you base your judgement on nonsensical vengeance or human intelligence. There was a time when animals were put on trial. Executing these lions was just as futile. Reason and the spirit of justice should acknowledge that they merely behaved like lions and were blameless.

So the massacre of the four lions was not only pointless but detestable. It would have been quite sufficient to enter the enclosure in a field car or other closed vehicle, chase the animals away, pick up the two victims and transport them to hospital. A cool-headed approach to the situation might have saved all six lives.

16

Malika Attacks

I have never been able to recall this tragic incident with indifference. As time went by, however, I began to wonder if I had the right to pronounce so harshly on the recklessness of others. I have already mentioned several instances where I myself courted disaster in a rather foolhardy way. I too have played the lion tamer on occasion, and not just because veterinary considerations demanded it. I did so for fun – an admission which does not make me entirely guiltless.

This puts me in mind of a story I intended to forget, perhaps because it is a source of dissatisfaction rather than pride. I was treating a rather grumpy lioness named Malika, who belonged to the trainer Jim Frey and used to work with him at the Jardin d'Acclimatation circus in Paris. The poor creature had good reason to be grumpy. She was suffering from cerebellar ataxia, a condition of the nerve centres which affected her coordination. She had fits of clumsiness, and sometimes staggered and missed her footing when she jumped, but she could still lash out like lightning when she chose to.

I was giving Malika injections of Besredka's serum into the skin itself, which was quite a performance. A lion's skin is well over a quarter of an inch thick and extremely tough. The introduction of 2 cc of serum necessitated my pressing so hard on the piston of the syringe that it hurt my palm, but it was Malika who suffered most from these injections, which must have smarted a lot.

Early in the course it was still possible to lure her to the bars and tether her there so that I could inject her, but she quickly caught on. As soon as she saw me coming she fled to the back of her cage and refused to budge.

Subterfuge was the only answer. Instead of showing myself

on arrival, I notified Jim and his assistants, who coaxed Malika into the wire mesh tunnel leading from her living cage to the circular working cage. There they trapped her between two doors. Unable to escape, Malika finally became resigned to her fate and stopped struggling. To her, the pain I inflicted on her defenceless body could only have seemed a token of superiority. In accepting the injections, she was also accepting my personal domination.

The ascendancy I wielded over her encouraged me to put on a show which might have ended in disaster. I was then associated with a weekly television programme entitled *Nos amies les bêtes*. Jim Frey's lioness seemed to rate an appearance, but it was decided for the cameraman's sake to shoot the sequence in the circular cage rather than the tunnel.

The time chosen was the interval during a Sunday afternoon performance attended by a thousand people. While I made myself scarce, the lioness was released into the big circular cage with her team mates, whose presence allayed her suspicions. They were then sent back through the tunnel. Armed with his whip and stick, Jim Frey directed the lioness to her usual place.

Enter the vet. At once, Malika froze on her stool.

But how was the cameraman going to work? Would he stay outside the cage? No, he said, he couldn't do a decent job from there. Oh well, let him come inside with me – there was nothing to fear. Caught between me and her trainer, the lioness couldn't fail to toe the line.

We were all inside the cage now. Malika, perched on the stool with her ears flattened, presented her hindquarters to me with a now habitual air of resignation. Jim Frey stood at her head, armed with another stool, while the cameraman stationed himself to one side. My syringe was filled with red wine for the sake of better visibility. It had, in fact, been arranged that I would only go through the motions this time. All set? The camera whirred. As if for a real injection, I took a fold of the thick skin on Malika's back between my fingers, applied the syringe and slowly expelled its rosy contents, which seeped into the fur on the side away from the camera.

'No good,' said the cameraman, 'your hand was masking the syringe.'

We did it again. I pinched another fold of skin and faked another injection, but the second take was no good either.

Malika was still rigid with fear. Although a little alarm-bell had started ringing in my head, I was too preoccupied with camera angles to pay any real attention. The cameraman had followed me into the cage without a moment's hesitation. I wasn't going to tell him to call it a day and come back next week, so we tried a third take.

Meanwhile, a couple of things had been going on in Malika's head too. She had begun by awaiting the stab of pain that established my authority and her own submission. She felt me take her skin between my fingers – the preliminary sensation – but nothing happened. Nothing happened the second time, nor the third. The imaginary and lilliputian bonds that had restrained her suddenly snapped. She recovered her freedom of movement in a flash.

Abruptly, she swung round on her stool and faced me. Crouching on all fours with her lips drawn back and her fangs bared, she emitted the sort of belly-roar whose very echoes are enough to make you swoon with terror: it was a prelude to the charge.

The cameraman jumped back, fell to the ground and passed out. I don't remember what Jim Frey did, but the lioness now had her back to him. It was all up to me.

I simply shouted 'Malika!' and raised my arms, palms outwards, above my head. I shouted sternly but not fiercely in a voice whose steadiness I can vouch for. It was an instinctive reaction, of course, not deliberate.

That was all. The roar died at once and the leap never materialized. Malika's charge had been nipped in the bud. She backed off slowly, still growling but relieved – as her whole demeanour conveyed – of pent-up aggression. We had escaped with a fright and could think ourselves lucky that she had not altogether recovered her freedom. A man standing erect, made to seem even taller by his raised arms and reinforced by a voice which called her to order and reminded her of previous injections, had held her in check after all. Last but not least, her movements were slightly impaired by ataxia.

I had felt no fear. Luckily for me, predicaments of that kind only clear my mental decks for action. My imagination ceases to function. I am instantly poised for attack or defence. If the lioness had leapt I should not have been a passive victim. She might have been too quick for me, but I should at least have tried to dodge. Physically, I was by far the weaker; mentally,

253

I was still the stronger. This, coupled with her infirmity, may explain why Malika failed to charge.

I got off without a scratch. Although I would be prepared to swear that my pulse beat no faster during the ordeal, I was not very proud of myself. I had been reckless. I had agreed to run a risk whose true extent could not be gauged. I was professionally and personally concerned to protect animals and preserve their dignity, yet I had agreed to use an animal's rump as a film prop. Who knows if Malika meant to punish me for that transgression too? It is true that I committed it in a good cause, on behalf of a programme designed to interest the general public in animals and help them understand and love their 'inferior' brethren, but the fact remains that my behaviour contained an element of bravado.

That said, can all risks ever be avoided by someone who has daily dealings with wild animals? Before resigning from the Mediterranean wildlife park I had stocked it with a certain number of animals including three elephants. They were three particularly difficult and unwanted females which had been passed from circus to circus like hot potatoes, not captured in Africa or Asia for the park's adornment. One of them, whom we have already met, had broken a companion's spine with blows from her trunk or head. It was not long before she caused another stir, this time in the summer of 1975, by negotiating the safety ditches and ravaging some local orchards.

Karim was twenty-eight when I saved her. She at once presented us with numerous problems. Our relations were complicated by the fact that nobody knew her 'language' or what words she was used to hearing in what tongue. The first time I approached her and tickled her tummy she promptly did her best to lie on me. Another time she tried to crush me against a wall. I only just escaped on each occasion. At one stage we had to move her from the shed where she was temporarily housed to her permanent quarters over a mile away. This operation entailed coaxing her on to a mobile platform drawn by a bulldozer. Ropes, words of encouragement and curses all proved equally ineffective – Karim didn't want to know. Though well aware that her trunk might flatten us at any moment, how could we help exposing ourselves under these circumstances? After a whole day's wearisome and fruitless exertions, she abruptly changed her mind. I had treated her to a final bombardment of elephant words in French, English and German. One of them got her moving – I can't remember if it was '*Schnell!*' or 'Go!'

But Karim was not the worst of the bunch. Two other females, Sabu and Nyemen, joined us later. Although they had become exceptionally vicious after the death of their trainer, his wife tried to work them herself. A blow from a trunk had consigned her to a plaster jacket which immobilized her entire spinal column from the neck to the coccyx.

During their first night with us, Sabu and Nyemen half-demolished the sheet-metal door of the elephant house, fought each other and generally raised hell. Tethering them was quite a problem. Rather than ask someone else to risk it, I did the job myself.

Sabu, the most ill-natured, was a small but sturdy female. She started by attacking me on the elephant hill. I fled with her in hot pursuit. The ground sloped, fortunately, and she slipped and fell. Feeling that she had made a fool of herself, she saved face by investigating one forefoot with her trunk as though there was a stone in it. I realized that she had meant to be playful and throw a scare into me, not attack in earnest, so I went back and spoke to her, stroked her eyes and gave her some bread and apples. Having once struck up a friendship we remained on good terms from then on.

My relations with Nyemen turned out equally well. Her favourite trick was to trumpet like a bugler. She soon condescended to perform it in my honour, so I benefited from her pride and satisfaction. It was, incidentally, after one such recital that she consented to let me hobble her.

I am still further convinced by my relations with these three she-devils that one can often come to terms with animals that have killed or injured their trainers. There is no doubt that the animal world, like the world of man, contains some whose congenital defects of character are beyond correction. On the other hand, one accident is not enough to prove an animal incorrigible or justify its destruction on the grounds of a single unfortunate blow with trunk or paw.

By dint of a little friendship and psychology, I got on friendly terms with my three elephants. I also persuaded them to live in peace together. My secret lay in recognizing that one of them was boss – Karim, the biggest and strongest – and that we had to protect Nyemen, the weakest, from the malicious attentions of Sabu, who was always stealing her fodder. The solution, which seemed simple once I hit on it, was to rearrange the elephant house so that Karim occupied the central or dominant position with the other two elephants flanking her. This suited all of them admirably. It is interesting to note that Nyemen, for so long the weakest of the trio, eventually gained in size and weight to such an extent that she took over the leadership.

17

Reflections on Zoos and Wildlife Parks

Reverting to my earlier questions: what about zoos, wildlife parks and 'reserves' where groups of so-called wild animals live in semi-freedom? Are they desirable or reprehensible? Am I now entitled to pass judgement on them?

I have seen much that is bad: the haphazard proliferation of self-styled zoological establishments designed to exploit public disquiet just when ordinary people are becoming aware of threats to nature and wildlife; the intrusion of business interests and the futile destruction of numerous animals; ignorance and incompetence, pain and suffering.

So there is bad in the midst of good. An oryx disembowels a dromedary, a she-elephant breaks her neighbour's spine, zebras trample baby gnus to death . . . These things should, perhaps, be entered on the debit side, but wouldn't similar tragedies have occurred in the natural state? Did they happen because the animals concerned were living in an artificial environment, albeit carefully devised, which had been imposed on them by man?

Even the best of intentions can be unproductive or disastrous, as I myself discovered while trying to establish a wildlife park of my own. I saved four lions from death when they were young and tried to provide them with a miniature paradise, yet they were slaughtered. I wanted to rear cheetahs for breeding purposes, but no young were born. What did I accomplish by enabling twenty-odd cheetahs to sun themselves on the Côte d'Azur? I merely uprooted them from their native savanna and helped to boost a trade that was already claiming numerous victims. And what of my grand design for a colony of gorillas on the French Riviera? This was a recurrent dream of mine: a large expanse of water, three islands linked by drawbridges, houses for the winter – how well they would have bred in such an environment! I would have acclimatized a whole range of new vegetation for their benefit. We had already planted three hundred palm trees in the park. Birds which had made themselves scarce, apparently feeling that they would not be safe for quite a few years, started to come back to our area. Our plans had been drawn up and studied in every detail, but there were no gorillas. Circumstances and difficulties of all kinds conspired to prevent their acquisition. I never fulfilled my dream: a breeding colony on the periphery of France and Europe which might have compensated, however inadequately, for the slaughter that was going on elsewhere.

But how far should criticism be carried? What about those two little cheetahs offered for sale in Somalia and bottle-reared by my wife – weren't they a point in my favour? Wasn't it better for them to live in an enclosure under the Mediterranean sun than die in their country of origin? Must one always look on the dark side? After all, I had probably seen and aided the birth of more zoo animals than ever succumbed to accidents or disease. The zebras had trampled the baby gnus to death, but we quickly put things right. We had failed to save the big male bison, but it was thanks to us that another bison – and not the last – came into the world one Whitsun afternoon.

What if we were on the right track after all, despite our blunders and miscalculations? One brand of extremists unreservedly condemns anything that resembles a zoo. According to them, it serves no useful purpose and is merely a penal colony for animals wrested from their natural environment. Immoral from the human standpoint, it offers our fellow men a degrading spectacle, constitutes a peculiarly loathsome form of exploitation and panders to the vile instincts of those who relish the sight of suffering.

Extremists of another complexion will reject these humanitarian strictures. Set up as many zoos as you like, they say. Animals exist to serve man, the lord of creation. Our superiority entitles us to exploit them in our own way. Hypocrisy is unworthy of us. If we condemn zoos, why not equally condemn horse racing, cats in our homes, dogs in our gardens and all forms of human domination over animals?

In my view, neither attitude is tenable. I believe that in this sphere, as in others, wisdom prescribes a middle position:

bad zoos are reprehensible and good zoos fulfil a useful, indeed, necessary function, but good can exist in that which is evil just as evil may exist where good predominates.

Even the role played by bad zoos has not been wholly valueless. They have helped to alert the public to the conditions in which wild animals are kept. The sight of wretched creatures crowded into frightful cages can exert a salutary effect on public opinion. Not long ago I received a letter from a woman complaining of the conditions in a French provincial zoo. Her attention had been drawn to them by Professor Grzimek of Frankfurt. He, in turn, had received a letter from a German diplomat who, on visiting the establishment, was shocked to see how its inmates lived. Bad zoos have themselves stimulated this sensitive attitude, which is something of a novelty in my country, by exhibiting jaded and pathetic animals to hundreds of thousands of visitors. It is on their premises that the latter have detected a silent plea for help, not only on behalf of animals incarcerated in cramped cages, but for all those whose freedom on our planet is being gradually eroded – all those who are more and more often stalked, hunted, devoured by starving villagers, sold on the international market or ousted from their natural environment by the march of civilization and a galloping human birth rate.

Showcases devoted to animal misery, bad zoos have also been a forum where emaciated lions, dejected bears and many other wretched creatures can appear as mute and pitiful advocates of a great cause: that of nature in distress and wildlife slaughtered by man.

The genuine zoo is one element in a deliberate endeavour by man to salvage what he can of the world of wild animals, which is being irresistibly destroyed by mankind as a whole. For human beings at large, the retention of contact with animals is not only therapeutic but essential to their own equilibrium.

The destruction of wild animals was not, in fact, ordained by man. It is happening not because of him but in spite of him. The more discerning members of the human race have a consequent duty to prevent it, and a few cautious moves are already being made to that end.

It is hardly futuristic to regard the genuine zoo as one means of resisting this pernicious trend. Contrary to what might be supposed, zoos are not responsible for depleting the world's natural reserves. That form of depletion is calculable and controllable. The fundamental threat to wild animals is human demographic pressure. The ever more numerous, anarchic and aggressive presence of man throughout the world, together with his growing needs, is spawning cultural and industrial developments injurious to their natural habitats and remaining places of refuge. Their natural larders are, for instance, being destroyed by the roads traversing Amazonia, by major land-clearance schemes, by the advent of vehicles of all kinds. It is not absurd, therefore, to speculate that one day – and sooner than we think – wildlife parks may be the sole repositories of species extinct in the areas which used to be their original habitat. As for Africa, only the initiate can conceive of the immense changes that have taken place there. 'It didn't matter where we went,' I was recently told by the wife of a safari enthusiast, 'there was nothing left.' Ten years ago, I myself toured a large expanse of Central Africa without meeting a single herd in country that used, until lately, to support a large animal population. Even the crocodiles had gone.

Will it be possible to preserve wild species under these conditions, if not in artificial reserves, at least in wildlife parks of suitable design? This form of conservation has already been provided for certain species, notably birds, but there is still far to go. In future, zoos may be the sole surviving abode of the panther, tiger and cheetah, eland, antelope and many others.

No one would dispute that natural game reserves in the animals' places of origin are more beneficial, effective, authentic and desirable. It would seem, however, that additional safe-guards for certain animal groups or species should be provided elsewhere, perforce in the shape of man-made reserves. Some may protest that a tiger in a zoo is nothing but a shadow of its former splendid self. My reply to them is that it is still a tiger and a reservoir of tiger genes. It might even prove possible to reintroduce the species to the wild after the last tiger has vanished from the last remnants of jungle on our planet – though it is, of course, preferable to set aside fully protected reserves where the animals can be truly at home.

I once witnessed an experiment of this kind. The plan was to transport some zoo-born lions to Senegal, where lions have become almost extinct. The zoo in question owned a group of lions reputed to be Senegalese. Like others of their kind, they had bred extremely well in captivity, so ten cubs were schooled for resettlement in Africa. This meant isolating them for a certain length of time. The keepers did not handle or go near them unless it became absolutely necessary, and their meat was thrown to them in the hope that lack of human contact would make them wilder and facilitate their return to nature.

One fine day they were flown to Dakar. It was planned to turn them loose in the Niokolokoba Reserve, nearly four hundred miles from there. After another trip by air, the first two lion cubs from France were released in a bend in the Gambia.

Considerable thought had been devoted to their mode of release. The river was deeply embanked at this point, and the lush vegetation bordering it sloped gently upwards to the savanna. There were plenty of birds and small animals but no adult lions that might have threatened the lives of our settlers from the Ile-de-France.

As an aid to survival, some sides of beef were left at the top of the river-bank. Arrangements had also been made to keep the immigrants supplied with food for a certain period. Last of all, we left them their cage so that they could take refuge inside if they wanted. Persuading them to leave it was quite a job. They obviously felt no urge to sample the dietary delights of the African savanna, and it took a lot of shouting and waving to dislodge them. At last they consented to remove themselves to the shade of a thornbush not far away, where they sat down and idly watched our departure.

I have little faith in the outcome of their adventure. Judging by what happened to the rest of the cubs, their prospects were poor. The other eight were released near a group of buildings containing the offices of the game reserve, in a fenced enclosure designed to hold giraffes but open at the bottom. Putting them there was tantamount to releasing them straight into the savanna, but they showed no urge to roam. Though well on the way to adulthood, they preferred to hang around for their rations.

The eight young lions were later installed in a neighbouring enclosure hardly bigger than the one in their land of origin, and the next thing we heard was that the game reserve authorities had found them so troublesome that all eight had been returned to Dakar in cages. Whether or not their little escapade in the Niokolokoba Reserve had given them a taste for freedom, they escaped. Instead of being peacefully recaptured, they were machine-gunned to death. It would have been better had they never left their native zoo in the Bassin Parisien.

Did this failure prove the impossibility of resettling wild animals in their ancestral habitat? Not at all. The only reasonable inference was that the operation had not been conducted as it should have been. The lions were too young. The adaption of two-year-old adults would have presented no difficulty. They would soon have found food and stopped waiting for handouts, and would not have been in danger of attack from any other animal. One day, perhaps, a fresh attempt will be made under more favourable conditions.

Some people may question the point of all these endeavours. Why move heaven and earth to preserve a few lions and tigers? What use are they? Can't we dispense with them perfectly well? Are we really so much the poorer for losing the diplodocus and the dodo? If he has to, the man of tomorrow will be able to adapt quite easily to a world without animals.

I am not that man. The human race has never yet dispensed with animals, and I doubt if it can do so without courting self-destruction. Man's attitude to animals is a test. He belongs to an animal species himself. If he cannot preserve the life of other animals he will fail to preserve his own.

In any case, man's estrangement from animals as a result of industrial and urban life is only one side of the coin. Not only in the developed countries but, to an increasing extent, elsewhere as well, he is making manifold attempts to restore contact with them. Never have our cities been inhabited by as many cats and dogs. Never has nostalgia for unspoiled natural beauty been so pronounced. We have no need of horses, yet riding clubs are multiplying. Hundreds of thousands of visitors drive many miles to see colonies of flamingos in the Camargue and elsewhere. Television documentaries on wildlife are legion. Zoos provide one means of restoring contact between man and beast. The wild animal is not essential to man's subsistence. It supplies him with no food or drink, but it does remind him that the world contains certain elements of beauty. Aren't these indispensable, even today? Wouldn't we be irremediably the poorer if a day came when the tiger or jaguar ceased to prowl through our minds and hearts?

So the zoo has a dual mission to conserve species and effect a *rapprochement* between man and beast. Failure to fulfil that mission is the real danger. A zoo of high quality is expensive to run and requires public support. To survive at all, it needs some form of patronage. Local communities can ensure the survival of zoos worthy of the name and turn them into cultural enterprises. The question is, do they want to? Some countries have developed such a 'zoophilous' attitude that these ventures, though limited in number, function satisfactorily under the watchful eye of public opinion and local authorities. Good will and a favourable climate of opinion are essential to the existence of zoos that conform to human and animal needs alike.

It is a matter for collective responsibility. Are we capable of the effort of insight and foresight necessary to the establishment and long-term maintenance of these 'artificial' wildlife reserves? Are we capable of recognizing and protecting the real interests of the human race in this respect? We have to make up our minds about what we want to be.

To toy with the preservation of wild animals on our planet would be even worse than permitting their extinction. Half measures are worse than no measures at all. Animals do not live by halves; they either live or die. The community's obligation towards them is the same as that of an individual towards his dog. It is shameful to take a dog home because you think you like animals, only to abandon it because it costs too much or takes up too much of your time. It would be just as inadmissible to want zoos but fail to supply their needs.

Although animals on which human progress has imposed artificial living conditions stand in need of us, it is probable that our own need for every kind of animal is even greater. The interdependence of species and individuals enables us to recognize the need for biological tolerance so that each individual's mission – life, reproduction, death – can be fulfilled under conditions of general equilibrium. Peace and the preservation of the freedoms for which we cherish a firm attachment are equally dependent on respect for all living creatures. Useless violence can only give rise to upheavals whose scope and magnitude escape our control. As for me, my obligation towards the animal remains the same whether it lives in a circus, zoo or 'reserve': to aid its survival and improve its lot, whenever possible and at whatever cost to myself.

Once, when I happened to be attending a large gathering dedicated to bird conservation in the Palais de Congrès at

263

Juan-les-Pins on the French Riviera, I received an urgent midnight telephone call from a woman journalist. According to an agency report, a shipload of animals had just been driven aground on some rocks in the Bab el Mandeb straits between the Gulf of Aden and the Red Sea. The crew had been saved by a French naval vessel from Djibouti, but some twelve thousand zebras, goats, sheep, dromedaries, horses and cattle were dying in the ship's half-flooded holds. It was appalling to think of so many creatures slowly expiring of hunger and thirst: could nothing be done to save them too? I had to do something, but what?

The French authorities at Djibouti, who had already gone to great lengths to save the ship's crew, could do no more. Almost insoluble problems were presented by the task of boarding the stranded ship and transferring the terrified animals in the middle of a storm. The idea of saving the crew and abandoning the animals shocked me profoundly, but whom could I turn to on a Saturday evening?

Then I had an idea. I knew the Americans maintained a well-equipped team in Eritrea for the recovery of spacecraft at sea. What if I appealed to their initiative and good will? From Juan-les-Pins I at once telephoned the US Embassy in Paris. The ambassador was not there at that hour on a Saturday evening, nor were many of his staff, but I eventually got hold of a senior aide. As I had hoped, she reacted in a prompt and favourable manner. Her country would be glad to do something on behalf of such a worthy cause, but the decision to mount a rescue operation rested with Washington and US headquarters at Frankfurt. She immediately phoned the competent authorities but could not promise any firm response before Monday. I found this admirable enough in itself, and naturally undertook to hold myself in readiness. Volunteers would have to be lowered aboard to handle the animals and net them if it became necessary to lift them off by helicopter. The storm showed no signs of abating, so the chances of transferring them by boat seemed slender.

But Paris had not been idle either. I learned that some journalist friends had contacted the War Ministry in my name and received a favourable hearing. The French authorities were ready to provide six helicopters for the rescue operation. What was more, numerous volunteers had already written to the newspapers offering their services, and I was able to get in touch with several of them.

So the operation quickly took shape. Considering the number of animals that might already have died of fright, thirst and suffocation in the holds of the stricken ship, every day and every hour counted. Before long, however, politico-legal complications arose. It seemed that, under international law, the vessel was not a wreck open to salvage. We learned that it flew the Saudi Arabian flag and that the cargo belonged to Saudi dealers.

We also discovered very soon that all the trouble we had gone to was an apparent waste of time. The storm that had been raging in the Red Sea quickly subsided and all the interested parties – shipowners, dealers, etc. – prepared to unload the animals into dhows from the neighbouring coast. I nonetheless believe that our efforts in various quarters, not to mention those of the press and the authorities at the War Ministry, the US Embassy, Frankfurt and Washington, were not entirely wasted. A threat to the existence of some wretched dromedaries and zebras had seemed important enough to well-meaning individuals, and even to official bodies, to warrant a considerable expenditure of time, effort and material resources. It was one of those human demonstrations in favour of the animal which bid us have faith in the future.

The essential thing is to do what we can and a little bit extra. Not long ago, repairs to an old hernia confined me to a hospital bed for ten days. My wife had forbidden any professional calls to my private ward, so the lions and tigers made no summons. A week after my operation, she herself reintroduced me to the world of animals. A young elephant belonging to Mary Chipperfield, who was showing it at the Cirque Jean Richard, had developed a prolapsed rectum, or portion of gut protruding from its anus. Michèle's first attempt to reach me at the hospital had failed, so she took it upon herself to visit the circus with my qualified woman assistant. The surgery was inundated with patients, notably a bitch in her sixty-sixth day of gestation but showing no signs of whelping. Michèle told herself that the elephant would not take them long. They would replace the gut and hurry back for a Caesarean on the bitch.

But things went badly. Michèle described the situation on the phone. As usual, the elephants were females. The one with the prolapse was moving about a lot, shuffling from foot to foot and moving a good yard sideways each time. She was diagonally hobbled, foreleg to hindleg, but this was insufficient. Working on her hindquarters was dangerous under these circumstances. The patient not only stamped her feet but turned her head to investigate the women with her trunk and tusks, which, since she was an African elephant, were long and pointed. There were also her neighbours to contend with. One of them had already explored my assistant's arm with her trunk. She didn't even notice, being engrossed in her work, but Michèle was perturbed. 'We're *all* going to end up in hospital by the time we're through,' were her precise words.

Having helped me to treat them in the past, Michèle had a good working knowledge of elephants and was well aware how dangerous they could be. In particular, she had had dealings with Sabu, the female which severely injured the wife of her trainer. Sabu had more than once gone for Michèle and tried to grab her, so she was doubly wary of the elephant with the prolapse.

I soon discovered that the risks were aggravated by something else: an atmosphere of scepticism which threatened to make treatment even more difficult. Michèle told me that the elephants' wooden platform had not been cleaned or strewn with fresh straw before her arrival with my assistant. This meant that the two women had to circle the patient on bare boards slippery with excrement. One slip might have been fatal. If an elephant feels tempted to sit on you, hospital is the least of your worries: you have to be scraped off the floor with a shovel.

According to Michèle, this negligence implied that the circus people had no faith in them – that they regarded them as second-class citizens and were submitting them to casual treatment which 'the' vet would never have tolerated for a moment. Although she had asked them to hold the elephant while they did what was necessary and keep her tusks and trunk away from them, they complied in a very halfhearted manner. She had also asked them to hobble the hindfeet tightly, but they seemed to think this a futile precaution. Meanwhile, my assistant bravely continued to administer antispasmodic injections beside the ear, heedless of the possibility that these lax conditions might encourage the elephant to react in a dangerous manner.

Lying in my hospital bed, I could picture the alarming situation as vividly as if I were there. I knew the elephant handlers well. They were rough diamonds with a tendency to be hard on women. It must have tickled them to watch these two at work: one of them blonde, in patent leather shoes and a sweater; the other – Michèle – small and dark, stomping around in my outsize rubber boots, which she had hurriedly pulled on before leaving for the circus. My assistant was a qualified veterinarian of long experience and my wife had spent ten years with me learning the business the hard way, but they were women, and that was that.

After wading around in the dung for a while, Michèle and my assistant reviewed the problem. Although the gut could always be replaced, it wouldn't hold. My deputies recommended general anaesthesia and suturing, but even that provoked argument. They were scathingly informed that the gut had been restored to its proper place without an anaesthetic in New York. Of course, they retorted, but the trouble would recur sooner or later. My assistant, who was starting to lose patience, insisted that the gut would not hold and proved her point three times in quick succession. She rolled up her sleeve and pushed the intestine back into the elephant's rectum, but it popped out again each time.

It was bitterly cold that day, $-5°C$. The two women's town clothes were stiff with frozen dung and urine. They came to the conclusion that I should have to take a hand myself. Time was going by, and they had to think of the little bitch and her Caesarean. There was nothing for it but to summon the vet from his bed. *Then* the circus people would see whether or not an anaesthetic was called for . . .

Michèle was right. The demands of elephant and woman brook no refusal, so I knew where my duty lay. It was only a week after my operation. I still felt a little shaky but was in fair general shape. All I had to do was slip out quietly and try not to bump into the surgeon, who was a personal friend, or he would bawl me out with a vengeance.

Making sure that the dressing on my belly was securely in position, I pulled on my clothes and swathed myself in a muffler and overcoat. Then I hailed a cab and headed for the circus.

The housework had been done by the time I got there. The wooden floor had been swept, hosed and covered with fresh straw. They brought me a chair in which I sat like a general directing an offensive from his desk. The two combatants, my wife and my assistant, had previously discussed

267

the situation with me at a safe distance from the battlefield of which both bore traces from head to foot. Inquiries soon disclosed that the patient was not suffering from a classic prolapse. When she rose on her hindquarters, all the perineal viscera, which are very substantial in an elephant, imposed an excessive strain on the animal's insufficiently developed musculature. The trouble would lend itself to long-term treatment, but we first had to deal with the immediate situation by pushing the organs back into place and reinforcing the anus with layers of stitches.

I handled the easy part, which was to inject the elephant with some of my miraculous American knockout drops. This ensured peace and an opportunity to work at leisure. The elephant obediently went to sleep and I returned to my chair. All the real work was performed by my assistants. Sprawled like their patient in the clean straw, which did not stay clean for long, they triumphantly replaced the errant intestine and inserted a preliminary row of stitches around the anus to constrict it a little. These purse-string sutures could not, in fact, be pulled too tight because elephants pass stools the size of miniature footballs and must not be hampered in their natural functions.

The latent antifeminism of the male staff around us, who found it hard to accept that a woman could bury her arm to the shoulder in an animal's backside, had evaporated. As far as they were concerned, we were all boys together. The work the women were performing on the elephant had ceased to be woman's work. Watching them as they scrambled around in the straw on all fours or lay at full stretch in their efforts to master the displaced intestine, the male spectators found it a huge joke. Masculine superiority reasserted itself, and they began to exchange snide remarks.

As for me, comfortably ensconced in my armchair, I had time to indulge in a few reflections on elephants and the human race. The subject had more than once been raised by Michèle, who is a subtle psychologist though sometimes a little biased against the opposite sex. Why should circuses and zoos always keep female elephants? Because the trainer is a man and thinks he can dominate females more easily? Because he imposes his putative male superiority on the female of the species? Because he is afraid of tackling the male? Ridiculous prejudices, according to my wife, but is she right? Could a team of bull elephants be handled like females? Experience alone can answer that question. One thing is certain: mixing the sexes would be impossible because a bull in must is beyond control. Besides, how would bull elephants in circuses react to the proximity of women at certain phases of the menstrual cycle? The male animal is reputed to respond exclusively to the sexual signals transmitted by the female of his own species, but numerous observations have shown me that matters are rather more complicated, at least in the case of mammals such as dogs, lions and elephants. Sacha, the lion I mentioned in an earlier chapter, became genuinely enamoured of Michèle at certain well-defined times, and we have already heard the story of the oryx fascinated by the female dromedary. The sexual signals emanating from the female of various species may be more closely related than we think. I have been personally and quite unmistakably teased by a young she-elephant while examining her during ovulation, not just once but on several occasions, so it may not be wholly absurd to wonder how bull elephants might react to female human riders at certain times of the month. Many mysteries remain to be solved in this respect.

My wife and my assistant finally completed their work. I felt proud of them and rather ashamed of my spotless overcoat and gleaming shoes. Michèle, whose face bore the marks of her battle in the dung-smeared straw, grimaced at me as she wiped them off. We decided to guard against a recurrence of the elephant's trouble by making her a special belt – a sort of truss – for use when required to rise on her hindlegs. More importantly, I prescribed exercises designed to strengthen the muscles in question.

The best thing, of course, would have been for the elephant to avoid all excessive physical strain in future. Although this was just what my friend the surgeon had told me with reference to my own abdominal weakness, it hadn't deterred me from sallying forth with a dressing on my tummy. I was no more of a free agent than the elephant.

'And now,' said the women, 'we'd better get back to the clinic and do that Caesarean. They must be biting their nails.'

18

A Pardon from the Poodle

When am I happiest, bending over the chest of a little York-shire terrier and bisecting a rib one third the thickness of a matchstick, or craning into an elephant's mouth with a hammer and chisel, trying to extract a molar twice as heavy as the dog itself? Which interests me more, a Caesarean performed on some tremulous little bitch belonging to Madame X or the prolapsed rectum of one of nature's giants; the marital prob-lems of the Pinscher or those of the bear, Elizabeth Taylor's Lhasa Apso or the mongrel brought me by a sewerman who had rescued it from the drain where some kind soul had left it to die?

I seem fated to shuttle between one world and another, to commute between the wide open spaces of 'Africa' in the Ile-de-France and my clinic in the middle of Paris, to treat Enzo the Pekingese and Tambo the tiger with heart trouble, Madame Durand's beloved alley cat and an anonymous princess's pampered Yorkshire terrier – to take an interest in the strongest and weakest, and not in the animal kingdom alone. Although the animal must always be my prime concern, how can I fail to heed the owner for whom it feels so close an attachment?

But owners can range from the wealthy English lady who charters a special plane for the benefit of her sick dog to the shop assistant's son who turns up at my surgery in tears over his cat. I fully accept, therefore, that I am also fated to run an everlasting race, not only from one animal to the next but from beast to man and man to beast.

The smallest domesticated animals occupy just as important a place in my personal and professional life as the biggest and strongest lions, tigers, rhinos and others.

Bigoudi, a small black long-haired dog weighing some

twelve pounds, was the offspring of a miniature poodle and a mongrel. He belonged to the laundryman at Courchevel, my favourite skiing resort, in the days when it was less thronged with people and cars. The resort had yet to celebrate its tenth anniversary, and the few dogs that lived there all winter were free to roam at will. One of them was Isidore, a mischievous wire-haired terrier from La Potinière, who used to hang around the bottom of the Loze ski lift. Having found a girl skier, preferably a novice, he would scare her into letting him grip one of her sticks between his teeth and hitch a free ride up the mountain.

One Christmas when icy roads made sudden braking impossible, Bigoudi was knocked down by a car. He wasn't killed, but his hindlegs were paralysed. The laundryman took him to the veterinary college in Lyon and was advised to keep the dog in his basket for several weeks in the hope that complete rest would effect a natural cure. When Bigoudi's master showed him to me at the end of February, I saw that paraplegia was well established. The dog could not stand on his hindlegs, so I had him x-rayed by the local doctor. We found that he was suffering from a fracture of the spinal column between the last dorsal and the first lumbar. The fracture had set at an angle of 60°. At the time, I thought Bigoudi was done for. A paralysed dog might just as well be dead.

At the end of my holiday I took Bigoudi to Paris with the intention of trying surgery. The injury to the spinal medulla was not too serious. With luck, I would restore the vertebrae to their normal position and Bigoudi's recovery should be relatively complete. One Sunday morning I and my entire team set to work. Using a hammer and chisel, both of them small and delicate, I broke the calluses around the spinal fracture. We could detect no injury to the medulla once it was exposed. Placing a prepared metal plate aganst the spinous processes, we fixed it with screws and stiff wire splints which passed beneath the ribs so as not to perforate the pleura. Everything went perfectly, and there were no postoperative problems in the way of pneumothorax.

Bigoudi spent three months' rehabilitation in a plaster and wire mesh jacket. His recovery was very slow, but we all felt pleased and enthusiastic at the success of our surgery even though re-education demanded plenty of patience.

Late one afternoon I was called to the phone by a lady who

271

lived in rue Saint-Ambroise, boulevard Voltaire, on the sixth floor of a building without a lift. She insisted on a house call and I agreed because she was phoning on my brother Jean's recommendation. She was pregnant and my brother Jean was attending her, so she had consulted him about the bitch in the hope that he might be able to help. I got to my clients' small apartment at 11 p.m., well after the close of surgery hours. My patient, an eight-year-old red setter bitch, was lying on a camp bed suffering from general paralysis. She was incontinent and unable to swallow. Her owners, Monsieur and Madame P, wiped her muzzle and anus every two or three minutes with an unending supply of cotton-wool swabs. Their only means of keeping her alive was to force-feed her. Despite medical care the bitch had been in this condition for almost three months. Infected with a neurotropic virus producing a complex form of distemper, she had passed through the digestive and pulmonary phases before its development could be arrested. Once she became paralysed, her mistress consulted several vets and the teaching staff at the Maisons-Alfort veterinary college. Without exception, they had quite justifiably recommended euthanasia. Everything was tried, but to no avail. Madame P and her husband were distraught with grief. The red setter was the couple's mascot. She had been an accompaniment to their courtship, engagement and marriage, so the thought of losing her seemed inconceivable.

Madame P, who was a teacher of English, presented me with a detailed case history which confirmed that the dog could not have received better treatment. I told the couple that I regretfully endorsed my colleagues' conclusions: there was no hope. The couple responded that they were prepared to do everything humanly possible to give the dog one more chance to live. Would I accept the case? If treatment proved unsuccessful, they would then put the dog down. Looking at the sorry scene before me, I thought it over for several moments. I suggested to the husband, who was an engineer and a practical type, that I might teach him how to administer intravenous and intramuscular injections. He quickly agreed to try, so we went off together to fetch the necessary drugs from the surgery. That night we gave the patient her first injection. Next day her clonic spasms ceased. Two days later she was able to swallow. On the fourth day she managed to rise on her forelegs. Within ten days, she had made a complete recovery.

Urinary incontinence persisted, but only for a few months.

I don't know why this miracle happened, because I had tried the same treatment in a number of similar cases with a ninety percent failure rate. Perhaps most of the credit was due to providence. Madame P celebrated her baby's christening by sending me an enormous box of sugared almonds. My brother, who actually delivered the child, only got a modest little carton.

Mustapha's kneecap subjected my grey matter to rather more of a strain. Mustapha was a tabby cat. Even if he had been just that, his patella would have claimed my full attention, but he also happened to be the beloved companion of a big-hearted and talented man, the writer Joseph Kessel.

Mustapha had dislocated his right knee. After being plastered for six weeks, the limb was found to be bent and immobile. It was at this stage that Kessel brought him to my surgery. From the worried look on his face, I saw at once that Mustapha figured prominently in his life.

Working on an elephant's molar the size of your fist is one thing. A cat's kneecap, which is no bigger than the smallest of shirt buttons, calls for a somewhat different approach. This one proved to be completely displaced. It had slipped round behind the knee into a postero-external position. The joint was seized up and the ligaments surrounding it had become retracted. The whole thing needed patching up.

I dissected. I severed the ligaments so as to free the joint and sewed them together again, reinforcing them with small pieces of fascia taken from elsewhere. Fascia (or aponeurosis) is the sheet of tendinous tissue, or whitish-looking skin, which a butcher removes from meat to make it more presentable. Then I replaced the patella, sewed up the wound, plastered the leg again and waited for a fortnight.

No good. As soon as I removed the plaster I saw that my repair job was not holding. I decided on another solution: if Mustapha's ligaments refused to knit, I would make him some new ones.

Back went Mustapha for a second session on the operating table. This time I had decided to use nylon thread, of which I had an assortment of the finest gauges ready for use. I made two little holes in the patella, inserted my thread and drew it tight. Then I pierced the two condyles of the femur, inserted one end of my thread through each, and – hey presto! – there were my two lateral ligaments. A simple knot flush with the two little holes sufficed to hold them in place. The kneecap was now attached on both sides. I adjusted the tension so that it would remain in its notch while sliding easily. The paw had plenty of play and the 'ligaments' appeared to be holding. I closed the wound, hoping that my second attempt would be a success.

Mustapha remained with me under observation for several days, but there were no postoperative problems. Joseph Kessel and his wife, Michèle, who inquired after the patient's progress daily, soon came to fetch him home. Their reunion was an orgy of purring and stroking. The cat told them all about his trials and tribulations while they told him how much they had missed him. After a few days' recuperation at their Paris apartment, Mustapha resumed tree-climbing in the country. That was nearly ten years ago. He is still happily running around on his patched-up knee.

In gratitude Kessel kindly inscribed his latest book for me with the words: 'In loyal friendship from Mustapha and his master – or rather, slave.'

Small dogs are afflicted with the same ills as large. The only difference is one of dimension. Imagine using plates, pins or screws to repair a tibia the size of a matchstick and broken in several places – imagine the labour and instruments required to deal with a slipped disc in the dachshund, Pekingese or Yorkshire terrier, not to mention a fractured jaw or pelvis. All these repairs demand a conjurer's dexterity on the part of the veterinary surgeon.

Still on the subject of watchmaker's work, I have also been treated to some awkward and interesting moments by a Yorkshire terrier's rib. This tiny long-haired dog is a highly refined product of the breeder's art. The smaller it is, the more it is prized by the dog fancier. The male champions most in demand for breeding purposes weigh less than two pounds. Cradled in the arms of a film star like Elizabeth Taylor, with its long hair full of ribbons, a Yorkie becomes an article of adornment like a jewel. In the hands of a vet who has manicured an elephant or pulled a tiger's tooth the day before, it poses obvious and sharply contrasting problems. When he has to open the chest of such a minute creature, he does well to banish the mental and muscular habits which professional familiarity with nature's giants tends to instill in his head and hands. This transition from one scale to another is a renewed test of mental agility and manual adaptation to radically different conditions. It is also an excellent antidote to monotony and routine.

The Yorkshire terrier in question belonged to the wife of a well-known Parisian restaurant owner. A fragment of chicken bone had lodged across his gullet in the thoracic region, an extremely dangerous position. The splinter of bone in need of removal was wedged in front of the diaphragm, on a level with the heart. It reposed close to the aorta, the main artery, and the lungs. In short, I had to work among the dog's vital organs. As for the gullet itself, this presented special difficulties. Opening the oesophagus exposes it to substances which are liable to contaminate the wound and produce infection. If it is swabbed too vigorously, the excessive pressure will cause bleeding. It also happens to be an organ which heals with difficulty once opened. Care must be taken to avoid damage to the gastric nerve, which passes close to it, and postoperative drainage is required to eliminate the various secretions that continue to be produced. Finally, closing the chest again entails a risk of pneumothorax, a pocket of air in the pleural cavity.

In fact, perfect closure of the thorax can be conveniently effected only if the initial cut has been made in the correct manner. This is a very delicate procedure, and one which cannot be fully described without pictorial illustrations and an appropriate commentary. Suffice it to say that the chest must be opened in such a way as to enable the surgeon to achieve a perfect seal, not only of the thorax but of the pleura or membrane lining its interior. The surgical trick, which may in itself convey some idea of the difficulties posed by the rest of the operation, consists in entering the thorax by splitting a rib lengthwise after peeling off the periosteum. The problem with a Yorkshire terrier is that the said rib, far from resembling a nice pork chop, is incredibly fine: as long as a matchstick but less than half as thick. To split it you have to propel the point of a scalpel down its full length with gentle – very gentle – taps from a miniature hammer. Caution is the watch-word: miss your aim by so much as a millimetre and you may damage a vital organ like the heart or lung. After surgery, observation and postoperative care, the little dog with the chicken bone no longer in its throat was duly restored to its mistress. All went well, but I doubt if she ever guessed what a concerted sigh of relief went up when the operation was over.

In the case of Pamela, Elizabeth Taylor's Yorkie bitch, the situation was serious but less dramatic.

The star was coming to Europe to make a film, escorted as usual by an entourage comprising of three children, eight dogs, various secretaries and the rest of her personal court.

Pamela, who was brought to see me by one of the aforesaid secretaries, had a large bald patch between her ears. Being two inches in diameter, the ugly circular expanse of bare grey skin covered well over half her skull and called for cosmetic surgery.

Working on such a tiny head was awkward. By stretching the skin to hide the scar, I would run two risks: too much tension in one direction would raise the little dog's eyebrows; too much in the other would draw her ears together. Either of these alternatives would have given her a funny expression, so I decided to preserve her facial balance by drawing the skin upwards from the neck and affixing it.

The whole operation was to be completed at one go, and I kept Pamela under observation for a fortnight. Happily, the little head seemed to be healing well. Pamela fell in love with my wife, like most other animals, and trotted between her legs from one end of the clinic to the other. She showed no resentment at having to rub shoulders with mongrels ignorant of the splendours of Hollywood, and was finally returned to her mistress. All that remained of her operation was a fine line well hidden by her hair and a faint air of surprise on her ever so slightly rejuvenated features.

I treated a number of Miss Taylor's pets for ailments of varying severity, and I also delivered several of their 'offspring'. She was fond of distributing them – a Lhasa Apso to Georgia, her hairdresser, a Yorkie to one of her secretaries, and so on – but her generosity was tempered with a peculiar loyalty to the animals in question. She liked to be surrounded by lots of people and animals, and giving away a favourite pet was a signal mark of friendship and esteem. She sometimes gave away parents as well as young, but she never did so at random. The recipients had to be worthy of her gifts, and she continued to watch over the latter's welfare.

One day a new client presented himself at my surgery with a beige-coloured crossbreed – a hint of Alsatian plus a dash of something else – which was walking on three legs. I was away, so my locum examined the dog instead.

I had, in fact, entered hospital some days earlier after repeatedly postponing my admission because I was inundated with urgent cases and temporarily without an assistant. I was eventually prodded into a decision by the sheer pain which so often compelled me to sit down while working. I diagnosed the trouble myself: a hernia – my peritoneum was being pinched between two knots of muscle.

It was hard to find a locum at the height of the holiday season, but I managed to get hold of a young colleague who agreed to spare me four days in mid-July. If four days was all he could give me, that would have to do. I phoned a surgeon friend, booked a private room and got myself put on his next morning's list. Technically, I was supposed to be admitted the same afternoon.

The morning and afternoon sped by. Emergency followed emergency, and the night brought yet another: a Scotch terrier with eclamptic convulsions. I dashed to the rescue. By this time it was 4 a.m.

I finally reached hospital at 9 a.m., was given a pre-anaesthetic injection and went straight down to the theatre.

The surgeon wanted to take my appendix out at the same time. Out of the question, I said, I had to be out in four days flat. No, he insisted. I was going to have my appendix removed and spend a week inside. No arguments.

I bowed to the inevitable. My locum would manage the extra few days somehow. On the fifth day I received a call from the surgery. Our new client with the beige-coloured crossbreed was on the premises at that moment.

My locum had examined the dog and found it to be suffering from coxofemoral dislocation. In other words, the upper end of the thigh bone had escaped from the cup-shaped depression in the pelvis where it normally resides.

After x-raying the hip, my young colleague had proposed putting the bone back into place and keeping it there with a plaster cast. Michèle, who knew I had my own ideas on the subject, took the locum aside and asked him to phone me. Reduction would not do the trick on its own, she said. The dog needed surgery or there would be a recurrence.

Unlike the condition of the elephant which drove me from my hospital bed twelve years later, after an operation for the same hernia, the dog's condition was not serious enough to warrant my taking risks. It could wait a few more days until my own stitches were removed.

The crossbreed's owner seemed rather disconcerted. A major operation? Was that really necessary? Was there no alternative? None whatever, my wife insisted. She had seen me operate in several similar cases. Without surgery, the dog would be bound to suffer a relapse – false joint, permanent limp, pain and discomfort.

I was absolutely categorical on the subject. We fixed an appointment for five days later, or the day after I left hospital. The thought of spending three solid hours on my feet at the operating table barely crossed my mind.

At that stage, coxofemoral dislocations in the dog – dislocated hips, in common parlance – were usually reduced with or without an anaesthetic. Sometimes the capsular ligament was stitched and the limb plastered. Attempts had even been made to attach the head of the thigh bone to the hip with a form of hinged screw, but that allowed only limited mobility. If the dog raised its leg sideways, as opposed to moving it back and forth, the screw twisted or snapped. I had seen victims of such accidents with their hindlegs comically but pathetically frozen in mid-air. In fact, no current method was wholly satisfactory.

My own idea was to fabricate a ligament – one end inserted in the head of the femur and the other in the cotyloid cavity which essentially holds the thigh bone in place – out of some tough but flexible substance which would allow all-round mobility. After considering the merits of various plastics such as acrylic fibre (Teflon was not in everyday use at this stage), I came to the conclusion that rolled wire gauze of a special stainless quality was the perfect answer to my problem.

The trick was to insert a plate in the pelvis (in other words, inside the abdomen), pierce the base of the socket, drill a hole in the head and neck of the femur, emerging below the trochanter, and attach the other end of my metal ligament. Gauging the correct angles called for great accuracy.

Léon came through the operation well. Indeed, he was in such fine fettle when his owner came to collect him that I detected a whiff of suspicion in the air. What was the client thinking? Did he imagine I had simply given his dog a few pills and confined myself to reducing the dislocation by hand? To make matters clear, I showed him my x-rays on the screen and described the operation in detail. He could easily pick out the plate and metal 'ligament'. His dog had undergone elaborate and intricate orthopaedic surgery. If he still wasn't satisfied, I would gladly submit the case to a leading expert on human surgery.

Léon's owner protested vehemently. The whole idea was absurd; he had the fullest confidence in my professional integrity. Besides, he had mentioned the case to one of his friends, Professor Y, who was a physician, not a vet. Professor Y had examined Léon himself and knew that the dislocation was not a minor matter. The client thanked me cordially and bore Léon off to his car. Seeing the dog in his arms, I could not help warming to the man despite my irritation.

While dining at a restaurant with some friends a few days later, I was treated to a surgical anecdote about a dog with a dislocated hip. Just imagine, one of our colleagues had actually done such and such . . . I chuckled to myself and went on eating my entrecôte Bercy with relish. Needless to say, the feat referred to was my operation on Léon. I let the speaker continue, prompting him with a few questions.

My friend was a man of many contacts. I learned through him that Professor Y had put the joint back into place himself, just as my locum originally planned to do. The operation had been performed at my client's private house in Neuilly with a friend of his – another prominent member of General de Gaulle's entourage – acting as veterinary nurse and helping to hold the dog while it was anaesthetized on the kitchen table, but it was no use. The dislocation had recurred, and that, my friend explained, was how Léon came to be entrusted to the vet who had finally operated on him.

I played the mystery man for a little while longer, then modestly confessed that he and I were the same person.

Some days later Professor Y telephoned to ask if he could inspect Léon's x-ray file. I was genuinely pleased to receive his congratulations.

Twelve years after that, I bumped into some friends near Fontainebleau. They had just rented a house, and I learned in the course of conversation that its former owner was Monsieur X, my distinguished client, who had lived there for some time.

'He used to have a dog called Léon,' I said.

'But of course,' my friends replied, 'we know the one you

mean. He's living with some neighbours of ours.'

I went to see Léon. My ex-patient was now fifteen. His master had died in the interval, but he was still very much alive and trotting around on four legs without a trace of a limp.

Small or large, the animal visitors to my surgery bring their owners with them as well as their ailments. The former are not the least of my professional interests, because the cat or dog reveals the man.

Nobody could have called the capped and booted sewerman who stumped into my surgery an important figure. Clasped to his chest was a dirty and bedraggled little dog with a great big sore on its leg. He had retrieved it from a sewer not far from the manhole through which somebody had dropped it.

We promptly bathed, disinfected, treated and comforted the foundling under the watchful gaze of our sewerman. 'I mean,' he kept on saying, 'you'd have to be a real swine to ditch a poor little brute like that . . .' It wasn't the first patient he had brought us. He usually took any live animals he found to the local police station for forwarding to the *Société Protectrice des Animaux*. Where this one was concerned, he wanted us to treat it; he didn't know why. Perhaps he was going to keep the dog himself.

He unzipped one of the pockets in his dungarees and pulled out a wallet. When we told him there was no charge he seemed quite taken aback and thanked us profusely. There would have been no haggling over the fee in his case.

Even more touching, perhaps, was the case of the woman in very humble circumstances who worked at a factory in the north of Paris. She came to see me accompanied by her fourteen-year-old son, who was carrying a female cat. Their concern for the animal was only too obvious. The mother explained that she had taken it to 'somebody' who had offered to operate for a very reasonable fee. Unfortunately, she could not manage it at present. Her son had been ill and her doctor had recommended a holiday in the mountains. That left no money to spare for the cat's operation.

The animal was suffering from metroperitonitis, so I performed a hysterectomy. The boy and his mother came to collect their pet after the operation. A few weeks later I received a postcard: 'Having a lovely holiday. The cat's fine and my son's better. Thank you.' Two months later they paid me another visit, just to show off their cat. Although I hadn't asked her for anything, the mother pressed a small sum of money into my hand. I accepted it with thanks. Some time later she sent me a second instalment. She ended by paying me precisely what she would have been charged elsewhere. Despite my silence on the subject, she felt she owed me a fee.

One day my surgery received a visit from two local inhabitants, a married couple of about fifty. The husband, a stout and imperious-looking gentleman, was holding a giant poodle on a lead. He angrily explained that he was sick to death of the dirty brute, which vomited and made messes all over the house. They wanted to get rid of him right away, so would I kindly give him a shot.

The woman was sobbing. I was no stranger to this combination of hardhearted husband and weeping wife. However, the woman could not have been totally cowed, because, in the midst of her tears, she said:

'Perhaps you'd take a look at him before you put him down. It may not be fatal.'

Examining the dog, I detected a large unyielding knot in his stomach. So that was it: the greedy beast had crunched up a lot of bones and failed to pass them.

'It's only an obstruction,' I said. 'I can operate quite easily.'

'Out of the question,' said the man, purple with rage now. 'Put him down.'

On that note he swept out, leaving me along with his dog and his wife, who was sobbing even harder.

'Listen,' I said, 'nothing's going to make me destroy this dog. I propose to keep the animal and treat him.'

Slightly reassured by this solution but still very distressed, the wife left.

I was then in the process of refurbishing my small ground-floor surgery. The window bay was open to the street and debris lay everywhere, so I was temporarily compelled to treat my patients in the basement. This was where I operated on the poodle. He responded well to surgery, and two days later he was trotting around and cocking his leg among the builder's rubbish on the ground floor. He could sally forth without having to ask anyone to open the door for him because there wasn't any door to open. His new environment was an obvious source of pleasure. Like the other dogs, he accompanied us back and forth between our home and the clinic.

Two days after the operation his mistress came to inquire after him, even though he had theoretically been put down. Seeing him very much alive, she shed a few more tears. A week later she returned, this time accompanied by her husband. They asked to see the dog.

'He looks fine,' the wife commented. 'You cured him, just like you said.'

The positions were completely reversed. Her tone was quite matter-of-fact, as though the poodle belonged to someone else. This time it was her big tough husband who lost his composure.

'Confound the dog,' he gulped. 'If only I'd known.'

And he started to weep – two or three great sobs which he unsuccessfully disguised as a fit of coughing.

I wasn't too keen to return the animal, but the owners insisted. They'd only brought him to me because there didn't seem to be any hope, they said, and I couldn't find it in my heart to bear them a grudge. They seemed genuinely fond of their dog after all.

Then came another reversal of roles: like Youyou, the poodle didn't want to go. He had turned his back when his owners entered the consulting room, and they had to make a tremendous fuss over him before he consented to be dragged rather than led away.

Two days later they brought him back. He was refusing to eat at home. We offered him a bowl of bread and meat, which he promptly devoured. Then he condescended to leave again with those for whom he had declined to eat just as they had denied his right to live. Next day they brought him back for another bowl of dog food at the clinic, and again he accepted it. He kept up this performance for a week before finally deigning to eat at home.

But he never entirely forgot the clinic. For years afterwards, whenever his master or mistress were walking him nearby, he would start tugging at his lead. He was a strapping great dog and very hard to hold, so they were sometimes towed inside. The poodle would scratch at the glass door and refuse to leave until he received a few pats and strokes.

The husband's initial attitude had been quite straightforward. Showing affection for a dog struck him as soft – something peculiar to women and unworthy of the male sex – so he had taken a hard-nosed line before finally yielding to his true emotions. At bottom, he was a very decent sort.

Some dogs have an extraordinarily good memory for acts of kindness, and there can be few greater kindnesses than a reprieve from death. I am convinced that the poodle grasped the whole situation. Being a highly intelligent dog, he managed to suppress his resentment and bestow forgiveness. Plenty of human beings would do well to take a leaf out of his book.

At about this time, I had dealings with quite a different dog. He was a very large Alaskan husky of herculean strength and fearsome aspect. His white and silver mask gave him a very intimidating appearance. Instead of barking, he howled like a wolf. He looked so much like a wild animal that people often got off the pavement when they saw him coming. All other dogs were his mortal enemies, and only a minority of human beings rated as his friends.

The husky's name was Sugar Bush, which my wife promptly Gallicized into Chouboubouche. His owner, a pleasure-boat builder, had imported him from Alaska by plane, but something was obviously wrong. He had kept no food down since his arrival six weeks before. Nothing agreed with him.

Sugar Bush was an awkward patient. It took a month's patient habituation at our surgery-cum-clinic before he became approachable. Even then, no other dog could be allowed within range or he would have killed it on the spot. My consulting room received many canine visitors, so this posed problems. On one occasion, when Michèle had attached his leash to my file-laden desk, a dachshund ventured a few steps in the husky's direction. Sugar Bush promptly charged, towing the desk and its cargo as effortlessly as he might have drawn an empty sledge down an icy slope in the far North.

Although we carried out every possible test, the patient's condition defied diagnosis. There were no discernible signs of infection, so what could be wrong? What if he wasn't ill at all? We put him on a diet to see, but his troubles persisted. Then we had an idea: Alaskan dogs are often fed on fish. We tried him with some, and it worked like magic. No more vomiting. Two days later we cautiously added some spaghetti. Sugar Bush kept the whole lot down. He became quieter and more tractable. We tried the same thing next day, and he licked his bowl clean.

This diet put an end to all his troubles and vomiting. Without really knowing why, we had hit the jackpot. After several more days of this exclusive diet, which would have been enough to sicken the most fanatical spaghetti-lover, I pronounced the husky's problem solved. His owner came to fetch him and we heard nothing more.

Ten years later a woman client phoned to fix an appointment. Fortunately, she was alone in the waiting room when my wife opened the glass door of my consulting room. Michèle just had time to see the woman desperately trying to restrain a monstrous great dog with a white and silver mask. 'Hey,' she said, 'that looks like Choub . . .' But Sugar Bush did not let her finish. He had already escaped from his terrified mistress, who was convinced that her dog was going to eat the vet. Michèle would have been upended if she hadn't been leaning against the door frame. Sugar Bush hurled himself at her. Braced on his hindlegs with his forelegs almost round her neck, he licked her extravagantly and emitted little whimpers of delight.

After a separation of ten years, Sugar Bush had recognized the bestower of the enormous bowls of spaghetti which had allayed his hunger and banished his troubles. It was not, of course, the spaghetti alone that provoked this display of affection but also the bonds that had developed between us at a formative period of his life.

Sugar Bush greeted me in the same enthusiastic manner. His mistress had brought him to see me about a sore on the groin. An attempt to consult a colleague nearer home had ended in disaster because the dog became so aggressive that the vet could not get near him. At that stage, her husband had remembered my existence. Fortunately, Sugar Bush remembered even better. He suffered my attentions gladly, rolling over on his back and allowing me to part his legs for a closer look. I was able to treat him without difficulty. Not long afterwards, I also dealt with his prostate. (Ah yes, ageing dogs have their troubles too!)

If Sugar Bush was dangerous, albeit more to other dogs than human beings, the fault did not in this case lie with his owners, who were charming. He simply had the temperament proper to his breed. Very often, however, a vicious dog is made so by its master.

This applied to the owner of a Pomeranian which persistently bit everyone including the man himself and even snapped in its sleep. Having paid several visits to hospital on the dog's account, the owner brought it to me in the hope that I could make it more sociable. I kept the animal under observation. All our efforts to ingratiate ourselves proved abortive, but I noticed that it became even more vicious when its master was present.

I asked him why they didn't part company. Heatedly, he launched into an elaborate and rather implausible explanation, the gist of which was that the animal had belonged to his late parents. The truth began to dawn on me. It wasn't the man who maltreated the dog so much as the other way round. He was a nervous and highly strung type – he confessed as much himself – so I strongly suspected that this lay at the root of the dog's irritability. My view was reinforced by something else the client let slip: he had owned other dogs, all of which had been equally aggressive. Since it was unlikely that the man's temperament would ever change, I predicted that his relations with the canine race would always remain strained.

I would not claim that a vet combines the functions of a psychiatrist with his own. It is obvious, however, that by bringing their animals along for treatment, or sometimes for destruction, people tell us a lot about themselves. In practice, this enables us to form a psychological picture of each client's family circle, determine the place of the animal or animals within it, and detect psychopathological flaws which a doctor might find it useful to know of.

I recall a youth of seventeen from the local high school who brought me his cat to spay. There was nothing wrong with her. I simply sterilized her by removing her ovaries and kept her under observation for a day or two.

What struck me about the boy was his profound air of sorrow. He visited the clinic daily and stroked the cat with tears in his eyes. I assured him that all was going well, but it was no use: he couldn't stop. 'I know, I know . . .' he muttered, over and over again. I later learned from his mother that her husband had died a few weeks earlier. Although the boy had greeted the death of his father dry-eyed, the sight of his live and healthy cat moved him to tears. Who or what was he really crying over?

In bringing me their animals to treat, some clients come in quest of treatment for themselves, and it is not only their souls which they involuntarily bare to the veterinarian's gaze.

I have already told how the farmer whose horse I cured as a young probationer absolutely insisted on my treating his ulcerated leg, but elderly peasants are not alone in requesting vets for services of this nature.

The businessman who brought me his cocker spaniel was not some medieval rustic. He solved his problems by appealing to reason, not quacks or sorcerers. That, I imagine, is why he asked me to look at his dog in the first place.

The spaniel's ears had been receiving treatment for a considerable time, but without any apparent success. They were completely purulent. I first tried bathing them under pressure with a special system of my own devising. Then I decided to open them. The operation, which was one of the first of its kind, went off without a hitch. After a month's treatment, the dog was cured. Highly delighted with my services, its owner left for the South of France.

A year later he telephoned from Nice to make an appointment. I glanced at the spaniel as soon as he and his wife walked into the consulting room. Quite calmly, he informed me that he hadn't come to see me about his dog, which was quite fit, but about his wife, who was in a very bad way. She had something wrong with her anus. After thirteen operations, she was almost suicidal. Having solved the problem of his spaniel's ears, I might well come up with the answer to his wife's complaint.

Should I have repudiated their trust? Should I have told them that a spaniel's ear and a woman's anus are two different things? Should I have taken refuge behind the law and lectured them on the illegal practice of medicine? Of course, but there are many shades of meaning and many different roads to honesty and prudence. Instinct and intuition sometimes prompt the taking of short cuts which bring you to your destination more quickly than the authorized route. Are you likely to be greeted by a policeman on arrival? Perhaps, but there are risks which can reasonably be undertaken.

Never fear! I didn't perform a fourteenth operation on my client's wife. Without even examining her, I took the liberty of forming a personal opinion and pointing her in the right direction. Having many friends in the medical profession, I was able to recommend one for whom a vet's opinion on a woman's anus was not wholly devoid of interest. He duly treated my patient – or, rather, the mistress of my ex-patient the spaniel – and the results were satisfactory. What does all this prove? Merely that a vet is an animal doctor and that man is an animal too. What a vet knows about the one may be useful to the other.

Even a hallowed embodiment of cinematic history may be moved to consult a vet instead of a doctor, be it only on a minor but unpleasant matter like a torn nail. For the sake of this nail, which could have been trimmed by the classiest specialist in Hollywood, Gloria *Sunset Boulevard* Swanson deigned to wait her turn among the cats and dogs in my cramped little waiting room in the Boulevard des Batignolles. Why? Because her daughter and son-in-law, Michèle and Bob, had told her I made a habit of delving to the bottom of problems, human as well as animal. In her view, as in that of the old farmer mentioned above, a man who knew how to treat animals ought to be able to do the same for human beings.

Artists are sensitive people with a good understanding of animals, which often figure largely in their lives. Anouk Aimée, who is a case in point, keeps a whole family of animals in London, where she has been living for some years. Once, while holidaying at Saint-Paul-de-Vence, she found a small stray cat. She adopted it and decided to take it back to England with her, forgetting that it would first have to spend six months in quarantine. Far from abandoning the idea, she spent six months worrying about the fate of her new foster child, making lengthy telephone calls to the quarantine station and paying regular visits until the day came when it could be legitimately welcomed to her large family circle.

Brigitte Bardot is another celebrated animal lover. Some years ago she was urged to take a public stand against cruel slaughterhouse methods. Her intervention proved effective and marked a turning point in this field.

We have since worked together on various animal protection schemes. At my request, she agreed to become patroness of the home run by the *Société Protectrice des Animaux* at Gennevilliers, near Paris. She celebrated its inauguration by taking in two abandoned ewes. In fact, the waifs and strays rescued by the SPA include monkeys, donkeys, hens and other birds as well as cats and dogs. I might add that Brigitte's passion for animals encourages her to crowd her own home with stray dogs – something which has led to a certain amount of friction with her neighbours . . .

In December 1974 she fulfilled her promise to me to appear in our televised Christmas programme entitled *Noël des*

Animaux. We had organized an adoption scheme in collaboration with a large number of other animal homes linked by telephone and television with the SPA centre at Gennevilliers. To launch this campaign, we got Brigitte to record appeals which were televised five or six times daily during the week before Christmas.

19

Love Life of a Yorkshire Terrier

Not the least important of my jobs consists in giving nature a helping hand. We have already seen that, like cattle and horses, the bear, gnu and bison cannot invariably breed without assistance. Often, however, maternity comes harder still to the tiniest of creatures, so a vet's services may be quite as necessary in the case of a two-pound Yorkshire terrier as in that of an eland weighing three quarters of a ton.

But all these little animals are faced with yet another problem which arises at the very moment of mating. It is not, of course, a problem peculiar to Pinschers or Yorkies. No individual, human or animal, achieves automatic success as a lover. I have remarked on the lion's prowess in this field, but I also pointed out that a rhinoceros, however redoubtable in appearance, may be hard put to it to achieve adequate penetration in spite of the two little fins on his penis. Where dogs like the Yorkshire terrier are concerned, man has created an additional problem. Fashion dictates that they should be as small as possible, and the answer is to breed from miniature sires. The male champions of this breed are lightweights, not heavyweights, but mating such a champion with a bitch appreciably larger than himself is anything but a foregone conclusion. In other words, he has to be assisted.

Generations of miniature marvels have thus been sired – if I may so describe it – by me personally. Either on my examination table or at the homes of the bride and bridegroom, I have manually officiated at grand and fruitful unions. These are no brief street-corner encounters of a type to attract disapproving glances from passers-by, but major ceremonies attended by guests and witnesses who behave with all the tact, respect and decorum obligatory in aristocratic circles.

The old Russian lady who made an appointment at my surgery on behalf of a Yorkshire terrier bitch had titivated her for the occasion: there were pink bows in her long hair, some of which cunningly set off the most important part of the bride's anatomy. She herself, the widow of a former goldsmith to the last Tsar, was all in black and dressed to kill. Her son, who also attended, wore a white carnation in his buttonhole. The old lady was in high spirits despite her four score years. So was the bride, which augured well for future developments. In these circumstances, dogs benefit as much as human beings from a warm and friendly atmosphere.

The little male was a true champion. Handsome and well built, he tipped the scales at just on two pounds. However, I soon discovered that he was a novice. On this day of all days, he literally wasn't up to it.

We disposed ourselves around my examination table in accordance with the complex ritual observed on such occasions. The old lady in black and her son with the white carnation stood at one end of the table, stroking the little bitch's head and lavishing every form of encouragement on her. I myself stood at the other end – the difficult end. My champion pattered up and down the table. He sniffed his bride, who was physiologically ready to receive him, cocked his leg and did a little wee (which was swiftly but ceremoniously wiped up), glanced at us, made a halfhearted attempt to mount, and then slid off again, performing a few movements with his hindquarters as if to assure us that we hadn't seen anything yet. We let him be, telling him that he was a regular Casanova and his bride a lucky girl. He looked highly delighted and wagged his tail, but that was as far as it went.

We couldn't afford to show the least hint of impatience or the dogs would sense it and become totally inhibited. Even now, the bride was looking less amenable and had sat down on her hindquarters as though tired of waiting. I decided to perform my party piece, for which ten fingers and two hands are barely sufficient. My left hand had to lift the bride and present her vulva to its fullest advantage while my right took hold of the bridegroom's backside, manipulating him gently to put him in the mood, and guide his penis towards its proper destination. This convergence of two hands may look quite simple but is really very tricky. It requires great dexterity and the patience of a saint. The target is minute and the male's little organ can elude your fingers. You have to be so kindly and considerate that, however diffident they are, the bride and bridegroom are eventually carried away by your own enthusiasm. You have, in a sense, to become more canine than they are themselves before they consent to be canine enough to perpetuate their delightful species.

That day, however, there was nothing doing. The old lady's tender words failed to stimulate the bride sufficiently for the scent of her ovulation to become irresistible to the bridegroom, just as my skilful caresses and powers of persuasion failed to galvanize the bridegroom into taking the initiative like a bigger dog – for the culmination of the process was, of course, his own affair. The game was declared a draw. We would have to try a different approach.

Working on the assumption that closer acquaintance might be more conducive to a happy union, I turned up at the bride's abode with the champion and his owners. After being shown into the drawing room, we began to flirt. I say 'we' because I joined in too. Even if they worked themselves up into a frenzy of excitement, the two little dogs would be unable to perform without my help. The more I participated in their preliminary frolics the more readily they would accept me at the crucial moment, so it was absolutely essential for me to worm my way into the couple's affections.

Our parlour game went on for nearly five hours, from about six in the evening to eleven at night, before the union was finally consummated. My champion played very hard to get. He had been granted carpet privileges for the occasion and took full advantage of them. His first act was to cock his leg against an armchair. He sidled up to his betrothed and sniffed her, cocked his leg again, lay down a few feet away, rose, trotted to the door and barked to be taken home, trotted back, took another sniff, and so on *ad infinitum*. I went down on all fours like the dogs. I played with them and chatted to them. Above all, I remained calm. I was not entitled to lose my temper or bemoan the passage of time. I not only did my job but managed to do it cheerfully, as if I had even more to celebrate than the principals. And a celebration there would undoubtedly be when we finally pulled it off: whimpers and caresses, licks and kisses.

However, final success was preceded by two more setbacks. The bridegroom suddenly prepared to do his duty. Quickly, I propped him at the right height and helped him to draw a bead on his target. Too late! He was so quick on the trigger that he missed altogether. Still, it was a step in the right direction. I gave him time to recuperate and muster his courage. We played for half an hour, then he had another shot. Missed again! Complete success was only achieved at the third attempt.

After this difficult trial run, my champion became a sire of note. He stopped playing hard to get and enthusiastically did all that was required of him. No longer in need of a drawing room, carpet and armchairs to get him going, he now seemed to find my examination table at the clinic an adequate nuptial couch. As for me, I became his undoubted accomplice. His mistress had only to say 'We're off to Klein's' and he started frisking at once, well aware that he was in for a good time.

Once on the table he would sniff his betrothed, circle her a couple of times and glance at me as if to say 'Shall we go?' All I had to do then was hold him in position by supporting his hindlegs on my palm. In spite of his good intentions and the experience he acquired, the operation remained a delicate one. I had to intervene at precisely the right juncture, not a second too soon nor a moment too late. Too soon and I dampened his ardour; too late and he missed the target. In fact, ejaculation occurred almost as soon as he started thrusting – within two seconds at most. He always beat my wife to the draw whenever she tried to assist him, a fact which led her to christen him 'the fastest gun in the West'.

In cases where nothing does the trick, there remains artificial insemination. The sire's semen is drawn off by hand and collected in the finger of a glove, then introduced into the female with a syringe. On one occasion, this manipulative procedure was carried out by a woman assistant of mine. Judging by the expressive movement he made as soon as he saw her next, the little champion cherished a vivid memory of what she had done to him!

There is something rather comical and touching about these matings of miniature dogs with their ribbons and fripperies, but persuading the bigger breeds to mate can be a nightmare. A celebrated general once consulted me about his bitch. She was not a lady's lapdog but a large and handsome Alsatian which suited his military image to a T. I and a woman assistant were to supervise the consummation of her nuptials. The dog was willing but the bitch, though properly in heat by all appearances, would have nothing to do with him. She resolutely sat on her posterior, growling and baring her teeth whenever we tried to stand her up. I did my best to distract her from the front by stroking her head and talking to her while my assistant tried to lift her recalcitrant hindquarters so that the dog could get near her, but it would have taken a crane. Meanwhile, her intended cocked his leg all over the place, sidled towards her, backed off, and finally gave up. A reluctant female is always discouraging to the male, probably because the specific scent emitted by her, which is at its strongest during ovulation, fails to reach an intensity sufficient to maintain his excitement. In the above case we were dealing with a 'frigid' female. The occasion was a flop, and we had to administer treatment before mating them at a later stage.

In some cases, matings sponsored by man are complicated by a phenomenon peculiar to the dog. Though not normally rigid just before copulation, the male's penis is sufficiently sustained by a grooved bone to allow penetration. Erection does not increase until the penis is inserted, however, and attains maximum intensity when ejaculation occurs. Given these factors, one can readily understand that the moment of penetration is a critical one because the penis is still in a slightly 'hesitant' condition. One wrong move, one psychological blunder, and everything subsides faster than if the penis had been fully erect.

However, nature has perfected a complementary mechanism to ensure that the semen reaches the uterus. The male is not allowed to withdraw as soon as he is inside and his ejaculation has occurred. The semen is projected towards the back of the vagina. If the penis withdraws at once, a good proportion of it will trickle back along the passage, which slopes downwards, and be expelled. Consequently, some form of retaining device is needed to encourage it to flow down the cervix into the uterus.

What provides this seal are two spongy protrusions forming part of the erectile body, one on either side of the penis. I mention this only because I have more than once been consulted by people who insist that their dogs have developed two extra testicles and must be abnormal. In reality, these two balls form the plug which prevents the penis from withdrawing too soon. This explains why dogs can be seen locked together after copulation. The plug normally holds for ten to twenty minutes and yields when erection ceases.

One way of hastening withdrawal is to pinch the male's nose, but it should be realized that pulling the 'cork' prematurely may render a mating unproductive. In the case of manually assisted matings, when the male is not always at his best, this seal may not be effected. You then dissuade the bitch from urinating and raise her hindquarters to ensure that the semen reaches its destination. A male Yorkshire terrier whose locking device has functioned correctly must be supported at the required height by hand or propped on a telephone directory, otherwise he may hurt himself.

If all goes well after these matings, the bitch will become pregnant and produce puppies. Whelping calls for greater supervision in the Yorkie than in other breeds. The bitch is so small – between two and six pounds in weight – that her genital passage is very narrow. The more puppies there are, the smaller they tend to be. This will facilitate their expulsion provided everything else is in order and the uterus can still contract sufficiently. If it cannot, a Caesarean becomes unavoidable.

Delivery may be just as difficult if a bitch is expecting only one or two well-developed pups too large for natural expulsion. Once again, a Caesarean may become necessary. A newborn Yorkie is a little sausage three to four inches long, an inch in diameter, and one-and-a-half to three-and-a-half ounces in weight. These dimensions are substantial relative to those of the dam. For comparison's sake, it may be recalled that a newborn bear cub is a foot-long sausage two-and-a-half to three inches in diameter, whereas its mother weighs eight or nine hundred pounds. This explains why Yorkie whelpings call for special care.

I have spent more than one night with a little expectant mother installed on a cushion beside my bed. To make doubly sure of not being overtaken by events, I leave one arm dangling over the side of the bed so that my fingers remain in contact with her and my sleep will be disturbed as soon as her contractions start. The little creature realizes that my hand is a source of help. Very often, her emergency call will take the form of a few little nervous licks. If I want to assist a normal delivery and save the firstborn from succumbing to stress, especially when the mother is primiparous, I have only a quarter of an hour in which to act. A midnight dash to the owner's house

294

could waste precious minutes and do irreparable damage.

In default of all else, I have to fall back on a Caesarean – an equally delicate task and one in which every minute counts if mother and young are all to be saved. To quote a typical case, I was telephoned at 2 a.m. by a doctor who owned a Yorkshire terrier bitch. He told me enough to convey that the puppies would not be born without assistance, so I woke Michèle and my assistant and drove them to the surgery. We arrived there at the same time as the doctor and his wife. I quickly examined their little bitch and decided to operate at once. A canine Caesarean requires a team of three, each with a predetermined part to play. My assistant disinfected and prepared the abdomen while Michèle secured the terrier's legs and I administered an intravenous anaesthetic. Three minutes later the puppies were out and squeaking lustily. They had not even had time to absorb the anaesthetic, but the speed of their removal provoked shock in the dam. The prompt administration of a drip soon put matters right. Mother and young had come through the operation safe and sound.

Helping to give life . . . Whenever I try to review almost thirty years of professional activity at a glance, this is what strikes me as the most satisfying aspect of my career. Giving life to the bear and the Yorkshire terrier, the lion and the gazelle, the tiger and the tabby cat – giving it, saving it and restoring it by a series of interrelated acts which can, at the same time, lend meaning to the life of a person devoted to animals.

Far from reducing that person to bestiality, the multiplying and safeguarding of animal life enhances his humanity. It is men, not animals, who are increasingly overpopulating the earth and speeding the day when, almost alone with themselves and their follies, they will have no recourse but self-destruction. Helping animals to survive – even, if need be, at the expense of certain human beings – may thus be one means of safeguarding humanity's own chances of survival.

I have always sensed this affinity, not only when helping to deliver a tiger, a lion or a litter of puppies, but also when my own children were born. It gave me supreme happiness to stand beside the obstetrician at the birth of my first child, Jean-François. A little boy, a little lion, a little bear . . . Life was bountiful. It was also homogeneous in its diversity. My animals were my children, and my child – my very own child, this time – came into the world in much the same way. Where was the dividing line between man and beast? I had never experienced such a keen sense of their kinship, their equality before the laws of life or their similar dependence on nature. Giving life to animals did indeed mean furthering the survival of man.

My twin daughters, Isabelle and Florence, were born on New Year's Day like the little eland whose arrival in the world nearly occasioned my own departure. My wife was very tired by the time she had carried twins to full term, but all went well. A few weeks later I paid a brief visit to London.

I discovered on my return – not before, because Michèle had refrained from worrying me about it on the phone – that something was wrong with one of the twins. Her nostrils were pinched and her mucous membranes engorged, she was losing weight, and her breathing was laboured. I was alarmed, especially as our regular paediatrician happened to be away. The one Michèle consulted put the child on breast milk, which she had to fetch daily from the only hospital in Paris where it could be obtained. Instead of improving, the baby's condition had deteriorated. After restraining myself for twenty-four hours, I decided to treat her like a puppy. I took her off breast milk and persuaded the doctor to administer antiseptic intestinal drops and an antiallergic. The baby rapidly improved and resumed a normal appearance.

A fortnight later we were due to go skiing at Courchevel, where I had rented a chalet. The twins were only two months old, and the one I was treating still had some trouble with her breathing. The doctors told me it would be madness to take them with us to an altitude of 6000 feet. Why? I had known a woman who gave birth prematurely up there. Unable to get her baby to the hospital in the valley, she kept it in its cradle beside an open window. If that child had prospered in the fresh air and sunshine, why shouldn't my own little human puppy do the same? All my practical and instinctive knowledge of animal life assured me that our baby daughter would do well at an altitude whose effects I had personally experienced. Something inside me said the mountains would do her good.

I was right. The baby benefited a great deal, and both twins were flourishing by the time we returned to Paris. Had I taken an excessive risk? Had I merely been lucky, or was it that I had learned to appreciate the needs of the human being by devoting so many years to the service of animals?

We may well have much to learn from our animal brethren. The fact that man has become man in the course of the millennia is due in no small measure to what they have given and we have taken, from the meat that sustains our bodies to the imagery that nourishes our dreams and visions. Our tendency during the past two or three centuries has been to reduce them to less than nothing, to regard them as soulless automata and assign ourselves an infinitely superior place in the natural hierarchy. Man confronted by man alone turns upon himself in a suicidal manner. In the last few decades, however, he has begun to re-adopt a humbler and more fraternal attitude towards his animal kin. A natural antidote to the human poison that threatens the whole of nature may possibly be at work in the heart of man itself.

I sometimes discern strange and moving signs of this trend. Take the clerk at the information desk in the gare Saint-Lazare in Paris. 'You're Dr Klein, aren't you?' he said. 'Mind if I pick your brains?' That an animal lover should have recognized me was not surprising in view of my frequent television appearances. But he wasn't worried about a cat or a dog. The object of his concern was a python – and don't run away with the idea that he was an eccentric. Nobody who dealt as calmly as he did with the impatient customer in the queue behind me could have been anything but better balanced than most! He not only felt friendship for a snake but was trying to understand life through the medium of that creature, and his fondness for animals had bred kindness and patience towards his own kind. Once an outlaw among living creatures and a symbol of evil, a serpent had come to be regarded as a friend by somebody with a rational cast of mind. It was a sign of the times, and indicative of a humbler and more tolerant attitude towards animals in general.

I find it no more surprising to be asked questions by the provincial post office clerk who often consults me about his reptiles or his cayman. Neither of the young men I have just mentioned does a job which has any connection with the creatures they keep, but both come into daily contact with people who are not always a good advertisement for humanity. Perhaps they derive a certain consolation from the society of reptiles . . .

Fortunately, human beings worthy of the name can be

encountered at any social level. The railroad employee and the post office clerk are hardly members of the jet set, but I once saw some wealthy and distinguished people display a no less humane attitude towards an animal – not a gorgeous or glamorous beast, either, but a poor old dying dog from which even a kindly person might have been forgiven for averting his gaze.

Although it would have been only too easy to abandon the animal to its fate, exceptional measures were taken to save its life. A rich man's luxury, some may say, but that is a facile verdict. The truth is that human concern and the human sense of kinship assumed a new dimension. The direct beneficiary was not man but a humble member of an 'inferior' species. To me, it seemed a renewed sign of human progress.

I was sailing to the United States aboard the liner *France*, during her maiden voyage in February 1962, when an English-woman telephoned me from Saint-Paul-de-Vence. She asked me to return and visit her there at my earliest convenience, all expenses paid. Why? In the hope that I could do something for her dog Sam, a thirteen-year-old boxer. She had already consulted three of my Riviera colleagues and summoned Professor Gordon Knight, her regular veterinarian, from London, but nobody had managed to diagnose the trouble. My name had been given her by two women friends.

My prospective client had a pleasant voice and considerable powers of persuasion, but I could not change my schedule overnight. Being inveterately interested in matters that seem to have no direct bearing on my work, I was going to Martinique to attend a medical congress. I promised to call on the lady at Saint-Paul as soon as I got back. She begged me to hurry and telephoned me several times during my stay in the United States.

I duly left for Saint-Paul as soon as I returned to Paris and was taken to see the patient on arrival. His mistress turned out to be an elderly but handsome woman with a gentle, kindly expression and an air of great distinction and elegance well matched by her luxurious house and grounds. It transpired that she was the wife of a prominent English barrister.

As for Sam, who occupied an eiderdown on a bed reserved for his personal use, he was an appalling sight. Emaciated and even older-looking than his years warranted, he could not stand unaided. What could I possibly do for an animal of his age and in his condition? The obvious thing was to put him out of his misery, but I had been summoned in the hope that I would try something. I examined every inch of him and found nothing. I compared my own meagre observations with the numerous analyses that had already been made. Still nothing. It looked as if I would be flying back to Paris as bankrupt of ideas as the rest.

More for psychological reasons than anything else, I suggested that Sam should be x-rayed. It seemed that the poor beast had been submitted to every possible form of examination but that, so there was an outside chance that I might find something.

Even this presented problems in view of the dog's condition. I did not have the equipment to x-ray him on the spot. That meant taking him elsewhere, but would he survive the journey? My client agreed that it was a risk worth running. I contacted a radiologist friend in Cannes, who offered to have Sam fetched by ambulance so that he could, if necessary, be resuscitated *en route*.

The dog reached Cannes safely – with me in attendance, of course – and was x-rayed at once. We examined the radiographs closely, but they told us nothing. The radiologist hung them on the screen and we pondered the situation. What on earth could be wrong with the dog? I paced up and down the room. Absentmindedly, I glanced at one of the films from some distance away. All of a sudden, something caught my eye. I strode over and took a closer look in front of the light. No, I was wrong, I hadn't spotted anything after all, and yet . . . I hung up the film again and returned to my former vantage point about three yards away.

I hadn't been dreaming. There was something there – a sort of shadow in the abdominal region, but very indistinct. As soon as I approached it vanished. To clinch matters, I asked my friend to examine the x-ray at long range too. He confirmed my original supposition: the suspicious shadow was there.

I now had something to go on. But what exactly did the shadow signify? Even after debating the question a dozen times and theorizing interminably with my friend the radiologist, I couldn't begin to hazard an answer. There was only one way of finding out for certain, and that was to operate.

Glad to be not entirely at a loss, I submitted the problem

to Sam's mistress. After a lengthy conference at the home of the person who had recommended me, we reached the following decisions: (a) I would send the x-rays to Professor Gordon Knight, the boxer's regular veterinarian; (b) if he approved an operation, I would perform it at my clinic but with him in attendance; and (c) if the dog were for surgery, he must be suitably prepared in Saint-Paul for the journey to Paris.

The British veterinarian telephoned his approval two days later. I had meanwhile left for Paris with my client's friend and a sample of Sam's blood in my suitcase. I had, in fact, decided that the dog should be given blood transfusions before his departure for Paris to help him withstand the journey and fortify him for the operation. Canine blood transfusions were somewhat exceptional at this time, at least in common veterinary practice.

Back in Paris, I did a cross match to ascertain whether the blood of my selected donors would be compatible with that of the patient. My client's friend took the supply back to the South of France, where a colleague from Cannes was to administer transfusions prior to Sam's departure. The same friend would continue them during his trip to Paris while I remained there and got everything ready for the operation.

This was scheduled to take place the following Sunday morning. Small as my surgery was, I would have no need to blush at its shortcomings in front of a distinguished foreign colleague. It had just been completely renovated. What was more, it boasted a handsome electric operating table of my own design and a theatre as well equipped as any in a hospital for human beings. Although I was still a small-time vet by his standards, I had to keep my end up in the presence of a leading British authority.

The whole company assembled at last. The dog arrived by special plane with his mistress and her husband while their chauffeur-driven Rolls followed by road. I was to be assisted by a friend of mine, Georges Leroy, an anaesthetist with veterinary and medical qualifications who has since become a professor of anaesthetics in human medicine.

The dog looked very sick, but no more so than before, so the transfusion must have helped him to hold his own. The English couple retired to the waiting room and left us to our work. We held a brief preliminary conference in English. I saw at once that Professor Knight was a charming, intelligent and humane person. Sam was lying almost inert on the operating table. Knight felt his abdomen. With wry British humour and a touch of irony which was typical of an experienced practitioner but did not belie his professional concern, he tweaked Sam's coat and remarked that it would all be over very quickly because the poor brute would never pull through.

I agreed with him, but we were there to attempt the impossible. Even if the dog died, he would die in battle. We decided to go ahead. Sam was anaesthetized by Georges Leroy. The moment had come. I handed the scalpel to Gordon Knight. He was not only a top man in his field but my senior and the patient's accredited veterinarian. It was not quite a repetition of the battle of Fontenoy – '*Messieurs les Anglais,* you fire first!' – but almost. The English general – vet, I mean – graciously declined the honour and handed the scalpel back. No, no, I had made the diagnosis, so I must operate. I was the boss, he would be happy to assist, etc.

It was all very pleasant and polite. A cynic might attribute this to Knight's certainty that the dog would die. If he took charge, he would bear the responsibility. If he did not insist on doing so, nobody could object because the operation was being performed on my initiative.

That left me holding the baby. I put a braver face on it than the butterflies in my tummy warranted. I was operating in front of a master, and probably to no avail, but at least we would discover the cause of the trouble. I opened the dog's abdomen. It was full of blood-tinged serous fluid. Just as I started to aspirate it, the patient collapsed. He was sinking fast. His mucous membranes paled, his respiration and heartbeat almost ceased, his blood pressure fell. Then Georges Leroy had a brilliant idea: he reversed the pump I had been using to draw off the fluid. Employing this heaven-sent item of equipment like a force pump, we injected as much blood as we could into Sam's jugular under pressure. Much to my relief, he revived.

Resuming my tour of his abdomen, I felt a sudden thrill of jubilation. I was in luck. In the course of our final conference on the case, I had advanced the theory that there might be a tumour somewhere even though it could not be detected by palpation. My hypothesis had been confirmed. The tumour was there at the base of the caecum, or blind end of the large intestine. It was a soft, spongy tumour, which explained why we had been unable to feel it when examining the patient, and this was responsible for all the fluid that had just been drawn off.

Another stroke of luck: the tumour was pedunculated, like an excrescence at the end of the appendix, and could easily be removed. I set to work, clamping and resecting – and again the dog started to go. Another collapse. I gritted my teeth. The poor creature mustn't be allowed to die on us just when there was a good chance of saving him. We quickly pumped some more blood into the jugular. An ordinary drip would never have done the trick, but injection under pressure worked wonders for the second time. The dog revived and his heart started to beat again. We went back to work.

Nearly over now. I made my sutures in inverted purse stitch and cleaned up. The patient was still holding his own. A few minutes later his owners were admitted to the theatre. We were pleased – and proud – to be able to explain what we had done and tell them that the dog had some chance of pulling through. The professor looked very satisfied too. He was just as fair and magnanimous as I guessed he would be.

The boxer was deposited in one corner of the theatre, still asleep. Who was going to look after him? My veterinary nurse, my assistant? None other than his mistress herself. Despite her age, the rich, handsome and elegant English *grande dame* camped in extreme discomfort at my surgery. She remained at her dog's side all around the clock, sleeping beside him on a mattress and living on sandwiches. Since she was there anyway, she did all she could to be helpful. She swept the floor, ironed aprons between appointments and generally showed herself a model of tact, discretion and loving kindness.

All that trouble for the sake of a dog? Some may suggest that the lady was a little on the eccentric side, to put it mildly. Wrong again. Although there are women who reserve their devotion for animals, usually to the detriment of their own kind, my client wasn't one of them. She had a husband who was equally fond of the old dog. She had children and grand-children who adored her. No, she wasn't suffering from any perverted maternal instincts. Her behaviour simply bore witness to a generous spirit, a great sense of responsibility and a love of life which was not limited to human life alone.

The boxer spent five days at my surgery. Meanwhile, his mistress had rented an apartment in the boulevard Maillot where he could convalesce within easy reach of me. I called there every day. The dog was improving steadily. No fever, no complications.

After a fortnight under observation in the boulevard Maillot, Sam was taken to convalesce in the greater freedom and fresher air of Saint-Germain, only thirty minutes away by car in case of emergencies. Finally, when the old boxer's state of health was such that he could trot gaily through the forest of Saint-Germain, his extraordinary mistress gave a dinner in my honour at the Hôtel Henri IV. I had been so enthralled by the whole case that I found it rather distasteful to end our connection on a financial note. Suffice it to say that the matter was settled at the end of dinner with all the grace and munificence I might have expected from a woman who could go to such lengths on behalf of a 'mere' dog.

Some days later, Professor Gordon Knight of the Royal Veterinary College sent me a congratulatory letter which touched me deeply. He also sent me a present of some Gillis forceps, a surgical instrument comprising a needle holder and scissors, having noticed during the operation that I did not possess such an article.

The boxer enjoyed a new lease of life. No serious problems arose until he died two years later, not of cancer but of acute uraemia.

I had several long conversations with his mistress about our common love of animals. At home in her English country house, she told me, her mornings were often enlivened by a delightful visitor. In summer, when she was breakfasting in bed with the windows flung wide, a squirrel had taken to climbing down the nearest chestnut tree, which almost brushed the wall, and hopping on to the windowsill. It gradually became bolder and ended by venturing on to her breakfast tray to nibble small pieces of toast. Before long, the kitchen was sending up a special breakfast of walnuts and hazelnuts for her guest.

One day the little creature disappeared. My client was heartbroken. Could somebody have killed it? Given that the grounds of an English country house are safer for squirrels than their equivalent in France, where we foolishly persist in slaughtering the little animals, this was unlikely. Perhaps it had fallen ill or been caught by a predator. Anyway, its presence was sadly missed.

303

One morning a few weeks later, the mystery was solved in an enchanting way. The squirrel suddenly reappeared on my client's windowsill. She felt sure it was the same one: only her old friend would have been so bold. After a moment it vanished into the chestnut tree, ignoring her muted invitations to stay. A few seconds later it was back, this time with company. There was another, smaller squirrel at its side, looking nervous and rather awkward. Within minutes there were no fewer than five squirrels on the windowsill. They must have been a mother and four youngsters reared in the neighbouring woods during her two months' absence.

My client held her breath, knowing that the slightest movement might scare them away. Would the mother remember? Would she pick up the threads of friendship where she had left them?

A moment or two later, all five squirrels jumped on to the bed and crowded around the tray. Tentatively, they applied themselves to the banquet and started nibbling.

20

Coexistence or Death

A human being and a handful of animals had re-created a little corner of paradise for their common delectation. Although I would not deny that such successes are exceptional, and that the relations between man and wild or even domesticated animals are seldom as idyllic, the squirrels' breakfast and the saving of the old boxer's life struck me as exemplary. They were yet another sign – and one that has repeatedly come my way – of the propinquity between man and beast.

I have been carrying this relationship to extremes for thirty years or more. My family and friends are well aware of my subordination to the world of animals. I may have been planning to meet a friend or take my children for a walk, but a telephone call from the owner of a sick old dog will put paid to all that: I have a spiritual need as well as a professional obligation to drop everything and run. If my life were not so satisfying, it might be described as a form of servitude. Animals monopolize me for three hundred and sixty-five days a year – nights too, very often. They lie in wait for me during my rare holidays and spells of leisure. There is always some friend's or neighbour's pet to tend, some reading to catch up on, some article to write, some television programme to rehearse.

We had planned to celebrate the eve of Michèle's most recent birthday by dining with some friends. At about four o'clock that afternoon somebody brought me a dog to examine for the first time. He was not only ill but dying, with a largish tumour of one testicle, which had failed to descend, and a prostate the size of a grapefruit. I was torn between destroying him, because his chances of recovery seemed minimal, and staking everything on an immediate operation. There was no question of waiting until the next day, so I decided to go for broke. I had urgent haematological tests made, which meant that we could not start operating until 7 p.m. Our perseverance paid off, at least from the patient's point of view. He left the theatre in excellent shape. Our new monitoring equipment had served us well, because – to crown everything – the dog presented cardio-vascular problems on account of all he had been toting around with him for the past few months.

It was 11 p.m. Our friends were offended. Even Michèle, who had assisted me and was acquainted with the circumstances of the operation, showed signs of annoyance. Perhaps they were right to be angry. My own nervous tension ebbed as fatigue took hold of me. In my heart of hearts, I felt content. I could hardly wait for tomorrow to come, just to see how my patient was doing.

Everyone knows I never make dinner dates on time. I accept as few invitations as possible, even important ones. How can I leave an open thorax or abdomen in mid-surgery? You can estimate the length of operations and programme them in advance, but what about the clients who descend on you without warning? Can you ignore them at the expense of the animals they claim to love? My team and I are permanently in the hot seat. Weighed against a social, family or business commitment, my patients always tip the scales.

Under these circumstances, how can the wide-ranging problem of human-animal relations not be fundamental to a person as monopolized by animals as I am? How can I fail to reflect almost constantly on the kinship or conflict between man and beast and the attitude of the former, whose destructive conduct seems to affirm that he can live without the latter?

Personally, I cannot live without animals. It was they who prevented me from subsiding into the limbo created within me by wartime bloodshed, by an awareness of unremitting persecution, by the knowledge that concentration camps had been succeeded by extermination camps and the belief that injustice, hypocrisy and deception were ever-present evils. Hovering on the brink of this dark void, in which disgust and rebellion mingled with the feeling that all was absurd or loathsome, that there was nothing to do but kill time, pretend to be busy and scoff at everything, I finally discovered a living, peaceful and unquestionable reality. My veterinary career, to which I very soon clung like a drowning man, conjured up an unexpected vision of personal deliverance. Cows, oxen and farm animals are not noted for being the most intellectually and emotionally stimulating of creatures. In caring for them, however, I found I was getting to grips with myself. By concentrating wholeheartedly on their ailments, sufferings and needs, I came to realize that I was not only gaining an insight into the nature of animals but rediscovering and accepting human nature as well – in other words, my own.

I felt that by tending the humblest of animals – an ox destined for slaughter or a donkey belaboured with a stick because it was 'only' a donkey – I was simultaneously defending a whole category of the human race. Because men so often treated their own kind 'like animals', it was my duty to tend and love animals as well as human beings or, if possible, even better. Jews, coloured or black people and dissidents were regarded as less than dogs in various parts of the world. By doing my best for some wretched old mongrel, I was showing solidarity with all the world's human dogs and, at the same time, mitigating my personal sense of shame at being a man. Thus, animals reintroduced me to humanity and, first and foremost, to myself.

I began to grasp the meaning of this close relationship through contact with pain and suffering – not only that of man reduced to an animal existence by the oppression of his fellow men but, above all, that of the animal itself. No vet can avoid being something of a philosopher in this respect. Picture me examining a sick cow. She refuses to eat, carries her head low and periodically emits a muffled groan. What's the matter with her? There are no outward signs of disease. She has no tendency to limp, no open sores or wounds on her body. I look at her and what do I see? A bovine countenance – in other words, something peculiarly inexpressive by human standards. For all that, I have to discover what it conveys. I have to mobilize my sensory and intellectual resources in order to read its message. Her mooing is significant, of course, and her occasional habit of turning to inspect her flank gives me at least some indication of where the trouble lies. What trouble? The cow won't tell me, but that's what I have to find out. As with the cow, so with the lion, monkey and dog. The quest is an ever-changing one because each species transmits a different message of pain whose decipherment requires a fresh effort of comprehension. This is what urges me on and impels me to plumb the depths of the animal nature. It is by analysing pain in animals as a means of identifying their ills that I have come to grasp something of their individuality.

What, apart from their ills, does the pain felt by a cow, lion or dog disclose? Not only that they are closely akin to us, but also – and I am not afraid to say it – that they possess souls. One Sunday not long ago, a woman doctor brought me her six-month-old Alsatian bitch. She was dying. I put her on a drip and examined her meanwhile. Her owner was still awaiting the result of some tests. I diagnosed a volvulus, or twisted loop of bowel. I opened the patient and found what I expected. There was nothing to be done. The volvulus was a triple one affecting over a yard of gut. It had strangulated the blood supply as well as the alimentary canal, causing congestion and necrosis in that part of the intestine. The animal was suffering from generalized peritonitis and could not be saved, even by drastic resection. With the consent of her owner, who, being a doctor, had attended the operation, we decided to end her sufferings. We did not bring her round, so the anaesthetic put her to sleep for ever.

I soon discovered the cause of the trouble. After conducting a thorough autopsy, I ascertained that the volvulus had not been occasioned by any organic disease or infection of a viral or bacterial nature. Two weeks earlier, my client had gone off with her two children and left her mother in charge of the household. The young bitch had been with the family from the age of two months. She was so attached, not only to her mistress but also to the children, that she could not bear to be parted from them. Grief and agitation had quite literally twisted her intestines into a fatal condition. Such was the message of this animal's pain and death. In this case, organic damage stemmed from the psyche, or what has for centuries been called the soul. Men are credited with souls but animals denied them. Speaking for myself, I was convinced by this animal's sufferings that she must have possessed one. Only those with souls can die of love.

Once I acknowledged the existence of such a soul – or psyche – in a dog and, in varying degrees, all other animals, they seemed infinitely closer to us and infinitely more deserving of our duties and responsibilities towards them. If the animal was a mechanism, as some religions and philosophies have asserted, man could dispose of it as he pleased. Even today, a Frenchman wields absolute power of life and death over his animals. I have the right to kill my dog if I so desire. French law merely forbids me to inflict unnecessary suffering. As for the animal, it possesses neither rights nor responsibilities. It rather resembles the 'lunatic', a creature who was for centuries treated like a dog and sometimes is today, except that we dare not get rid of him by killing him. Indeed, some countries evade even this restriction by variously disguised means, while others send people mad in order to eliminate them – as witness the psychiatric treatment administered to political dissidents in various parts of the world.

Our human tendency is to deny rights to those we cannot understand; to deny the humanity of 'madmen' because they differ from the rest of us, who comprise the society that made them different by making them sick; to deny rights and souls to animals because their psyche does not exactly resemble ours. But permanent contact with 'madmen' – or animals – teaches a person that fellow creatures whom he thought of as alien are really akin to himself. How can such a person fail to develop a new sense of duty towards them? He soon perceives, in the very depths of his being, that the relationship between himself and them is more one of brotherhood than superiority.

I can hear pessimistic voices raised in protest. Brotherhood? Ever since man's intellect enthroned him as lord of creation, he has persistently inflicted every kind of slaughter upon animals, not only to feed himself like any other predator but for the sheer perverted pleasure of killing. Discounting a few welcome exceptions, the real relationship between man and beast is less one of kinship than of lethal exploitation. Man has always been, and is more so now than ever, the executioner of the animal.

Such is the dialogue I have been pursuing for thirty years or more. I often surrender to pessimism, I admit. It is quite true that man's sense of responsibility towards animals remains very inadequate, to say the least, in spite of all the international conferences on wildlife conservation. International agreements and national laws are seldom enforced. The protection of marine fauna, in particular, is practically non-existent. The real state of affairs is concealed by a worldwide smokescreen. The International Whaling Commission is so undermined by politico-economic interests that it achieves nothing. Protected in theory, the whale continues to be exterminated in practice. One has only to see the trail of destruction left by Soviet and

Japanese factory ships, among others, to be convinced that, despite the good intentions of the few, humanity in general has yet to develop a responsible code of behaviour.

We have annihilated whole species and are still engaged in so doing. By invading the entire planet and multiplying without restraint, we are driving the noblest animals from their habitat and destroying them one by one. Our sole excuse is a further reinforcement of the pessimistic standpoint: if man executes beast, he does so because it is in his nature to be an executioner. We slaughter and exploit animals to death, but we do the same or even worse to our own kind.

We may be the lords of creation, but we may also be the most pernicious of the animal species. Ethologists engaged in the study of animal behaviour have sometimes ventured comparisons between man and rat. They have demonstrated that rat societies are in some respects similar to human. For instance, rats are fiercely tribal in their behaviour. They make short work of any stranger to their group. Like human beings, they are characterized by extreme intraspecific aggression. Like human beings, who abominate, imprison, expel or kill those who belong to other nations or espouse different ideologies and religions, rats drive away and if possible kill those of their own kind who have a different scent and do not belong to the same extended family or tribe. But even rats are capable of imposing certain restraints on their development and aggressive instincts. Within their own group, which may be very large indeed, they are easygoing and share their food. There is mutual toleration between young and old, strong and weak. Human beings have not yet reached this stage. It could thus be argued that man resembles a rat of the worst type.

I have often been tempted to think that, if I had to choose between man and beast, my choice would fall on the latter. It is a temptation I do my utmost to resist. I am still encouraged by daily and long-standing contact with animals and the human beings on whom they depend to believe that all is not lost. Although I am often inclined to abandon hope, I would still take a last gamble on the human race. If the devil, as it were, resided in our chromosomes – if the human race, after a brief efflorescence on our planet, were destined to destroy fauna, flora and, ultimately, itself – there would be no hope or remedy. But I believe that the debate between human wisdom and human folly is not yet closed. I believe there to be an incipient realization in man that he is nearing the great divide between survival and extinction. The instincts of animals protect them against the excesses into which man plunges, and I am enough of an optimist to believe that by dint of the exercise of man's vestigial instincts humanity will survive. It is clear that the survival or extinction of our species depends on our rediscovery of animal wisdom, and that, in turn, implies a knowledge and acknowledgement of creatures that merit our respect and protection.

The threat of extinction requires us to learn from the animal and, above all, to gain a profound awareness that human beings are animals too. Personally, I have never failed to perceive this in my contacts with innumerable members of other species. If I have so often sensed a current of communication passing between me and my dogs, lions and monkeys, it is not because of our mutual differences but because we all possess something in common: our animal nature.

Based upon my daily experience, this conviction has been reinforced by ethological studies. When man feels a shiver run down his spine at the sound of a scream or a trumpet-call, the emotion he expresses is undoubtedly human but also, and primarily, animal. His shiver is that of the agitated chimpanzee bristling at a prospective foe. We are, in fact, only one branch of the phylogenic tree whose other ramifications are the chimpanzee and gorilla, orang-utan and gibbon. Our animality is written in our chromosomes. Made in collaboration with Dr de Grouchy's team at the Necker Hospital in Paris, a study of karyotypes (chromosomal charts) in man and the anthropoids led us to determine the karyotype of our common ancestor. It may be mentioned in passing that we came across a Mongoloid gorilla on this occasion. Its Mongoloid characteristics could not be discerned from its appearance or behaviour, as in man, but were revealed – as in man – by its chromosomes.

We owe our humanity to the animal, not only because we ourselves are evolved animals but because, from time immemorial, animals have played a leading role in the development of our humanity. They have fed and clothed us. Our dreams, myths and gods are inseparably linked with them. Our very language teems with animals: a 'dog's' life, a 'wolfish' stare, 'catty' behaviour, and so on. Our subconscious contains a whole bestiary which contributes to the development of our human personality. We cannot dispense with animals even today, when the gulf between us is wide. We not only feed on them, like our ancestors, but sacrifice millions of them for the sake of scientific projects of all kinds. Although dogs are exterminated on various pretexts in other parts of the world, they have never been so numerous in my own country, where their presence is as much in demand as that of other domestic animals.

Today more than ever before, animals are performing functions of great importance on our behalf. Again I can hear the pessimists. Yes, they say, sacrificial functions for the benefit of man, not of themselves or nature as a whole. What you term a function is quite simply the brazen exploitation of animals by man. The animal's function in circuses, zoos, wildlife parks and any place where it is kept in semi-captivity is to be a victim of man, neither more nor less. This is a valid objection, but only in part. Man being what he is, it would be unrealistic to reproach him for exploiting the world and its fauna for his personal benefit. He can, on the other hand, be urged not to lop off the branch that supports him – not to commit the folly and absurdity of destroying the natural heritage on which his own existence depends.

In this sense, it is no more realistic to reproach him for exhibiting animals in circuses, zoos and natural or artificial reserves. It is, however, legitimate to demand that he does so under conditions which guarantee their survival, comfort and dignity. To the extent that these conditions are observed, I feel that the animal's exercise of this particular function is fully justified. I remain convinced that circuses, zoos and 'reserves' fulfil a useful role by reminding us of the animal's existence. Of course it lives in captivity in such surroundings, but freedom to an animal is as relative as it is to the human being.

It is also true that such establishments put animals on display 'for money'. This is not, however, the last word to be said on the subject. As we have already seen, professional enthusiasm and affection for animals may often prevail over other considerations; indeed, there are some who take their cultural role so deeply to heart that they neglect their own interests. 'Send the animals back where they came from; liberate them from man.' In my opinion, those who take such a line are mistaken. The fewer man's contacts with animals and the smaller his realization that human life is linked with theirs, the less concerned he will be for their survival. Going even further, I submit that the present existence of circuses and zoos is essential to the future existence of open spaces inhabited by wild animals.

But the animal's principal function today may be to remind man of the elementary conditions of his own survival at a time when he is losing sight of them. It is no mere accident that so many ethological studies are now in progress or that researchers in the field of bionics are striving to plumb the mysteries of the extremely delicate sensory resources available to animals with a view to placing them at the service of man. There is a growing awareness that animals have much to teach us.

First and foremost, they remind us of the biological importance of the pair and the family. Only those who have heard a baby cheetah fret itself to death when separated from its mother can comprehend the full strength of a bond which human societies now deem themselves able to disregard or even break as a deliberate act of policy. Like any young animal, the cheetah cub reminds us that the human baby is also an animal which requires a great deal of affection if it is to avoid grave damage, first to its own existence and later to that of others. Man is the vehicle whereby affection is transmitted, like genes, from one generation to the next. He who has not received it will be unable to pass it on. Instead, he transmits a deficiency which gradually disrupts his social environment and the generations that come after him. Any human society which repudiates these biological family foundations is necessarily abstract and artificial. It is doomed to the evil it disseminates.

Animals teach us that social equilibrium is geared to the fulfilment of certain elementary needs in which a crucial role is played by the mother, parents, family and family group. Experiments conducted by authorities such as the American psychologist John B. Calhoun have demonstrated how, under certain circumstances, the disintegration of bonds and family rites in a community of rats will bring about the total disintegration of that community and the death of its members. Males can be observed violating the taboos associated with mating rites and forcing themselves on females in season without regard for their wishes. Females thus impregnated become incapable of carrying their offspring to term, either

313

aborting or dying before they can give birth. Mother rats normally transfer their litter to a place of safety, one by one, if danger looms. Deserted by this instinct, they abandon and lose track of them. The baby rats become dispersed and are soon devoured by their elders. In the ensuing general disorder, some rats become introverted, seek refuge in inactivity, never stir from their corner of the cage, even starve themselves to death. The majority, however, become hysterical and run around all day like mad things. High-ranking males are attacked, the hierarchy dissolves and internecine strife rages. In the end, not a single member of the original community survives.

Interpretations of this type of experiment are necessarily complex. Everything seems to decay, however, as though the loss of the reproductive instinct designed to preserve the species had not only halted the group's development but caused social disintegration and the death of those with the ability to breed. Some will object that rats and human beings differ. I wouldn't bank on it. We can at least ask ourselves whether the loss of this primal instinct and the rejection of the framework essential to its fulfilment – in other words, the pair and the family – will not eventually lead to the disintegration of human society.

Animals and animal communities show us that they possess regulatory mechanisms which limit their development in certain circumstances, which curb intraspecific aggression and prohibit excesses of individualism and selfishness. They activate altruistic instincts and maintain them by educative means. They know nothing of consumption for consumption's sake, killing for the sake of killing. Animals kill to eat and do not eat more than hunger prescribes. Even the big cats display this natural wisdom. At sunset, when the sated lion comes to drink at the waterhole, the other animals do not scatter in alarm. They know they have nothing to fear.

Every observation of animal behaviour confirms that animals set us a good example. Their instincts are never bad. The only 'wild' animal, pejoratively speaking, is man. There are no 'vicious' animals except in the sense attributed to that word in the ironical statement: 'This animal is vicious: it defends itself when attacked.' Contact with animals never fails to convince me that they exemplify what is best in ourselves: our animal instincts, which are good by definition. Their society re-educates us in devotion to the family, the duty owed to children, the virtues of forbearance and forgiveness. I would recall the story of the giant poodle: after showing resentment towards the owners who had first rejected him and then taken him back, he finally consented to forget the past and accept their food.

Because we are animals ourselves, and because animals have much to teach us, I believe that this new alliance between man and beast is founded on reality. I believe that, far from being a pious hope or product of hypocrisy, it is becoming translated into fact. Take contraception, for example. Whatever its negative effects on the individual, the family and society, it may also represent an instinctive control mechanism. By employing such methods to limit its alarming proliferation, humanity may be rediscovering one aspect of the animal's age-old wisdom.

I would further submit that, despite the ignorance and recklessness of mankind in general, some individuals and nations are gradually adopting a new and better attitude towards animals. To paraphrase a well-known aphorism, we are now beginning to say: 'I am a man and nothing animal is alien to me.' The battle has yet to be won, but we at least have an inkling that we shall not preserve ourselves without preserving nature and the animals it has engendered over millions of years. We must either coexist with animals or die with them.

While remaining an executioner of animals, man is also striving to tend, love and preserve them. Will good prevail over evil? We can only hope so, but it is too easy to stress what is bad. My intention in this book has been to illustrate the bonds between man and beast rather than their points of difference, their living union in nature rather than the destruction of one by the other.

I should prefer to leave the last word to a man who has taught us a great deal, the biologist Jean Rostand. 'One of my most firmly held beliefs,' he writes, 'and one of the rare things of which I am well nigh certain, is that the difference between us and animals is only relative, a difference of quantity, not quality; that we are of the same stuff and substance as the beast . . .'

Thanks to the existence of 'this solidarity, this continuity between the animal kingdom and the human domain', to quote Rostand again, I can affirm with gratitude that it is animals as much as human beings – not only those I have tended and loved, but all those whose existence on our planet is linked with that of humanity – that have made me what I am: a man.